THE
COMPREHENSIVE
GUIDE TO THE
SAT®

MARKS PREP

The Comprehensive Guide to the SAT®

Senior Editors: Dan Hertz, Anthony Celino, and Shaun Stiemsma

Preface

Dear Student and Parent,

Thank you for purchasing this book, which provides proprietary content and highly effective strategies for each part of the SAT. Please take a few minutes to read this Preface and the Introduction that follows. They contain helpful background information and practical advice on how to best use this book in conjunction with the free resources provided by the College Board.

Nitin Sawhney
Managing Director, Marks Prep
nitin@markseducation.com

What Makes This Book Different?

The SAT contains very challenging reading comprehension passages and questions, a tricky Writing section, and a lot of algebra, some of which is not covered by many high school math courses. The material on each part of the test is still unfamiliar to many tutors and teachers who have had limited success in helping students improve. Overall, for many students and teachers, the new SAT is more resistant to improvement than the ACT.

With carefully constructed strategies for each question type on the new test, Marks Prep tutors have simplified preparation for the SAT. Using these strategies, our students taking the current SAT have achieved percentile improvements in average scores similar to our students who took the old SAT and ACT. In this book, written after months of careful preparation, we lay out our methods with clear and accessible language so others who cannot access our tutoring services may benefit similarly.

In each section of this book (Reading, Writing, and Math), we have broken down the content of the test into highly effective, easily learned strategies followed by problem sets that reinforce those strategies. These materials have helped our students in the high school class of 2018 improve, on average, 212 points from baseline 10th grade PSAT test to final SAT test (1236 to 1448). On average, our students use approximately half the number of tutoring sessions recommended by other firms to achieve these gains.

Why Not Simply Take the ACT?

Many students can do very well on the ACT and should consider that test. However, the ACT, which requires students to work very quickly, particularly on the Math, Reading, and Science sections, is not the best test for every test taker. The SAT, in contrast to the ACT, has more involved questions, but also allows more time per question. Thus, it can be the better test for those who like to work carefully and not be rushed.

What Is Marks Prep?

Marks Prep is the test preparation and tutoring division of Marks Education, which provides tutoring, test preparation, and admissions counseling to students all over the world.

Each Marks Prep tutor is an experienced full-time educator and a top 1% test taker who sits for the SAT and other tests every year, in real test centers, along with our students. We use the knowledge gained from taking these tests and working with our students to write efficient strategies and materials for all the tests we tutor—from the SSAT and ISEE to the SAT, ACT, GRE, GMAT, MCAT, and LSAT.

The full-time tutors at Marks Prep have, for the past ten years, tutored hundreds of students each year across the United States and the world, via Skype and other platforms. Students who have worked with us for at least six sessions have, on average, improved their scores by 340 points on the SAT (pre-2015, from baseline 10th grade PSATs) and almost 7 points on the ACT. In contrast to many other firms, we use only actual College Board PSATs and real past ACTs for baseline tests. More specific score improvement data for all tests (including graduate school tests) are available on our website, marksprep.com.

We also work with several schools and non-profits to help them improve their students' standardized test scores and change college admissions outcomes and to thus markedly enhance their School Profile.

Table of Contents

How to Use this Book

In order to make best use of this book, you should either a) have scores from a recent actual SAT or b) first take a full-length timed diagnostic SAT, either from the College Board website or from our book: *Four Realistic SAT® Practice Tests*, available on Amazon. Please take the scores on each part of the test and write them on the first row of the table on page 7.

Then carefully review the errors from your test. This process should give you a good idea of your strengths and weaknesses and the areas you most urgently need to review. Next, use the table below to cover the areas that were weakest on your test.

Areas of Weakness	Focus on
MATH	
If you need improvement on Section 3 (the non-calculator section)	Pages 133–136 and 140–198
If you did relatively well on Section 3, but would like to improve on Section 4	Pages 199–240
READING	
If your score was low	The entire Reading section of the book, pages 9–36
If your score was low because you ran out of time	Page 12
If you struggled with Command of Evidence questions	Pages 15–17
If you struggled with Words in Context questions	Pages 18–21
WRITING	
If you could improve on Expression of Ideas (or the questions about meaning of the passage)	Pages 41–68
If you could improve on Standard English Conventions (grammar and punctuation questions)	Pages 69–114

After each layer of review, take another full, timed practice test from *Four Realistic SAT® Practice Tests* or from the College Board website. If using the website, please be sure to print the test out, so you can write on the test booklet. Writing out your work—on <u>all</u> sections of the test—is an important strategy. Then note your score on page 7 of this book, review errors on the practice test, and cover relevant parts of this book. Please reach out to us if you have any suggestions or questions.

SAT Score Tracker

Date	Raw Scores				Scaled Scores				
	Reading	Writing	Math—No Calc	Math—Calc	Reading	Writing	R/W Total	Math Total	Total Score

Tips for Peak Performance

The Week Before the Test

- **Get eight hours of sleep each night.** Remember, sleep makes you smart. Studies have shown strong links between inadequate sleep and many aspects of test taking including attention span, emotional intelligence, attention to detail and oral recall.

- **Eat lots of complex carbohydrates and healthy protein.** Breads, pastas and other complex carbs give you energy you will need for the five-hour marathon ahead of you.

- **Visualize carefully the test you are about to take.** Top performers (including athletes, actors and dancers) often use visualization to create a mental image of success. In your mind, create a detailed picture of the test—from section to section. Visualize yourself achieving your targets in each part of the test. As you do this, try to anticipate potential distractions (stress, a loud classmate, an overly watchful proctor, etc.) and then visualize yourself proceeding calmly and confidently through all such distractions.

The Night Before the Test

- **No studying past 9:00 PM.** Last-minute cramming leads to last-minute jitters, and it can keep your brain whirring long past the time you stop studying—which will keep you from falling asleep. Read a book for school, go for a run, or watch a movie. Do something fun that doesn't keep you up late. The idea is to be completely relaxed on test day.

- **Lay out your pencils, appropriate calculator, ID, Admission ticket, watch (with no beeps!), and a snack.** Check the batteries on your calculator. Granola bars are a good snack. So are PB&J sandwiches. Starbucks bottled beverages can help give some people a nice mid-test boost.

- **Go to bed!** If you can't fall asleep, don't worry. Just lying in bed can be very restful. Read a boring book, if you like. That might help put you to sleep.

Test Day

- **Wake up early!** Studies show that it takes the average person about three hours (after waking up) to function at peak capacity. The SAT begin around 8:00 in the morning. Try to wake up at least 2 or 2.5 hours before the test.

- **Get some aerobic exercise.** Because of the length of the test (including filling out forms and breaks, the SAT can last up to 4.5–5 hours), you can end up feeling quite brain-dead toward the end. Aerobic exercise oxygenates your blood and can help you to focus for longer amounts of time.

- **Get a big, healthy breakfast with some protein.** Try not to eat heavy foods that can be difficult to digest. Eggs and toast, cereal, bagels with cheese, and such foods generally work well. Remember, standardized testing is a stressful, draining process.

- **Dress in Layers.** Test centers can be very warm (A/C not working) or very cool (A/C cranked up!). If you wear several layers, you can adjust your clothing according to the temperature of the room.

- **Breathe.** Deep breathing is a great relaxation technique. It also helps in blood circulation. During the test, remember to stretch and breathe deeply often.

- **Fifteen minutes of Reading or Math in the morning.** Often students find that they are not completely awake for the first section of the test. Doing a reading passage on the morning of the test can help wake you up.

- **Test-day checklist**: Snack, Pencils, Photo ID, Watch (no beeps), Admission ticket, Appropriate Calculator (e.g. a TI–84).

- Go CRUSH the test!

Reading Test Manual

The Reading Test of the SAT is composed of five passages and at least two tables/graphs. One literary passage, two science passages, and two social science passages combine for a total of 52 questions to answer in 65 minutes.

Most reading passages are challenging, *so you have to read the passage carefully*. Also, because the answer choices are meant to confuse you, we strongly believe that for the best chance at a top score, you should follow an R–W approach: **Read** *and then* **Write** *about the passage and each of the questions*. This strategy has allowed thousands of our students to avoid the traps in the answer choices by basing their responses on their own understanding of the passage.

In the following pages, we will explain the R–W strategy, as well as special adaptations of this strategy to prepare you for three special question types.

Overview and Strategy

Passage Strategy

While the difficulty of these passages varies, all are rhetorically sophisticated. Each tests your ability to understand not only the ideas and facts presented in the passage but also the author's intention and rhetorical strategies. Thus, it is essential to read well and to answer each question carefully. The following three steps will help you to navigate both the complexity of the passages and the trickiness of the questions.

1. R – W 1: **Read** and **Write** about the **whole passage!**

   Read the entire passage carefully and actively.

   - It is important to read the passage carefully before you answer any questions. Start by reading the introductory note above the passage, which will often contain essential information about the date, author, genre and purpose of the passage. As you read, mark up the passage by underlining key ideas, circling names, dates, and figures, and noting confusing passages or unfamiliar terms. Actively reading the passage in this way will help to assure deep comprehension of the main ideas of the passage.

   Write down the main point of the passage *before* you move on to the questions.

   - Most passages have a main point, and writing it down in 5–10 words is a good way to check that you have understood the passage. One way to do this quickly and accurately is to ask write a topic in 3 or 4 words, and then write an action or description of what the author says about the topic in another 5 words or so. This strategy helps most students come up with a main idea that's neither too broad nor so specific or lengthy that it is not helpful.

   - For the literature passage, which is first on the test, write down, in a total of about ten words, the names of the key characters and what is revealed about their personalities or relationships. What you write down for the main point of the passage will almost always be directly useful on at least one of the questions, and knowing it well can help you rule out wrong answers on most questions, even when the question is about a specific detail.

2. R – W 2: **Re-read** and **Write** to **answer each question!**

   Read the question and **find** the answer in the passage by **reading** the relevant lines once more.

   - When you get to the questions, cover up the answer choices and find the answer to each question in the passage for yourself. Then, before you look at the answer choices, *always* **write down** the correct answer you have found. Remember to be literal: just copy over the language of the passage because the correct answer choice is often just a paraphrase of information in the passage.

   - Quite often the question will direct you to a misleading line number. In these lines, you will find the word or phrase that the question refers to, but, in most cases, the answer to the question is *not* in those lines. Read at least one or two sentences before and after the line(s) to which you're directed. In most cases, you'll find the answer to the question. If you can't find the answer, skip the question, bubbling in a placeholder answer and circling the question number so that you can come back to it later.

   - Many questions are based on understanding the intention, tone, etc. of the author. On those questions, you will need to **write** your own *inference* about the answer. Avoid making large inferential leaps: just write down your own explanation of the purpose, tone, etc. in a few basic words. If you cannot determine the answer to the question based on your own reading, just skip it, again circling the question and bubbling a temporary answer.

   - Remember, the answer-choices are there to confuse you. Avoid the temptation to look at the answer choices before you *write down* your own answer.

3   Compare the answer choices to the response you wrote down and choose the answer that best matches the idea you wrote down before looking at the answer choices.

- If you have gone through the first two steps, in many cases the correct answer will jump out at you when you look at the answer choices. If it doesn't, start by crossing out the answers you know are wrong, using both the main point of the passage and your own written answer to the question. If you're down to two answer choices, try to find the *incorrect* one, which will always have at least one or two words that are not indicated by the passage. Once you find the words that make the wrong answer wrong, you can confidently choose the one that's left!

- Remember also that in most cases, the correct answer is the less extreme of the two answer choices, and language of the answer choices is often very general, so don't fixate on how well the specific words of the answers match the answer you wrote at first, but on how the idea of the answer fits with the answer you found.

Time Saving Strategies

Section Management

The five passages on the SAT Reading Test vary greatly in their level of difficulty: many test-takers find one or two of the passages fairly easy, but often one or two passages will be almost prohibitively difficult, and it will take much more time to read these. In order to maximize your score, **focus on passages that you will be able to read quickly and understand thoroughly**. This ensures that you spend your time on the passages that will get you the most points.

Dates of Passages

Every passage on the SAT includes a brief introduction that gives some background information about the passage, its author, and its context. This information *always* includes the date of publication.

Thus far, every SAT released has at least *one* passage that was not written in the last century, and almost all test takers find such passages more difficult and time consuming. Always read the background information, and **simply skip any passage that is from the 1800s or earlier**. Do this passage last.

If you read quickly through the other passages, you will have extra time to read the older passages. And even if you use up most or all of the time reading the other passages, you will have skipped the passage that would have taken longest and would have most likely led to the most errors. So either way, by skipping the hardest passage, you maximize the number of questions you can answer correctly.

Types of Passages

Since every SAT Reading Test is made up of the same types of passages, you can also maximize your score by starting with passage types that are your greatest strengths. If you struggle with fiction, as many students do, don't start with the first passage. Even if it is fairly recent and you enjoy reading literary texts, it still often takes more time, and thus it can be a good passage to save for later or just to skip. The remaining passages are divided between science and history/social science, so you can also play to your strengths in completing these passages. For example, if you find science passages with unfamiliar terms and concepts difficult, you can complete the history/social science passages first. However, if you find political philosophy hard to follow or historical debates somewhat dry, you can start with science passages.

Question Management

Just as you need to choose which passages to focus on in order to maximize your score, so you must effectively manage how you handle specific questions on each passage in order to maximize your reading score.

Skipping

Every question on the SAT reading is worth the same amount; thus, if you cannot find the answer, **skip the question**! Circle the question number and grid in a random placeholder on your answer sheet. After you have answered the rest of the questions on the passage, come back and try the question you skipped once more. You may now know the passage better and be able to answer the question correctly, because the questions create a cohesive "story" of the passage as a whole.

REMEMBER: If you skip quickly, you give yourself time to attempt easier questions that come later in the test. The test tries to trick students into spending the most time on questions that they have the least likelihood of getting correct, so don't fall into that trap! Since each question is worth the same, there is no reason to agonize over a hard question if you have more easy questions yet to answer on the test.

Prioritizing Questions

Many students find it difficult to complete the full section in the allotted time. If you realize that you do not have enough time to read a full passage and answer all the questions, **find these specific question types that are easier to answer** without reading the passage. Here's what to look for:

- If the passage has supplementary materials like a graph or a table, answer questions on these first, as often several can be answered without reference to the passage (see pages 22–23 for more on how to answer this type of question).
- Most passages have 2 words-in-context questions (see pages 18–21 for more on these questions), and these can almost always be answered by reading only one sentence. Further, they always point you directly to the specific line the word appears in, so you don't have to search the whole passage to find the answer!

Most passages have at least a few other questions that refer to specific lines, and so you can also usually answer these fairly quickly. Be sure to read a few lines before and after the specified lines in order to answer the question, because line number references are often misleading if the information is taken out of context.

Final Note: Rereading

If you have daydreamed your way through the passage and get to the end and realize that you have no idea what it was all about, don't worry. This happens often, even to the best of us. However, DON'T give in to the temptation to go on to the questions anyway. The SAT reading requires that you really understand the passage, and so you will be setting yourself up for failure if you try to answer the questions.

Instead, go back and carefully read the first paragraph or two, until you are confident that you can write down the main point of the passage. Then go on to the questions.

Furthermore, the test provides enough time for most test-takers to reread portions of the passage in order to answer the questions. For example, if the question asks about the purpose of the fourth paragraph and you cannot remember it clearly enough just by looking back at it, then take the time to re-familiarize yourself with the material. Focus on the first sentence or two to understand how it relates to the rest of the passage, and then read the rest of the paragraph quickly and **write down** your answer.

Special SAT Reading Strategies

The general strategy outlined in the previous pages is useful for all passages on the SAT Reading Test, but there are three special question types that can be easier to solve if you use the specific strategies outlined on the following pages. Together, these questions account for about half the total questions on the test, and many students struggle more with these questions than any others. Thus, you will want to take the time to recognize these questions and master the strategies that will allow you to answer them correctly.

Command of Evidence Questions

These questions are the hallmark of the SAT, and most passages will have two *pairs* of evidence-based questions. These are recognizable by being in pairs, with the first question asking a difficult detail or interpretive question and the second giving four choices with line numbers referring to different parts of the passage, one of which is the "evidence" needed to solve the initial question.

Words in Context Questions

The SAT does not directly test vocabulary knowledge as it has in the past, so there is less need to spend a lot of time memorizing vocabulary words to prepare for the test. However, the test continues to test vocabulary by asking for the meaning of specific words and phrases—sometimes "hard" words and sometimes abnormal uses of common words—in the context of the passage.

Figure-Based Questions

Another feature of the SAT Reading Test is the inclusion of tables, graphs, and other figures that relate to the content of some of the reading passages. Usually, two of the five passages will include "supplemental materials" like these, and there will be several questions based on either the figure itself or the figure considered in conjunction with the passage.

Command of Evidence Questions

Most reading passages on the SAT will have two sets of paired evidence-based questions. On these pairs of questions, the first asks about the passage in some way—often a very difficult question—and the second asks where the best evidence for the answer to the preceding question appears within the passage.

For example:

1

Picard indicates that the process he describes in the passage

A) protects the traditional and ceremonial usages of threatened landmasses.

B) is rendered obsolete through the use of faster than light travel.

C) violates central tenets of the Federation.

D) dramatizes an insignificant but inevitable outcome of the described events.

2

Which choice provides the best evidence for the answer to the previous question?

A) Lines 12–17 ("Worf … honor.")

B) Lines 17–19 ("It … Vulcans.")

C) Lines 23–24 ("For … ourselves.")

D) Lines 30–34 ("We … travel.")

Note that these questions, although sequential, will not necessarily appear on the same page. Thus, it can be a good idea to mark these questions when you start answering questions on a passage, because many of them are *much* easier to answer if you look at the "evidence" in the second question before answering the first question.

The primary strategy for answering these questions is as follows:

1. Read the first of the two paired questions, and underline the key words in the question.

2. Then, *without looking at the answer choices to the first question*, go to the second question of the pair. Look for the answer to the first question by re-reading the lines indicated in the answer choices from the second question. Choose the lines that most clearly and directly answer the first question.

3. Then go back to the first question and find which answer paraphrases or best fits the information in your chosen lines, and then select that answer choice.

   NOTE: Sometimes, you may find that two or more of the options for the second question in the pair seem to answer the first question, especially if the first question is fairly open-ended or central to the passage as a whole. In order to handle this situation, work carefully to "pair" the answers for the first question with the line references in the second. Only one of the line references from the second question will "fit" with an answer from the first question, so you then can choose both answers together.

Command-of-Evidence Practice Passage

Questions 1–7 are based on the following passage.

The following excerpt is adapted from a speech given by the Fourteenth Dalai Lama upon receiving the Congressional Gold Medal in 2007.

Today we watch China as it rapidly moves forward. Economic liberalization has led to wealth, modernization and great power. I believe that today's economic success of both India and China,
5 the two most populated nations with long histories of rich culture, is most deserving. With their newfound status, both of these two countries are poised to play an important leading role on the world stage. In order to fulfill this role, I believe it
10 is vital for China to have transparency, rule of law and freedom of information. Much of the world is waiting to see how China's concepts of "harmonious society" and "peaceful rise" would unfold. In today's China, a state of many
15 nationalities, a key factor is how it ensures the harmony and unity of its various peoples. For this, the equality and the rights of these nationalities to maintain their distinct identities are crucial.

With respect to my own homeland Tibet, today
20 many people, both from inside and outside, feel deeply concerned about the consequences of the rapid changes taking place. Every year, the Chinese population inside Tibet is increasing at an alarming rate. And, if we are to judge by the example of the
25 population of Lhasa, there is a real danger that the Tibetans will be reduced to an insignificant minority in their own homeland. This rapid increase in population is also posing serious threat to Tibet's fragile environment. Since Tibet is the
30 source of many of Asia's great rivers, any substantial disturbance in Tibet's ecology will impact the lives of hundreds of millions. Furthermore, with Tibet situated between India and China, the peaceful resolution of the Tibet
35 problem also has important implications for lasting peace and friendly relation between these two great neighbors.

1.

According to the Dalai Lama, what does China need to do to maintain unity in its heterogeneous population?

A) Liberalize its economic systems to ensure equal distribution of wealth.

B) Develop greater transparency, maintain the order by fair statutes, and grant freedom of speech and unrestricted access to information.

C) Ensure that all people groups are treated equally and permitted to maintain their individual characteristics.

D) Maintain and promote an understanding of its long history and rich culture.

2

Which choice provides the best evidence for the answer to the previous question?

A) Lines 2–3 ("Economic … power")

B) Lines 3–6 ("I believe … deserving")

C) Lines 9–11 ("I believe … information")

D) Lines 16–18 ("For this … crucial")

3

The primary environmental concern regarding Tibet that the author addresses is

A) the possibility that the Chinese population in Tibet may overtake its Tibetan population.

B) the probable effect upon all of Asia if a growing population in Tibet pollutes its freshwater sources.

C) the likelihood that China will threaten the natural beauty of his peaceful homeland.

D) the scale of possible pollution because Tibet lies between the two most populous nations on the planet.

4

Which choice provides the best evidence for the answer to the previous question?

A) Lines 22–27 ("Every ... homeland")

B) Lines 27–29 ("This ... environment")

C) Lines 29–32 ("Since ... millions")

D) Lines 33–37 ("Furthermore ... neighbors")

5

Although the Chinese government protested the presentation of the Congressional Gold Medal to the Dalai Lama, some political analysts found the speech to be more conciliatory than confrontational towards China. Does the passage support this claim?

A) Yes, lines 3–6 ("I believe ... deserving") suggest that China has earned its prosperity.

B) Yes, lines 22–24 ("Every ... rate") show approval of China's expanding population.

C) No, lines 11–14 ("Much ... unfold") use quotation marks to show ironic indignation at Chinese policies the Dalai Lama sees as oppressive.

D) No, lines 33–37 ("Furthermore ... neighbors") indicate that the speaker considers Tibet more important than China and India.

6

According to the author, the resolution of Tibet's concerns impacts other nations because

A) it can serve as a model for nations with similar issues, so that others can learn from its success.

B) Tibet's location means that its peace will promote amiable relations between China and India.

C) it will bring economic benefits to nations throughout the world once its internal affairs are set in order.

D) the freedom and equality of all people anywhere impact the well being of free and equal people everywhere.

7

Which choice provides the best evidence for the answer to the previous question?

A) Lines 1–3 ("Today ... power")

B) Lines 19–22 ("With respect ... place")

C) Lines 24–27 ("And, if ... homeland")

D) Lines 33–37 ("Furthermore ... neighbors")

Words In Context Questions

Most reading passages on the SAT will have two questions on the meaning of individual words or phrases in context. These questions will ask about hard or obscure vocabulary words, words and phrases with odd or archaic meanings, and words with several possible meanings. To answer them, you must choose the word or phrase that best matches the meaning of the word or phrase as it is used in the passage. The answer will rarely be the most common meaning of the word, especially if it is an everyday word or phrase.

For example, consider the following text passage:

25   No humane being, past the thoughtless age of boyhood, will needlessly murder any creature which holds its life by the same tenure that he does. The hare in its extremity cries like a child.

 1

In line 27, the phrase "by the same tenure" most nearly means

A) in the same occupation.

B) with the same permanence.

C) under the same conditions.

D) for the same length of time.

Here is the strategy to use on these questions:

1. Read the question, but do not read through the answer choices, as recommended in the "R–W" strategy.

2. Go back to the passage and read the entire sentence in which the word appears. You may need to reread a sentence before and/or after the one in which the word appears for additional context. Use this context to determine what the word or phrase means in the context of the sentence.

3. Write down, next to the question, your own synonym for the word or phrase as it is used in the sentence. Don't worry about picking a perfect word or making sure that the part of speech matches, just make sure that you get the meaning of the word from the sentence itself. You should not look at the answer choices until after you have written down an answer.

4. After you have written in your own synonym, look at the answer choices and pick the word that most closely mirrors the word that you wrote. Be sure to cross out incorrect answers as you reject them, but **do not** reject answers simply because you do not know the meaning of the answer choice. Instead, if you eliminate all the answers you know are wrong, you may end up with only one left, or at least you will be able to make a more educated guess.

- If you are left with two possible answers that might fit, read each in place of the word or phrase in the sentence and choose the one that keeps the same meaning and tone for the sentence as a whole.

- If you cannot write in a synonym for the word or phrase because you don't know its meaning and the context does not seem clear enough to you, try to read each answer into the sentence and choose the one that makes the best sense in the context of the passage. However, *only* use this technique if you *cannot* write in your own word, because often an answer choice will make the sentence as a whole make sense but is not a good synonym for the specified word.

Words In Context Practice Passage

Questions 1–19 are based on the following passage.

The following passage is adapted from P.G. Wodehouse's *My Man Jeeves*, published in 1919.

I'm not absolutely certain of my facts, but I rather fancy it's Shakespeare—or, if not, it's some equally brainy lad—who says that it's always just when a chappie is feeling particularly top-hole, and
5 more than usually braced with things in general that Fate sneaks up behind him with a bit of lead piping. There's no doubt the man's right. It's absolutely that way with me. Take, for instance, the fairly rummy matter of Lady Malvern and her son
10 Wilmot. A moment before they turned up, I was just thinking how thoroughly all right everything was.
    It was one of those topping mornings, and I had just climbed out from under the cold shower,
15 feeling like a two-year-old. As a matter of fact, I was especially bucked just then because the day before I had asserted myself with Jeeves— absolutely asserted myself, don't you know. You see, the way things had been going on I was rapidly
20 becoming a dashed serf. The man had jolly well oppressed me. I didn't so much mind when he made me give up one of my new suits, because Jeeves's judgment about suits is sound. But I as near as a toucher rebelled when he wouldn't let me
25 wear a pair of cloth-topped boots which I loved like a couple of brothers. And when he tried to tread on me like a worm in the matter of a hat, I jolly well put my foot down and showed him who was who. It's a long story, and I haven't time to tell you now,
30 but the point is that he wanted me to wear the Longacre—as worn by John Drew—when I had set my heart on the Country Gentleman—as worn by another famous actor chappie—and the end of the matter was that, after a rather painful scene, I
35 bought the Country Gentleman. So that's how things stood on this particular morning, and I was feeling kind of manly and independent.
    Well, I was in the bathroom, wondering what there was going to be for breakfast while I
40 massaged the good old spine with a rough towel and sang slightly, when there was a tap at the door. I stopped singing and opened the door an inch.
    "What ho without there!"
    "Lady Malvern wishes to see you, sir," said
45 Jeeves.

"Eh?"
    "Lady Malvern, sir. She is waiting in the sitting-room."
    "Pull yourself together, Jeeves, my man," I said,
50 rather severely, for I bar practical jokes before breakfast. "You know perfectly well there's no one waiting for me in the sitting-room. How could there be when it's barely ten o'clock yet?"
    "I gathered from her ladyship, sir, that she had
55 landed from an ocean liner at an early hour this morning."
    This made the thing a bit more plausible. I remembered that when I had arrived in America about a year before, the proceedings had begun at
60 some ghastly hour like six, and that I had been shot out on to a foreign shore considerably before eight.
    "Who the deuce is Lady Malvern, Jeeves?"
    "Her ladyship did not confide in me, sir."
    "Is she alone?"
65   "Her ladyship is accompanied by a Lord Pershore, sir. I fancy that his lordship would be her ladyship's son."
    "Oh, well, put out rich raiment of sorts, and I'll be dressing."
70   "Our heather-mixture lounge is in readiness, sir."
    "Then lead me to it."

1

In line 2, the word "fancy" most nearly means

A) decorated.
B) special.
C) imagine.
D) pretend.

2

In line 4, the term "top-hole" most nearly means

A) excellent.
B) overcome.
C) closed.
D) empty.

3

In lines 6–7 the author says "Fate sneaks up behind him with a bit of lead piping" to suggest

A) that one can be murdered at any moment.

B) Fate is a tricky plumber.

C) something bad and unexpected can happen any time.

D) no one can escape the final end of death.

4

In line 13, "topping" is closest in meaning to

A) being immature.

B) very good.

C) uncertain.

D) putting above.

5

In line 16, "bucked" most nearly means

A) blithe.

B) thrown off.

C) tied up.

D) tired.

6

In lines 17 and 18, the word "asserted" is closest in meaning to

A) affirmed the truth about.

B) claimed superiority over.

C) spoken up for.

D) served.

7

In line 27, the word "matter" most nearly means

A) issue.

B) materiality.

C) substance.

D) importance.

8

In lines 31–32, the author uses the phrase "set my heart on" to suggest

A) his romantic feelings.

B) his complete dependence upon a certain outcome.

C) his passion for mundane concerns.

D) his mind was made up.

9

In line 34, the word "painful" most nearly means

A) difficult.

B) damaging.

C) gratuitous.

D) aching.

10

In line 43, the word "without" means

A) lacking.

B) bereft.

C) outside.

D) alone.

11

In line 50, the word "bar" most nearly means

A) clog.

B) fasten.

C) segregate.

D) disallow.

12

In line 54, the term "gathered" most nearly means

A) amassed.
B) grabbed.
C) united.
D) surmised.

13

In line 55, the word "landed" most nearly means

A) arrived.
B) struck.
C) fell.
D) birthed.

14

In line 57, the word "plausible" most nearly means

A) appreciable.
B) believable.
C) able to be molded.
D) clear.

15

In line 60, the word "ghastly" is closest in meaning to

A) like an apparition.
B) frightening.
C) loose.
D) appalling.

16

In context, the phrase "shot out" as it is used in line 60–61 is intended to convey that the narrator was

A) literally fired forth.
B) symbolically darkened.
C) ironically withstood.
D) unceremoniously dropped off.

17

In line 63, the phrase "confide in" most nearly means

A) trust in.
B) reveal to.
C) depend upon.
D) suspect about.

18

In line 68, the word "raiment" means

A) clothing.
B) food.
C) disguise.
D) drizzle.

19

In line 70, the phrase "in readiness" most nearly means

A) located conveniently.
B) dependably constructed.
C) set for use.
D) able to be understood.

Figure-Based Questions

The reading section of the SAT will ordinarily have two passages with "supplemental materials," including graphs, charts and tables. Usually, about five questions are based partly or entirely on those figures. When working with graphs, charts, and tables on the SAT Reading Test, complete the following steps:

1. Focus on the variables listed and the types of data being recorded. Circle or underline the title as well as the axes if the source is a graph or the column headings if it is a table. Pay attention to the scaling on graphs— look out for notes like "in billions" or indications that a graph is drawn not to scale.

2. When reading a question that asks about material on a chart, graph, or table, underline key terms in the question, and find where these terms are represented on the figure. Often, questions will contain multiple **true** answers, only one of which answers the actual question. Underlining key information in the question will help you focus on the details needed to answer the question correctly.

3. After you have read and underlined words in the question, go back to the graph to find the relevant data and circle it.

4. Use the answer choices to eliminate wrong answers. You may need to refer to the text of the passage as well as the figure itself to answer some of these questions, so reread relevant portions of the passage, if needed.

   - Be careful about language involving percentages. A larger percent does not necessarily mean a larger number if they are not drawn from the same total!

Try It!

Table 1

Nebula Class	% Deuterium atoms	% Helium atoms
1	1.7	4.8
2	2.8	3.9
3	3.2	3.3
4	4.0	3.2

1

Based on the data in Table 1, which choice best represents the difference in the percentage of deuterium atoms and helium atoms in a Class 2 Nebula?

A) 0.1%

B) 1.1%

C) 1.2%

D) 3.1%

Figure-Based Questions Practice Set

Answer questions 1–3 based on the table and passage excerpt below.

Tibetan regions population in China in 2000	Total Population (in millions)	Chinese Population (in thousands)	Tibetan Population (in thousands)
Tibet Autonomous Region (TAR)	2.62	157	2,427
All Tibetan Regions	13.5	7,500	6,000

The following excerpt is adapted from a speech given by the Fourteenth Dalai Lama upon receiving the Congressional Gold Medal in 2007.

With respect to my own homeland Tibet, today
20 many people, both from inside and outside, feel
deeply concerned about the consequences of the
rapid changes taking place. Every year, the Chinese
population inside Tibet is increasing at an alarming
rate. And, if we are to judge by the example of the
25 population of Lhasa, there is a real danger that the
Tibetans will be reduced to an insignificant
minority in their own homeland. This rapid
increase in population is also posing serious threat
to Tibet's fragile environment. Since Tibet is the
30 source of many of Asia's great rivers, any
substantial disturbance in Tibet's ecology will
impact the lives of hundreds of millions.
Furthermore, with Tibet situated between India
and China, the peaceful resolution of the Tibet
35 problem also has important implications for lasting
peace and friendly relation between these two great
neighbors.

1

In lines 23-24, the speaker claims that by 2007 the population of Chinese settlers within the TAR is increasing "at an alarming rate." Based on the data above, what must be true about the population of the TAR at the time of the speech?

A) The Chinese population in the region was over 157,000,000.

B) The Tibetan population was less than 2,000,000 in the TAR.

C) There were more than 157,000 Chinese people in the TAR.

D) The Chinese population was more than 7.5 million in all Tibetan regions.

2

According to the data in the table, approximately what percent of the total Tibetan population is in the TAR?

A) 20%

B) 30%

C) 40%

D) 60%

3

Based on the passage and the data in the table, which of the following must be true?

A) In 2000, there were more than 157,000 Chinese people living in the TAR.

B) The total population in all Tibetan regions was less than 13.5 million by 2007.

C) The Chinese population in all Tibetan regions accounted for more than half of the total population in 2007.

D) The Tibetan population in the TAR was less than 2 million in 2007.

Sample Reading Passages

Social Science

Questions 1–11 are based on the following passage.

This passage is adapted from a speech delivered by First Lady Hillary Rodham Clinton on September 5, 1995, to the United Nations 4th World Conference on Women, held in Beijing, China.

If there is one message that echoes forth from this conference, let it be that human rights are women's rights and women's rights are human rights once and for all. Let us not forget that among
5 those rights are the right to speak freely and the right to be heard.

Women must enjoy the rights to participate fully in the social and political lives of their countries, if we want freedom and democracy to thrive and
10 endure. It is indefensible that many women in nongovernmental organizations who wished to participate in this conference have not been able to attend or have been prohibited from fully taking part.

15 Let me be clear. Freedom means the right of people to assemble, organize, and debate openly. It means respecting the views of those who may disagree with the views of their governments. It means not taking citizens away from their loved
20 ones and jailing them, mistreating them, or denying them their freedom or dignity because of the peaceful expression of their ideas and opinions.

In my country, we recently celebrated the 75th anniversary of Women's Suffrage. It took 150 years
25 after the signing of our Declaration of Independence for women to win the right to vote. It took 72 years of organized struggle, before that happened, on the part of many courageous women and men. It was one of America's most divisive
30 philosophical wars. But it was a bloodless war. Suffrage was achieved without a shot being fired.

But we have also been reminded, in V-J Day[1] observances last weekend, of the good that comes when men and women join together to combat the
35 forces of tyranny and to build a better world. We

have seen peace prevail in most places for a half century. We have avoided another world war. But we have not solved older, deeply-rooted problems that continue to diminish the potential of half the
40 world's population.

Now it is the time to act on behalf of women everywhere. If we take bold steps to better the lives of women, we will be taking bold steps to better the lives of children and families too. Families rely on
45 mothers and wives for emotional support and care. Families rely on women for labor in the home. And increasingly, everywhere, families rely on women for income needed to raise healthy children and care for other relatives.

50 As long as discrimination and inequities remain so commonplace everywhere in the world, as long as girls and women are valued less, fed less, fed last, overworked, underpaid, not schooled, [and] subjected to violence in and outside their homes,
55 the potential of the human family to create a peaceful, prosperous world will not be realized.

Let this conference be our and the world's call to action. Let us heed that call so we can create a world in which every woman is treated with respect
60 and dignity, every boy and girl is loved and cared for equally, and every family has the hope of a strong and stable future. That is the work before you. That is the work before all of us who have a vision of the world we want to see for our children
65 and our grandchildren.

The time is now. We must move beyond rhetoric. We must move beyond recognition of problems to working together, to have the common efforts to build that common ground we hope to
70 see.

---

[1] V-J day refers to "Victory over Japan Day," the anniversary of the day in which Japan surrendered, in effect ending World War II.

1

It can reasonably be inferred from the passage that at the time it was written, the problem of women's inequality

A) had been and continued to be a significant issue in the United States and the world due to denial of equal rights and discrimination.

B) was of significant importance only from a historical perspective, because women had achieved suffrage, so that inequality was no longer a pressing concern.

C) was on the rise due to complex social and genetic factors that were not then fully understood, but had led to systematic prejudice.

D) would likely be solved through the specific steps delineated in the passage, which would be enacted gradually to create meaningful change.

2

The author most likely repeats the phrase "it means" in the third paragraph in order to

A) clarify the limits of the scope of her definition of the term "freedom."

B) convey with increasing intensity the importance of maintaining a free society.

C) provide a list of rights included in freedom as well as behaviors that are prohibited where freedom thrives and endures.

D) reference violations of freedom committed on specific occasions by other countries.

3

In line 36, the term "prevail" most nearly means

A) influence.

B) persuade.

C) defeat.

D) persist.

4

Which of the following would be most in conflict with the author's description of the concept of freedom (lines 15–22)?

A) Sentencing convicted criminals to the death penalty

B) Jailing citizens based on their violent expression of ideas and opinions

C) Penalizing citizens for holding certain dangerous and antisocial viewpoints

D) Allowing people to organize and assemble for open debates

5

The author references "Women's Suffrage" (line 24) in the United States in order to

A) compare an event in American history with the current situation in another country to show how that country's women can succeed.

B) provide a concrete example of one result of the fight for women's equality and emphasize the significance of this right for women.

C) demonstrate that women are capable of fighting bloodless battles because of their more emotional and compassionate demeanors.

D) illustrate one specific technique that can be used to nurture equality in both authoritarian and democratic nations.

6

In this passage, the author advocates most directly for

A) bold, collaborative reform.

B) courageous decisions on an individual level.

C) consistent but gradual policy changes.

D) working to change men's view of gender.

7

Which choice provides the best evidence for the answer to the previous question?

A) Lines 1–4 ("If there … for all") and lines 37–40 ("But we … world's population")

B) Lines 7–10 ("Women must … and endure") and lines 30–31 ("But it … being fired")

C) Lines 46–49 ("And increasingly … other relatives") and lines 50–56 ("As long … be realized")

D) Lines 42–44 ("If we … families too") and lines 66–70 ("The time … to see")

8

The primary rhetorical effect of the list provided in lines 52–54 ("valued less … their homes") is to

A) exemplify the consequences of inequality on women from least significant to most significant in determining quality of life.

B) explain the nuances of gender inequality and encourage careful and deliberate debate on the status of impoverished men and women.

C) illustrate a multitude of effects of inequality on women to demonstrate the importance of solving such inequality.

D) compare and contrast these conditions to those of women in the United States prior to Women's Suffrage and implicitly support suffrage.

9

Based on the passage, which choice best reflects the relationship between women's equality and the cause of liberty throughout the world?

A) The first is substantially more important than the second.

B) Advancements in the first may negatively impact the second but still must be attained.

C) Advancements in the first are necessary to ensure attainment of the second.

D) Neither is likely to be achieved in the near future.

10

Which choice provides the best evidence for the answer to the previous question?

A) lines 7–10 ("Women must … endure")

B) lines 24–31 ("It took … fired")

C) lines 32–37 ("But we … world war")

D) lines 57–62 ("Let us … future")

11

The author's use of the word "rhetoric" in line 67 most nearly means

A) persuasive language.

B) making a point without expecting or desiring a response.

C) words without action.

D) working together.

Science Passage

Questions 12–22 are based on the following passage and supplemental material.

This passage is adapted from Brittany Linkous' "Misconceptions and the Spread of Infectious Disease," published by the Federation of American Scientists Public Interest Reports in 2014.

New and improved medical treatments for infectious diseases are vital to improving global health security; however, public education is equally important. Myths and misperceptions
5 regarding infectious diseases have detrimental effects on global health when a disease outbreak occurs. While it may seem that this problem is isolated to remote regions of the developing world, neither infectious diseases nor misconceptions
10 regarding them are explicitly confined to certain areas.

Outbreaks can be highly disruptive to the movement of people and goods, often leading to increased regulations and restrictions on travel and
15 trade to reduce the potential for further spread of disease. The Severe Acute Respiratory Syndrome (SARS) epidemic in 2003 was but one of the numerous examples in which international travel was disrupted. The disease quickly infected
20 thousands of people around the world and disrupted national economies. Due to the rapid transmissibility of SARS, the World Health Organization (WHO) issued a travel advisory in effort to reduce the international public threat. In
25 2001, the United Kingdom experienced a detrimental hit to the agricultural sector as foot-and-mouth disease spread throughout livestock. Because of the highly transmissible nature of the disease (which affected cattle, pigs,
30 sheep, and goats), the government banned all exports of live animals, meat, and dairy products. Later that same year, the tourist industry estimated that businesses lost nearly $421 million U.S. dollars.

35   In the developing world, pneumonia, diarrhea, malaria, measles, and HIV/AIDS are some of the primary causes of death, especially among children. This is in part attributable to socioeconomic factors that prevent people from
40 having access to routine health services and immunizations. Poor nutrition and unsanitary living conditions also place people at risk. Among children in Africa, the death rate from measles, a viral respiratory disease, has reached an average
45 rate of one per minute. Yet, in the developed regions of the world, measles is commonly treated through immunizations.

Tetanus, an infection caused by the bacteria *Clostridium tetani* (which is ubiquitous in the
50 soil), is common in developing areas where unsanitary medical techniques such as use of contaminated medical bandages continue. Although proper sanitary resources are often scarce in these regions, lack of supplies is not
55 the only cause of disease transmission as proper sanitation techniques could have mitigated transmission. Due to the lack of education about public health, sanitation, and the mechanisms of disease transmission, the spread of infectious
60 diseases like tetanus continues.

Despite modern medical advances and technology, developed countries are also susceptible to infectious disease outbreaks. These outbreaks have been due in part to the
65 misconceptions about vaccines and anti-bacterial drugs that have been used to deter the spread of infectious diseases. Some individuals have the perception that antibiotics are a "cure-all," but this view has led to people taking antibiotics when they
70 are not needed. This overuse has allowed the emergence of antibiotic-resistant strains of bacteria. Vaccines are also misunderstood: this was evident in the recent reemergence of pertussis, also known as "Whooping Cough," in the mid-1970s
75 when Great Britain, Sweden and Japan reduced their usage of the pertussis vaccine due to a common fear of vaccinations. The effect was immediate and drastic—there were over 100,000 cases in Great Britain, 13,000 cases in Japan, and
80 3,200 cases in Sweden. The United States witnessed a similar outbreak in the northwest region of the country in 2012, when over 17,000 cases emerged shortly after an increased rate of vaccine refusals for pertussis. While no vaccine is
85 100% effective, it is evident that popular misconceptions regarding infectious diseases and their spread can have detrimental repercussions on the populace and need to be addressed head-on.

Education, early detection, and access to
90 vaccines are all essential in containing and

preventing the spread of disease in a globalized society. Although myths and misconceptions have hindered their effectiveness, vaccinations can drastically reduce the chances of contracting many
95 diseases. Additionally, developing and utilizing programs that educate the public regarding the implications of infectious diseases and treatments

pertaining to them will significantly reduce the spread of disease. While making better medical
100 practices and medicines available will help to combat the transmission of infectious diseases, there is no substitute for better public health education.

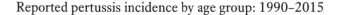

Reported pertussis incidence by age group: 1990–2015

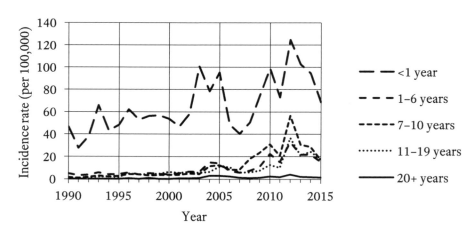

Adapted from the Centers for Disease Control and Prevention Website

---

12

The main purpose of the article is to

A) offer a comprehensive survey of infectious diseases through history and across the world.

B) inform readers of the importance of understanding the nature of infectious diseases and how to treat them.

C) persuade readers that vaccines and antibiotics are the best solution to all global public health issues.

D) dissuade readers from believing that infectious diseases are only a problem in developed countries.

13

As it is used in line 26, "detrimental" most nearly means

A) fiduciary.

B) complementary.

C) fatal.

D) harmful.

14

The author mentions the 2001 outbreak of foot-and-mouth disease in the UK as an example of

A) the kinds of problems created by people misunderstanding infectious diseases.

B) the ways in which economic factors can affect the spread of infectious diseases.

C) the impact that infectious diseases can have on global economies and trade.

D) mistaken ideas about responding to outbreaks of infections.

15

Which choice offers the best evidence for the answer to the preceding question?

A) Lines 4–7 ("Myths ... occurs")

B) Lines 7–11 ("While ... areas")

C) Lines 12–16 ("Outbreaks ... disease")

D) Lines 21–24 ("Due ... threat")

16

As it is used in line 49, the word "ubiquitous" most nearly means

A) pervasive.

B) constant.

C) located.

D) global.

17

The author claims that one side effect of the overuse of anti-bacterial drugs is that

A) outbreaks of pertussis have become more widespread.

B) more developed countries are now more susceptible to diseases than in the past.

C) some bacteria have begun to develop resistance to antibiotics.

D) children's natural resistance to strains of bacteria has weakened.

18

Which choice offers the best evidence for the answer to the preceding question?

A) Lines 53–60 ("Although … continues")

B) Lines 63–67 ("These outbreaks … diseases")

C) Lines 67–70 ("Some … needed")

D) Lines 70–72 ("This overuse … bacteria")

19

The author mentions that "no vaccine is 100% effective" (lines 84–85) primarily to

A) warn parents against using vaccines to prevent disease in their children.

B) clarify the risks associated with over-vaccinated populations.

C) qualify the strength of a recommended solution to the spread of infectious diseases.

D) question the wisdom of the widespread acceptance of vaccination as an aspect of public health policy.

20

The graph reveals that pertussis cases in the United States

A) are almost all in those less than 1 year old.

B) were nearly eliminated in 1990 but have gradually grown to the level of an epidemic.

C) are more common among infants than adults.

D) are due to the failure of vaccines to protect public health.

21

The graph offers support for the information in the passage in that

A) the incidence of cases of whooping cough spikes in 2012.

B) both reveal an inverse relationship between the number of people vaccinated and the number of pertussis cases.

C) 2007 marks a 10-year low for the incidence of pertussis among those younger than 1.

D) the outbreak of SARS in 2003 is clear in an increased incidence for all age groups.

22

Based on the argument in the passage and the information in the graph, the author would be most likely to investigate which of the following hypotheses about pertussis?

A) Was there a decrease in pertussis vaccinations between 2002 and 2005?

B) Were anti-bacterial drugs overused to treat pertussis in 1993?

C) Are adults less likely to develop pertussis than infants?

D) Are people from different parts of the United States more or less likely to develop pertussis based on their local climate?

Literature

Questions 23–32 are based on the following passage.

The following is from the novel *The Beautiful and the Damned* by F. Scott Fitzgerald, published in 1922.

Fifth and Sixth Avenues, it seemed to Anthony, were the uprights of a gigantic ladder stretching from Washington Square to Central Park. Coming up-town on top of a bus toward Fifty-second Street
5 invariably gave him the sensation of hoisting himself hand by hand on a series of treacherous rungs, and when the bus jolted to a stop at his own rung he found something akin to relief as he descended the reckless metal steps to the sidewalk.
10 After that, he had but to walk down Fifty-second Street half a block, pass a stodgy family of brownstone houses—and then in a jiffy he was under the high ceilings of his great front room. This was entirely satisfactory. Here, after all, life
15 began. Here he slept, breakfasted, read, and entertained.

The house itself was of murky material, built in the late nineties; in response to the steadily growing need of small apartments each floor had
20 been thoroughly remodeled and rented individually. Of the four apartments Anthony's, on the second floor, was the most desirable.

The front room had fine high ceilings and three large windows that loomed down pleasantly upon
25 Fifty-second Street. In its appointments it escaped by a safe margin being of any particular period; it escaped stiffness, stuffiness, bareness, and decadence. It smelt neither of smoke nor of incense—it was tall and faintly blue. There was a
30 deep lounge of the softest brown leather with somnolence drifting about it like a haze. There was a high screen of Chinese lacquer chiefly concerned with geometrical fishermen and huntsmen in black and gold; this made a corner alcove for a
35 voluminous chair guarded by an orange-colored standing lamp. Deep in the fireplace a quartered shield was burned to a murky black.

Passing through the dining-room, which, as Anthony took only breakfast at home, was merely a
40 magnificent potentiality, and down a comparatively long hall, one came to the heart and core of the apartment—Anthony's bedroom and bath.

Both of them were immense. Under the ceilings of the former even the great canopied bed seemed
45 of only average size. On the floor an exotic rug of crimson velvet was soft as fleece on his bare feet. His bathroom, in contrast to the rather portentous character of his bedroom, was gay, bright, extremely habitable and even faintly facetious.
50 Framed around the walls were photographs of four celebrated thespian beauties of the day: Julia Sanderson as "The Sunshine Girl," Ina Claire as "The Quaker Girl," Billie Burke as "The Mind-the-Paint Girl," and Hazel Dawn as "The Pink Lady."
55 Between Billie Burke and Hazel Dawn hung a print representing a great stretch of snow presided over by a cold and formidable sun—this, claimed Anthony, symbolized the cold shower.

The bathtub, equipped with an ingenious
60 bookholder, was low and large. Beside it a wall wardrobe bulged with sufficient linen for three men and with a generation of neckties. There was no skimpy glorified towel of a carpet—instead, a rich rug, like the one in his bedroom a miracle of
65 softness, that seemed almost to massage the wet foot emerging from the tub....

All in all a room to conjure with—it was easy to see that Anthony dressed there, arranged his immaculate hair there, in fact did everything but
70 sleep and eat there. It was his pride, this bathroom.

23

Throughout the passage, the author's style is best described as

A) psychologically complex.

B) curtly pragmatic.

C) blissfully oblivious.

D) lavishly descriptive.

24

The author refers to "his own rung" in lines 7–8 to indicate

A) the means by which Anthony climbs down from the bus.

B) the stop closest to Anthony's apartment.

C) Anthony's sense of possession of the bus route.

D) the feeling that resonates within Anthony as he rides the bus.

25

As it is used in line 25, the word "escaped" most nearly means

A) absconded.

B) avoided.

C) departed.

D) emerged.

26

As it is used in line 31, the word "somnolence" most nearly means

A) bewilderment.

B) tiresomeness.

C) seriousness.

D) leisure.

27

The passage's description of his apartment suggests that Anthony is

A) fastidious about his appearance and refined in his tastes.

B) defined entirely by his love of possessions.

C) shrewd in buying only the very best furnishings.

D) lonely, feeling incomplete because he has no one to love.

28

The narrator says Anthony's apartment is where his "life began" (lines 14–15) because

A) he always desired to stay there, uncomfortable leaving the safe and cozy space it provided.

B) it was where he took his morning meal, hosted guests, slept at nights, and more.

C) it sustains him and provides him with all he needs, acting as a surrogate parent.

D) it is an allegory for his life, with each room presenting a different aspect of his existence.

29

Which choice provides the best evidence for the answer to the previous question?

A) Lines 15–16 ("Here … entertained")

B) Lines 18–22 ("in response … desirable")

C) Lines 55–58 ("Between … shower")

D) Lines 67–70 ("All in … there")

30

The description of the pictures on the wall of Anthony's bathroom (lines 50–58) serve primarily to

A) exemplify the lighter atmosphere of the bathroom relative to the bedroom.

B) mock the pedestrian tastes of the day.

C) clarify the attributes Anthony finds attractive in women.

D) contradict Anthony's view of himself.

31

Based on the passage as a whole, the most important part of the apartment to Anthony is

A) the bathtub, because he loves to read his favorite books while soaking in the tub.

B) the front room, which allows him to impress guests with his Chinese art and decadent furniture.

C) the bathroom, which he sees as almost magical in nature.

D) the bedroom, due to both its size and its comfortable bed.

32

Which choice provides the best evidence for the answer to the previous question?

A) Lines 29–36 ("There … lamp")

B) Lines 43–45 ("Both … size")

C) Lines 59–62 ("The bathtub … neckties")

D) Lines 67–70 ("All … bathroom")

Challenge Passage

Questions 33–44 are based on the following passage.

This passage is adapted from a speech regarding the United States Constitution given by Benjamin Franklin at the 1787 Constitutional Convention.

Mr. President:

I confess that there are several parts of this constitution which I do not at present approve, but I am not sure I shall ever approve them; for having
5 lived long, I have experienced many instances of being obliged by better information, or fuller consideration, to change opinions even on important subjects, which I once thought right, but found to be otherwise. It is therefore that the older
10 I grow, the more apt I am to doubt my own judgment, and to pay more respect to the judgment of others.

Most men indeed as well as most sects in religion, think themselves in possession of all truth,
15 and that wherever others differ from them it is so far error. Steele, a Protestant, in a Dedication, tells the Pope, that the only difference between our Churches in their opinions of the certainty of their doctrines is, the Church of Rome is infallible and
20 the Church of England is *never in the wrong*. But though many private persons think almost as highly of their own infallibility as of that of their sect, few express it so naturally as a certain French lady, who in a dispute with her sister, said "I don't know how
25 it happens, Sister, but I meet with nobody but myself, that's always in the right." "Je ne trouve que moi qui aie toujours raison."

In these sentiments, Sir, I agree to this Constitution with all its faults, if they are such;
30 because I think a general Government necessary for us, and there is no form of Government but what may be a blessing to the people if well administered, and believe farther that this is likely to be well administered for a course of years, and
35 can only end in Despotism, as other forms have done before it, when the people shall become so corrupted as to need despotic Government, being incapable of any other.

I doubt too whether any other Convention we
40 can obtain may be able to make a better Constitution. For when you assemble a number of men to have the advantage of their joint wisdom, you inevitably assemble with those men, all their prejudices, their passions, their errors of opinion,
45 their local interests, and their selfish views. From such an assembly can a *perfect* production be expected? It therefore astonishes me, Sir, to find this system approaching so near to perfection as it does; and I think it will astonish our enemies, who
50 are waiting with confidence to hear that our councils are confounded like those of the Builders of Babel;[2] and that our States are on the point of separation, only to meet hereafter for the purpose of cutting one another's throats.
55 Thus I consent, Sir, to this Constitution because I expect no better, and because I am not sure that it is not the best. The opinions I have had of its *errors*, I sacrifice to the public good. I have never whispered a syllable of them abroad. Within these
60 walls they were born, and here they shall die. If every one of us in returning to our Constituents were to report the objections he has had to it, and endeavor to gain partisans in support of them, we might prevent its being generally received, and
65 thereby lose all the salutary effects and great advantages resulting naturally in our favor among foreign Nations as well as among ourselves, from our real or apparent unanimity.

Much of the strength and efficiency of any
70 Government in procuring and securing happiness to the people depends on *opinion*, on the general opinion of the goodness of the Government, as well as of the wisdom and integrity of its Governors. I hope therefore that for our own sakes as a part of
75 the people, and for the sake of posterity, we shall act heartily and unanimously in recommending this Constitution (if approved by Congress and confirmed by the Conventions) wherever our influence may extend, and turn our future thoughts
80 and endeavors to the means of having it *well* administered.

On the whole, Sir, I can not help expressing a wish that every member of the Convention who may still have objections to it would, with me, on
85 this occasion doubt a little of his own infallibility and, to make *manifest our unanimity*, put his name to this instrument.

---

[2] This refers to the biblical story of the failed attempt to build a tower to reach heaven.

33

Based on the passage, how does the author most nearly view the Constitution?

A) It must be revised before it is to take effect so that it will adequately provide the necessary tools for governing the state.

B) Although it would not likely gain approval from the King, it has garnered unanimous support among members of the Constitutional Convention.

C) While perhaps flawed in some ways, its ratification remains a necessary step in providing for the establishment of a unified government.

D) Its remaining flaws are insignificant in themselves, but its passage is undesirable because it will inevitably lead to despotism.

34

Which choice provides the best evidence for the answer to the previous question?

A) Lines 28–38 ("In these … any other")

B) Lines 41–45 ("For when … selfish views")

C) Lines 60–68 ("If every one … unanimity")

D) Lines 82–87 ("On the whole … this instrument")

35

The overall tone of this passage is best described as

A) persuasive.

B) scholarly.

C) zealous.

D) disappointed.

36

In lines 4–12 ("for having … of others"), the author suggests that aging

A) is an unfortunate but necessary and inevitable aspect of life for himself and others.

B) has made him willing to change his opinions over time due to the increased access to new and different information.

C) provides him with a wealth of knowledge and experience that cannot be accumulated in any other way.

D) leads to individuals strengthening their opinions over time except when they are presented with new information.

37

According to the author, the Church of Rome and the Church of England are

A) essentially identical in theology.

B) highly differentiated in their treatment of certainty.

C) both bureaucratic and hierarchical.

D) ironically similar in their notions of infallibility.

38

The primary rhetorical effect of the French lady's quote in lines 24–27 ("I don't know … raison") is

A) to contradict the idea that the doctrines of infallibility held by the listed churches are fundamentally the same.

B) to emphasize the importance of the issue of infallibility in sects both religious and secular.

C) to highlight Benjamin Franklin's skills and expertise developed through his involvement in international affairs.

D) to extend the issue of infallibility beyond churches and other organized groups to private individuals.

39

In line 35, "Despotism" most nearly means

A) monarchy.

B) chaos.

C) tyranny.

D) leadership.

40

The intended effect of the question in lines 45–47 ("From such … expected?") is

A) rhetorical, in order to suggest a clearly negative answer.

B) dramatic, in order to reveal the author's unexpected answer.

C) inquisitive, in order to open the audience to new line of consideration.

D) uncertainty, to show the author's genuine pursuit of the unknown.

41

Which of the following would be most in conflict with the author's views based on lines 47–60 ("It therefore … they shall die")?

A) Because the constitution provides for a new and different form of government, other countries anticipate its failure.

B) The Constitution's flaws should be debated locally and globally so that the best possible version can be passed.

C) Different states hold various and contradictory interests, causing tension in the Convention.

D) While not flawless, the Constitution is the best possible governing document in the current situation.

42

In line 63, "partisans" most nearly means

A) divisive government leaders.

B) anarchists against the unity of the state.

C) zealots for personal ideals.

D) followers of a particular view or faction.

43

In lines 60–87 ("If every one … this instrument") the author focuses on unanimity primarily because

A) individual doubts are irrelevant in any collective decision.

B) the members need to be united in accepting the constitution in order to begin the task of successfully governing.

C) allowing multiple opinions undermines unity and eliminates the possibility of successful rule.

D) it will extend America's influence and improve reputation throughout Europe and the world at large.

44

Which choice provides the best evidence for the answer to the previous question?

A) Lines 60–63 ("If every one … of them")

B) Lines 69–73 ("Much of the … Governors")

C) Lines 73–81 ("I hope … administered")

D) Lines 83–85 ("every member … own infallibility")

Writing and Language Test Manual

The SAT Writing and Language Test is composed of four passages with 44 questions of two types:

Expression of Ideas questions test your understanding of basic rhetorical and compositional elements based on your comprehension of the reading material.

Standard English Conventions questions test your knowledge of specific grammar and usage rules.

Overview and Strategy

Each passage on the SAT has 11 questions of two different types: Expression of Ideas (6) and Standard English Conventions (5). The two types require different approaches, so it is important to recognize them.

Expression of Ideas (EOI)

These questions assess your **rhetorical, compositional,** and **organizational skills**. These questions can be answered by using contextual clues within the passage, and the correct answer must be chosen based on either the **meaning** of the words or **principles** of effective composition: they are *not* based on grammar rules.

Standard English Conventions (SEC)

These questions test your knowledge of **standard grammatical conventions**, such as the accepted rules for punctuation, sentence structure, word usage, idioms, subject-verb agreement and more. Most questions feature an underlined portion of a passage that can range from one word to an entire sentence. You must decide whether to keep the underlined part as it is or to choose one of three possible revisions, based on which best conforms to the academic standards for written English.

Strategy

1. READ!
   1.1. READ the entire passage as you answer questions rather than skipping from one underlined section to the next. Especially for EOI questions, having the entire context of the passage is **essential**.
   1.2. READ at least to the end of the sentence of the underlined section before answering any question. Often, even on grammar questions, an answer can seem to be correct when you first read it, but something *after* the underlined portion makes it an error.
2. IDENTIFY what is being tested on each question.
   2.1. Identify the question as EOI or SEC: if there is a specific question before the answer choices, it is an EOI question, and you need to follow the directions in the question, using the strategies in the following pages. If there is no question, go to 2.2.
   2.2. Specify the exact rule or principle, such as comma usage or redundancy.
   2.3. For every question on which you are not sure what is being tested, circle the question in the test booklet and return to it when you have finished the rest of the passage.
3. MARK directly on the test booklet to ELIMINATE answer choices.
   3.1. Cross out what makes each wrong answer incorrect, so that you are specifically attending to the small differences between answers.
   3.2. If there are two elements being tested on a question—such as apostrophe use and verb form—deal with each error one at a time, starting with the one you know better.
4. When in doubt, READ IT OUT.
   4.1. If you are stuck between two answer choices, read the entire sentence in your head and choose the one that "sounds" better.
   4.2. Many students use this method as their primary approach to this section, but it will lead to many errors on questions you could otherwise get correct, so *only* use this strategy if you are stuck!

Writing and Language Strategy Flow Chart

Refer to this flow chart to help you navigate the questions on the SAT Writing and Language Test

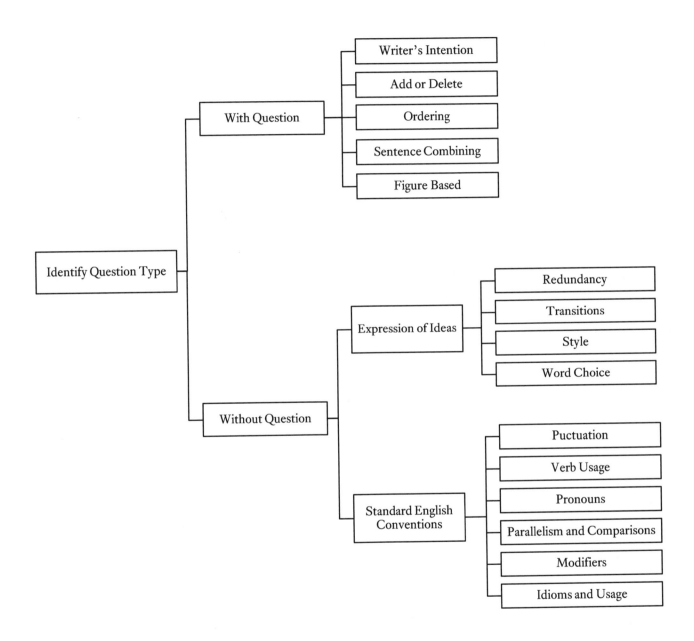

Expression of Ideas

The SAT Writing and Language Test offers more contextual, reading-based questions—called "Expression of Ideas" on the test—than rule-based grammar questions. Thus, it is essential to read the whole passage carefully in order to have a clear sense of the content, style, and purpose of the passage as you read it. There are a few types of Expression of Ideas questions that you will want to familiarize yourself with, all of which will be covered in depth in the following pages:

"Questions" Without Questions   These questions look just like grammar-based questions, so the trick is to recognize them!

Writer's Intention Questions   These questions ask which choice best accomplishes some specific purpose that the writer wants to accomplish.

Add/Delete Questions   These questions ask whether to take out an underlined section or add a phrase or sentence, usually with two "yes" options and two "no" options, each with different reasons.

Ordering Questions   These questions require you to put a sentence in the correct place in a paragraph or to put a paragraph in the correct place in the passage as a whole.

Sentence Combining Questions   These questions ask you to combine two separate sentences into one clearer and more concise sentence.

Figure-Based Questions   These questions ask about figures included with the passage, usually in connection with what is written in the passage.

"Questions" Without Questions

The standard format for questions on the SAT Writing and Language Test actually has no question: it simply lists four options for an underlined part of the passage. Nearly all Standard English Conventions—grammar-based—questions are in this format; however, some Expression of Ideas questions also use the same format.

Here is a strategy for these questions:

1. When you come across a question without a specific question, you *must* first determine whether it is a Standard English Conventions (grammar) or Expression of Ideas (context) question. One key to differentiate between the two question types is that *all the answer options for Expression of Ideas questions will be grammatically correct.* These questions only test your rhetorical skills and contextual understanding of the passage and do not ask you to correct grammatical errors.

2. Once you have identified the question as an Expression of Ideas question, identify the exact principle being tested by the question. There are four main concepts tested by questions without questions: style, redundancy, transitions, and word choice. Knowing these types can help you to recognize them!

Style

Style questions ask you to evaluate the style of a certain phrase in the context of the passage. Is the phrasing too technical? Colloquial? Awkwardly worded? Too wordy? Try to understand the tone of the passage and then determine which of the choices provided best fits with the tone of the rest of the passage. Don't be tempted by answers merely due to difficult words—if the style is less formal, then long, difficult words are not in keeping with the style of the passage!

Style—Try It!

Though many may disagree, the movement toward greater transparency in the war on terror is gathering momentum.

1

A) NO CHANGE
B) is really picking up speed as it heads into the last turn.
C) seems unequivocally to be resistant to gravitational and frictional forces limiting its acceleration.
D) is running wild and kicking it into high gear.

Redundancy

Redundancy questions ask you to consider what details are repetitive in an underlined section. You can often recognize these questions by noticing that some answer choices include content that others cut out. Eliminate answer choices that are internally redundant or include information contained elsewhere in the sentence or the paragraph. *Sometimes, the information that makes what is underlined redundant comes **after** the underlined portion, so be sure to read at least to the end of the sentence before choosing.* The right answer will be the most concise answer that still contains all relevant information.

Redundancy — Try It!

Without a doubt, the meat industry 2 of the future will undoubtedly be unable to maintain its current practices in the coming years.

2

A) NO CHANGE
B) of the next generation will not certainly be able
C) will not be able
D) will not be able, in the future,

Transitions

Transition questions require you to choose a single word or phrase that most effectively connects two parts of a single sentence, clarifies the movement from the end of one sentence to the beginning of the next, or leads the reader from the close of an earlier paragraph to the start of a new one. Be careful to differentiate these questions from those testing sentence structure: if all the answer choices are grammatically the same, you need to consider the meaning of the words to choose the correct answer. These transitions signal the trajectory of the paragraph or sentence, so consider the relationship between the sentences or paragraphs they connect in order to answer these questions correctly. Ask yourself:

- Do the two parts create a contrast?
- Does the second offer more evidence for the same idea as the first?
- Does the second part offer the next step in a process?

Once you know the relationship, choosing the best word is usually quite simple!

Transitions — Try It!

According to Hans Gruber writing in *Rocking Roll*, if Ian Anderson, a singularly talented flutist and vocalist, had not lost his range and tone, he would have continued his meteoric rise to the heavens of rock and roll. 3 Indeed, many fans believe that his unique combination of raw musical talent and showmanship would have led to stardom greater than that achieved by any other human being.

3

A) NO CHANGE
B) Surprisingly,
C) Therefore,
D) However,

Word Choice

Word choice questions can be based on grammar or context, so distinguishing between the two is crucial. Standard English Conventions word choice questions test your knowledge of the correct usage of a word pair such as **affect** vs. **effect** (See "Idioms and Usage" on page 108 under SEC). In contrast, Expression of Ideas word choice questions are all grammatically correct and test your knowledge of the contextual appropriateness of a word. In order to solve these questions, read the whole sentence and choose the answer that is most logical and suited to the point being made in the sentence. If you are not sure of the exact meaning of some of the word choices, start with those you know, and eliminate all those that don't work. If one of the words you *do* know works in the sentence, choose it rather than an unknown word; if none of the words you know suit the sentence well, choose the unknown word (or one of them) and move on.

Word Choice—Try It!

Of the bombardment of big-budget blockbusters released in the wake of the *Star Wars* franchise, many of the films are, in themselves, well-made and thoughtful films, but they have had a cumulative effect of silencing many kinds of voices.

4

A) NO CHANGE
B) extremity
C) superfluousness
D) abundance

Questions Without Questions Practice Set

Jethro Tull: The Best Band You're Not Listening To!

Although many critics argue that other groups, such as the Rolling Stones and the Beatles, are more influential than "the Tull," [1] however, there can be no debate that the band's lyrics are [2] superior to those of all others, even those of the Stones and the Beatles. [3] The poetry of songwriter and lyricist Ian Anderson is in an entirely different realm of literary merit than the [4] mean verse composed as accompaniment to the repetitive and catchy tunes of most bands. [5] Thus, instead of relying on a repeated chorus and fragmentary expressions of sentiment, Anderson's lyrics are always full of allusions, layered ironies, and complex themes, all of which [6] challenge listeners as much as the finest lyrical poetry that has ever been written in English.

1

A) NO CHANGE
B) furthermore,
C) consequently,
D) DELETE the underlined portion

2

A) NO CHANGE
B) better even than those other, more influential bands, the Stones and the Beatles.
C) better than any other band's, even bands more popular than they are.
D) the best.

3

A) NO CHANGE
B) Therefore, the
C) Inevitably, the
D) Actually, the

4

A) NO CHANGE
B) sinister
C) simple
D) base

5

A) NO CHANGE
B) Rather than
C) Indeed, just
D) Theretofore, not

6

A) NO CHANGE
B) multivalently engage every auditor
C) mess with audiences
D) bug people

[7] Nonetheless, any song the band wrote could be cited as [8] a useful illustration of the poetic power of the band's [9] lyrics, for a popular song like the classic "Thick as a Brick" will suffice. It criticizes [10] the insipid ignorance and thoughtlessness of the mass of modern people for being neither thoughtful about their own lives nor knowledgeable about the world around them. Creating a timeless [11] image, Anderson alludes to classical mythology: "Believe in the day! / The Dawn Creation of the Kings has begun / Soft Venus (lonely maiden) brings the ageless one."

7

A) NO CHANGE
B) However, every
C) Any
D) In any case, a

8

A) NO CHANGE
B) an adept picture
C) an illustrious incident
D) a pictorial instance

9

A) NO CHANGE
B) lyrics; thus,
C) lyrics, yet
D) lyrics; moreover,

10

A) NO CHANGE
B) the oblivious foolery of
C) the silly and obnoxious stupidity of
D) DELETE the underlined portion

11

A) NO CHANGE
B) illusion,
C) morality,
D) mirage,

[12] Therefore, turning to the mundane reality of contemporary existence, Anderson finds that "Cats are on the upgrade / Upgrade? Hipgrave. Oh, Mac." No sensitive listener can fail to recognize his or her own culpability in the contrast, confirming Anderson's contention that his listeners are "Thick as a Brick" even as they are woken from their [13] tripping foolhardiness by the song's call to "rise up from the pages of … comic-books."

[14] Additionally, with the band's combination of instrumental virtuosity and lyrical brilliance, few rock groups in history can approach the genius of Jethro Tull in either one of these [15] spaces. Their star burned too brightly to burn long, but no star before or since has burned brighter.

12
A) NO CHANGE
B) In contrast,
C) For example,
D) Still

13
A) NO CHANGE
B) somnolent obviousness
C) worn-out dumbness
D) sleep of ignorance

14
A) NO CHANGE
B) Nonetheless,
C) In conclusion,
D) However,

15
A) NO CHANGE
B) areas.
C) regions.
D) ranges.

Writer's Intention Questions

These questions have text prompts that ask you to accomplish a specific objective with the underlined text. For example, you may be asked to make things more concise, or you may be asked to make the phrase more vivid and detailed, or you may be asked to reiterate the main point of the passage. There is a wide range of questions you may be asked, but you always need to pay close attention to exactly what the question asks for.

Read over the question carefully and underline the key words that will allow you to choose the correct answer. Remember: *All of the answers will be grammatically correct, and many of them could be considered "good writing" based on the overall context, but only one choice will accomplish the question's objective.*

For example:

1. Which choice provides the most relevant detail?

    You want to underline the words "relevant detail" and then look over the answers and evaluate each *only* in terms of whether it provides a relevant detail. Only one answer will, and that is the correct answer!

2. Which choice best concludes the paragraph by re-stating the author's thesis?

    You might be tempted to underline "concludes the paragraph" as well, which would be fine, but the key to the question is to understand that the conclusion of the paragraph must re-state the author's thesis. In order to answer this question correctly, you must read the entire passage carefully so that you know what the thesis of the passage is.

Writer's Intention Questions — Try It!

However, once the door to paying athletes is opened, it is difficult to predict how the business and competitive aspects of college sports will be affected. Coaches will probably have to be paid less, players will become essentially employees rather than students, and **1** professional teams will continue recruiting from the top programs in the country. But from there, the changes could be even more dramatic.

1

Which choice best emphasizes the writer's position that there will be specific changes to college sports?

A) NO CHANGE

B) some teams will be forced to drop out of their leagues.

C) college education will be even more useful for future employment opportunities.

D) many other changes will certainly occur for many schools.

47

Writer's Intention Practice Set

Home or Office? Home AND Office!

    1 To many people, working from home seems ideal. You don't have to fight traffic to get to the office, you can work in the same clothes you exercise in, and **2** you can make the same amount of money. Although many people find that these benefits do dramatically improve their work life, **3** there are still questions about whether working from home rather than commuting to an office is really better.

1

Which choice provides the best introduction for the tone and content of the essay as a whole?

A) NO CHANGE

B) Everyone loves working from home, because a home office is a worker's paradise.

C) Working from home is a great way to avoid work and still make money.

D) You should try working from home: you'll love it!

2

The writer wants to provide a third apparent benefit of working from home that is similar to those discussed earlier in the sentence. Which choice best accomplishes this?

A) NO CHANGE

B) one can accomplish more in less time.

C) you don't have to follow an office schedule for your work time.

D) workers can still manage their time effectively.

3

The writer wants to end this paragraph by offering a specific outline of the rest of the essay. Which choice best accomplishes this?

A) NO CHANGE

B) other people have found drawbacks.

C) lots of employers don't like having employees work from home.

D) there are issues to resolve in terms of managing employees, collaborating on projects, and maintaining a work–life balance.

[4] One perspective that must be considered is the management angle. Technology helps managers to keep track of time for employees working remotely: [5] many managers require employees either to log into a shared "virtual space" when working or to track their own time with online tools. However, some managers have a difficult time effectively assessing the quality of the work-time logged by employees who work from home, because they cannot directly observe workers who are not in the same physical space. Further, the freedom from a 9–5 schedule for many work-from-home employees means that managers may not be available when they are working, and vice versa. [6] Since none of these problems are insurmountable, many offices that allow employees to work from home find that it is still helpful to require employees to come together for at least part of the work week.

Many companies have found ways to work around these common management issues, but collaborative work is another difficulty for a business in which employees work remotely. [7] Again, technological advancements can ease the cumbersome burden of collaborative efforts for employees who need to labor closely together on significant endeavors. Shared drives often allow

4

Which choice provides the most appropriate introduction to the main idea of this paragraph?

A) NO CHANGE

B) Managing remote employees is one of the unique challenges for offices with work-from-home employees.

C) Let us address the first challenging aspect of working from home: technology.

D) Managers hate having employees who work from home.

5

Which choice most logically completes the sentence with supporting details?

A) NO CHANGE

B) employees sometimes have to track their own time, which makes managers' jobs easier.

C) technology is a distraction for some workers, however, and so is also risky for companies.

D) some employees do not use technology in their work.

6

Which choice most effectively sets up the information that follows?

A) NO CHANGE

B) In order to try to address these kinds of issues,

C) Thus, requiring employees to work from a shared office space for some time is common, so

D) Nonetheless, if employees are able to,

7

Which choice best maintains the tone and style of the rest of the passage?

A) NO CHANGE

B) However, technology can connect remote workers who need to work collaboratively.

C) Tech to the rescue again!

D) For workers who insist on working from home, technology can help approximate, but never replace, working in the same office.

workers to access and edit documents simultaneously and [8] live video chatting allows employees miles—even thousands of miles—apart to work closely together. However, John McClane, an editor at a political magazine that creates articles and features [9] often authored by teams of 10-15 people, claims, "There is simply no replacement for having my colleagues across the hall from me. Not only is there palpable excitement in our office space as we work together, but there are also constant exchanges of creative thoughts and challenging ideas that make every project we do better than it could be if we were not working so closely together." Nonetheless, some companies have found ways to make remote office workers effective parts of team projects, [10] but others have employees work separately on their own major projects.

[8]

Which choice provides a second relevant example of collaborative technology?

A) NO CHANGE

B) workers can still work together at other locations that might be more convenient than their shared office space.

C) employees can plan to meet at regular intervals to compare and combine their work.

D) employees can often use their home computers to access programs needed to complete tasks.

[9]

Which choice provides the most relevant detail?

A) NO CHANGE

B) that present both sides of political issues,

C) commonly involving graphic representation of data,

D) that require great skill to craft,

[10]

The writer wants to close the paragraph by suggesting that face-to-face meetings are still valuable for collaborative work. Which choice best accomplishes this?

A) NO CHANGE

B) so face-face meetings are eliminated and time is saved for all employees.

C) and others do not need to have employees work together in person.

D) but many require employees to come together for critical parts of major projects.

Although these kinds of issues are commonly acknowledged as problems of working from home, many home-office workers are finding that, along with personal benefits, there are serious drawbacks. [11] Many employees find that their work is not as effective or efficient when they work from home. Though managers might fear that people working from home may not really be working, most employees find that they actually work more hours than they used to, because it is so "convenient" to work. For example, architect Richard Thornburg, who has worked remotely for four years after working from an office space for over a decade, found that he missed the feeling of leaving the office for the day, [12] so that every day seemed the same. To try to create a clear boundary between work and his own life, Thornburg explains that he has taken to [13] frequenting local coffee shops and libraries that offer private work spaces. Thornburg affirms that he feels "pretty zen" about finding a definite work space and time without "going bananas every day during rush hour."

As new technologies create new possibilities for work arrangements, both employers and employees will have to continue [14] to balance efficiency, teamwork, and productivity with convenience and personal priorities.

11

Which choice best sets up the examples that follow?

A) NO CHANGE

B) The same technologies that enable remote work also mean that employees never leave the office, because they are always connected through their computers and phones, so many feel they are never "done for the day."

C) One major concern for managers is the fact that they cannot directly observe their employees working, so many employees "pad" their work time.

D) These drawbacks are sometimes even more serious than employees realize when they first work from home instead of a shared office space.

12

Which choice best completes the sentence with an explanation that supports the main idea of the paragraph?

A) NO CHANGE

B) and the relaxing hour of time spent riding public transportation home.

C) which gave him a clear division between work time and personal time.

D) a feeling he missed when working from home.

13

Which choice best completes the sentence with a specific supporting detail?

A) NO CHANGE

B) waking up early to jog before work starts.

C) doing whatever he can to improve his work.

D) meeting with friends at bakeries and cafes.

14

Which choice best concludes the essay by summarizing the ideas about working from home?

A) NO CHANGE

B) to work from a shared office space.

C) to make special exceptions and arrangements in order for remote working to succeed.

D) to try harder if they want to work from home.

Add/Delete Questions

On the SAT Writing and Language test, you will also encounter questions that ask you if you should add or delete a clause or sentence from the passage. The four answer choices will provide you with "yes" or "no" answers followed by reasons for adding or deleting that portion.

Add

When faced with questions asking about adding a sentence or phrase, your primary question should be: "Is the part that we're adding relevant?" If it's irrelevant, adding something off-topic or redundant, you should not choose to add it and immediately cross off the "yes" answer choices. On the other hand, if it adds clarification of something that would otherwise be confusing or adds a new detail to support the main purpose of the paragraph, it should be added, and you can cross out both "no" answer choices. Usually, if you can make the decision about whether the element should be added to the passage or not, the justification for that answer is easy to choose, because often only one is even true or relevant to the sentence in question.

Add—Try It!

When the fresh sound of the Beatles took the world by storm, Jethro Tull began as just one among many of the British bands to rise to prominence. **1** The band released its first LP in 1968, but the record, influenced primarily by the blues roots of guitarist Mick Abrahams, would be almost unrecognizable to the band's later flocks of frenzied fans who came to love the flute-centered progressive rock of their monstrous hits "Aqualung" and "Thick As a Brick."

1

At this point, the writer is considering adding the following sentence:

> Other groups that became popular at the same time were the Rolling Stones, the Who, and the Kinks, while Herman's Hermits fell from favor, sounding old-fashioned and boring compared to the new sound produced by the Beatles and other new bands.

Should the writer make that addition here?

A) Yes, because it shows that the writer has a broad knowledge of the music of the period being discussed.

B) Yes, because it effectively introduces the ideas the reader needs to understand the importance of the following sentence.

C) No, because it shifts the focus from Jethro Tull to other bands who are less important to the passage.

D) No, because the information is implied in the previous sentence.

Delete

Similarly, when faced with questions asking whether to keep or delete a sentence or phrase, you want to consider relevance and redundancy as the keys to choosing the correct answer. Again, if the material is off-topic or redundant, cross out the "Kept" options, and choose the best explanation of the reason to delete. Be careful—often the information that makes the added element redundant comes after the underlined portion. On the other hand, if the passage would be unclear or confusing without the underlined portion or if it adds relevant support to the main point of the paragraph, cross out the "Delete" options and choose the answer with an accurate explanation of why the underlined part should be kept.

Delete—Try It!

The band released its first LP in 1968, but the record, influenced primarily by the blues roots of guitarist Mick Abrahams, would be almost unrecognizable to the band's later flocks of frenzied fans who came to love the flute-centered progressive rock of their monstrous hits "Aqualung" and "Thick as a Brick." Though the record was successful enough and critically well-received, it wasn't until Abrahams left the band that flautist and vocalist extraordinaire Ian Anderson was able to fully assert himself as a songwriter, a jazz flute virtuoso, and a singer of remarkable range and inventiveness: once Anderson did so, the band became the monolith of rock history it is known as today, producing unforgettable anthems like "Aqualung" and "Thick as a Brick," which are today so much a part of the soundtrack of our lives.

2

The writer is considering deleting the underlined portion (ending the sentence with a period). Should the writer make this change?

A) Yes, because the information in the underlined portion detracts from the paragraph's focus on the change the band went through from its humble origins to its titanic later success.

B) Yes, because the information in the underlined portion is provided elsewhere in the paragraph.

C) No, because the underlined portion provides information necessary to make sense of the following sentence.

D) No, because the underlined portion gives examples that provide context to explain the claim made earlier in the sentence.

Add/Delete Practice Set

The Billy Goat Gives Up the Ghost

In the history of sports, there has been no "curse" on any professional team quite like the championship drought that haunted the Chicago Cubs for over a century. **1** The Boston Red Sox, for instance, had a considerable drought, usually called the "curse of the Bambino," a nickname for Babe Ruth, when they didn't win the World Series for 86 years after trading Babe Ruth to the Yankees. The Cubs won back-to-back World Series championships in 1907 and 1908, and then went on the longest championship drought in the history of professional sports. **2** After these championships in 1907 and 1908, the team went to the World Series several more times in the first half of the twentieth

1

The writer is considering deleting the underlined sentence. Should the sentence be kept or deleted?

A) Kept, because it provides necessary context to understand the severity of the Cubs' championship drought.

B) Kept, because it gives a generalization that proves the claim made in the preceding sentence.

C) Deleted, because the information is easily inferred from the rest of the passage.

D) Deleted, because it takes away from the primary focus of the passage.

2

The writer is considering deleting the underlined phrase, adjusting punctuation and capitalization as needed. Should the writer delete this phrase?

A) Yes, because the information is already clear from the preceding sentence.

B) Yes, because it is too positive in its tone to fit with the rest of the sentence.

C) No, because the timeline of events in the paragraph would be unclear without this information.

D) No, because the information is essential to understand the scope of the "curse."

century, but they never won the series. [3] The Cubs were in the World Series and up 2 games to 1 over the Detroit Tigers. Game 4 was held at the Cubs' home stadium, Wrigley Field, and partway through the game, [4] William Sianis, owner of the Billy Goat Tavern, was supposedly asked to leave due to the smell of the goat he took with him to the game. Sianis allegedly responded angrily, declaring, "Them Cubs, dey ain't gonna win no more." The Cubs went on to lose the game. Emboldened by the success of his initial curse, Sianis, [5] his family claims, went on to send the following telegram to the team's owner: "You are going to lose this World Series and you are never going to win another World Series again. You are never going to win a World Series again because you insulted my goat."

Although the veracity of these

3

The writer is considering adding the following sentence here:

> The team's luck became even worse in 1945, after an alleged incident that led to what became known as the "curse of the billy goat."

Should the writer add this sentence?

A) Yes, because it explains why the Cubs' curse became known as "the curse of the goat."

B) Yes, because it effectively sets up the information that follows.

C) No, because it contradicts the main idea of the passage.

D) No, because it repeats information provided earlier in the passage.

4

The writer is considering adding the following phrase here:

> as the supposed story goes,

Should the writer add this phrase?

A) Yes, because it clarifies that the event is not known for certain.

B) Yes, because otherwise the reader would not know what the story is about.

C) No, because the lack of certainty regarding the event is clear from other parts of the passage.

D) No, because it contradicts information presented elsewhere in the passage.

5

The writer is considering deleting the underlined portion, adjusting the punctuation as needed. Should this clause be kept or deleted?

A) Kept, because it suggests that there is no physical evidence to support the existence of the telegram.

B) Kept, because the telegram's significance to the story would otherwise be unclear.

C) Deleted, because it introduces aspects not relevant to the story as told.

D) Deleted, because it contradicts information presented elsewhere in the passage.

events cannot be confirmed, the "curse of the billy goat" has certainly felt real to many Cubs fans for years. [6] However, the team finally went to the World Series again in 2016 and edged out the Cleveland Indians, [7] who also have been under a curse since their World Series victory in 1948, with the deciding game requiring extra innings to complete. Now, fans can celebrate the end of the longest curse in professional sports—and no goat can stand in their way!

6

The writer is considering adding the following sentence at this point:

> The Cubs were in the playoffs several times since 1945, often even within 1 game of making the World Series, but the team was unable even to get to the World Series for 71 years.

Should the writer make this addition?

A) Yes, because it provides context to explain why fans felt the curse was real.

B) Yes, because it provides a transition needed to understand the following sentence.

C) No, because the information is already clear from the previous sentence.

D) No, because this example contradicts the idea of the team being under a "curse."

7

The writer is considering deleting the underlined phrase. Should the phrase be kept or deleted?

A) Kept, because the phrase provides a relevant example to illustrate the significance of the victory.

B) Kept, because the irony of both teams being cursed is needed to understand the following sentence.

C) Deleted, because it contradicts the central claim of the passage.

D) Deleted, because it introduces unnecessary information.

Ordering Questions

Some questions ask you to reorder words or sentences in order to make the passage more logical and cohesive. When you reorder sentences you should try to think about both logical sequence and flow. Consider where the sentence fits into the greater narrative of the paragraph—is it introducing an idea? Concluding? Providing evidence? Transitioning? Also, consider how the sentence relates to specific parts of the other sentences in the paragraph.

For example, if the sentence in question has a pronoun (**he, she, you, it**…) or demonstrative adjectives (**this, that, these, those**) for which the previous sentence does not provide context, then the sentence in question is probably in the wrong place.

Sometimes it helps to read the paragraph with the sentence in each potential placement to determine what sounds the most natural.

NOTE: Two elements on these questions are often confusing to students—

- First, do not be fooled by the placement of the question—ordering questions within a paragraph are *always* at the end of the paragraph, but can refer to *any* sentence in the paragraph. To make sure you are dealing with the correct sentence, underline the sentence number in the question.
- Second, notice that sentence numbers appear *before* the sentence they identify, so that placing a sentence *after* sentence [2] does *not* mean adding it right after the number [2], but rather adding it after the end of the sentence labeled [2].

Ordering Questions—Try It!

[1] The impact of *Star Wars* on the landscape of the motion picture industry goes far beyond the financial success or critical reception of any one of the films. [2] Before the first *Star Wars* in 1977, the studio system was one in which executives worked primarily with specific directors who had a vision for making a particular kind of film or telling a particular kind of story. [3] Since *Star Wars*, movies have become an increasingly producer-centered medium, with franchise properties featuring reusable actors and replaceable directors making the most money and receiving the most attention from studios. [4] Ironically, the original *Star Wars* film was a typical representative of this system: it was a long shot for 20th Century Fox, the studio that produced it, because it was a film with no big-name stars in an unpopular genre by an unproven director, but Fox's president Alan Ladd was willing to bet on George Lucas' idiosyncratic vision. [5] In the last decades, studios have depended more and more on "tent-pole" movies, so called because they "hold up" the other films financed by the studio; in fact, in 2014, seven of the top ten movies in box office receipts were sequels, prequels, or spin-offs from existing franchises, and two of those "original" film series currently have sequels in production. 1

1

To make this paragraph most logical, sentence 4 should be placed

A) where it is now.
B) before sentence 1.
C) after sentence 2.
D) after sentence 5.

There are two other basic types of ordering questions:

1   Best place to add new sentence

These questions will provide a new element, usually a complete sentence, and ask where that element would be best added to the passage, usually within a single paragraph. These questions can also come at the end of the passage and provide possible locations throughout the entire passage to place the new sentence. The same strategies that will help you know where to move an existing sentence within a paragraph should be used to determine where to add the new sentence.

2   Best order for paragraphs

These questions will always come at the end of the entire passage, and they will ask about the arrangement of the paragraphs as a whole, rather than that of sentences within a paragraph. You can know that a question of this kind is coming when you see that all the paragraphs are numbered in the passage. Also, if the paragraph is in the wrong place, you will often recognize it as being out of place from the start, which can allow you to eliminate Choice (A) immediately.

To answer these questions, think about the arrangement of the passage as a whole: Is it ordered chronologically? Then place the paragraph in the proper order based on dates referenced in it. Is it ordered by cause and effect? Place the effect paragraph directly after the cause paragraph. Additionally, transition words can provide important contextual clues: If the paragraph begins with **However**, see which paragraph it is providing contrast to. If it begins with **Second**, put it between the paragraph offering the first reason/evidence and that offering the third (or last) reason/evidence.

Ordering Practice Set

Paragraph 1

[1] The scientific and technological developments of the Second Industrial Revolution helped Europeans conquer much of Africa during the 19th and early 20th centuries. [2] Superior weaponry, for example, gave imperial countries a distinct military advantage over native peoples who found it hard to resist in the face of modern rifles, machine guns and long-range artillery. [3] Advances in science and medicine also contributed to European domination. [4] Finally, improvements in transportation technologies facilitated the conquest of inland continental areas. [5] Steamboats allowed Europeans to travel up rivers in the interior of the African continent where once explorers and traders had been confined to coastal areas. [6] The development of quinine, for example, made it possible to penetrate tropical regions without succumbing to malaria and yellow fever. **1**

1

To make this paragraph most logical, sentence 6 should be placed

A) where it is now.
B) after sentence 2.
C) after sentence 3.
D) after sentence 4.

Paragraph 2

[1] Famine was a major killer in the primarily agricultural countries of Europe during the long 18th century (1670–1820). [2] In Sweden, for example, the death rate doubled from the epidemics and famine following the harvest failures of 1771 and 1772. [3] Poor harvests usually resulted from bad weather—too much rain or a very cold spring—which afflicted all regions at some time. [4] However, the consequences of a bad harvest and whether a poor harvest led to famine varied greatly across the continent. [5] Similarly, Finland lost one third of its population as a result of the famine in 1696–7. [6] In England, by contrast, although agricultural output fell behind population growth for most of the period between 1755–1820, no serious mortality crises occurred after 1729. **2**

2

To make this paragraph most logical, sentence 2 should be placed

A) where it is now.
B) after sentence 3.
C) after sentence 4.
D) after sentence 5.

Paragraph 3

[1] After herbicide resistance, the second most common application of genetic engineering in agriculture has been to create "insect resistant" crops. [2] To produce these crops, scientists have inserted into corn, canola, and potatoes genes that make the plants poisonous to insects. [3] These "toxic" genes are found in soil bacteria called *Bacillus thuringiensis*. [4] Proponents of genetic engineering argue that *B. thuringiensis* crops will reduce the need for insecticide and, therefore, protect the environment. [5] In addition to killing pests, genetically engineered *B. thuringiensis* crops are lethal to beneficial insects, including ladybugs, butterflies, and honeybees that pollinate crops. [6] However, environmentalists point out that there are negative implications for the environment of these crops. [7] Further, pest insects are also more likely to evolve resistance to the toxin *B. thuringiensis* if they are free to graze on hundreds of acres of crops exuding the toxin. `3`

`3`

To make this paragraph most logical, sentence 5 should be placed

A) where it is now.

B) after sentence 1.

C) after sentence 6.

D) after sentence 7.

Paragraph 4

[1] Although they have grown significantly in recent years, many cities in Latin America and Asia such as Sao Paulo, Singapore, Bombay, Manila and Jakarta have historical roots. [2] The growth of such centers was not a natural development reflecting modernization in the country but was rather a forced development intended to maximize the profits of imperialist concerns. [3] The colonial city was a hub to which resources from the rest of the country were channeled and in which the colonial administration was concentrated. [4] The consequence of this pattern was extremely uneven growth within the colony as resources and infrastructure were directed to one center, neglecting a large part of the country. `4`

`4`

The writer wishes to add the following sentence to this paragraph:

> These cities have evolved from colonial outposts that served as way stations for exporting commodities to imperial nations such as Portugal and England.

This sentence should be placed

A) after sentence 1.

B) after sentence 2.

C) after sentence 3.

D) after sentence 4.

Paragraph 5

[1] Wildlife Services is a federal program operated by the U.S. Department of Agriculture. [2] The program undertakes a diverse range of activities including the protection of aircraft and airports from birds and geese, the protection of crops from blackbirds and the protection of dikes from beavers. [3] Many of these activities are uncontroversial and reflect the mission of the program to provide "federal leadership and expertise to resolve wildlife conflicts to allow people and wildlife to coexist." [4] However, a large portion of Wildlife Services' budget goes towards its "livestock protection" program—a program that kills "predators" or animals such as coyotes, wolves, foxes, bears and bobcats that can prey on domestic sheep, goats or cattle. [5] The methods used to kill the animals include setting M-44 traps that eject sodium cyanide into animals' mouths and catching animals in steel leg holds. [6] Critics of the livestock protection program argue that it is not only inhumane but also ineffective. [7] Despite millions of coyotes killed by Wildlife Services over 90 years, the coyote population—the principal target of the program—is not only stable but has spread geographically from a dozen western states in 1913 into every state in the Union except Hawaii.

5

The writer wishes to add the following sentence to this paragraph:

> Independent studies suggest that coyote populations subject to culling produce larger litters, have higher pup survival rates, and breed more resilient and nocturnal individuals.

This sentence should be placed

A) after sentence 3.
B) after sentence 4.
C) after sentence 5.
D) after sentence 6.

Sentence Combining Questions

Some "Writer's Intention" questions will ask you to combine two underlined sentences into one coherent sentence. When encountering these questions you should think about not only how to convey the underlined information most concisely, but also how to best illustrate the relationships between the ideas. As you choose an answer choice consider:

1   Which choice is stated most clearly, directly and briefly? Choose it!
    The shortest answer is almost always correct!

2   What punctuation and transition words help combine the ideas? Remember that all the answers will be correctly combined, so think about the meaning of the choices, not the grammatical correctness!

3   Is all the information included necessary? Don't choose a sentence that is redundant or wordy!

4   Are the verbs active or passive? Active verbs are usually preferred!

Sentence Combining Questions—Try It!

Most voters see voting as a fairly private activity, something they do as a public duty, but not as a public declaration of their values. **1** People are free to make their voting choices based on whatever criteria they choose. Too many voters don't even know what criteria they are using when they vote.

1

Which choice best combines the two underlined sentences?

A) People are free to make their voting choices based on whatever voting criteria they choose; indeed, too many voters don't even know what voting criteria they are using when they vote.

B) Though free to vote based on any criteria, too many voters don't even know what criteria they are using when they vote.

C) Voting choices can be made by people based on any criteria they choose, and too many voters don't even know what criteria they are using when they vote.

D) People who are allowed to be free to make their voting choices based on whatever criteria they choose sometimes don't even know what criteria they are using when they vote.

Sentence Combining Practice Set

1. Jeremy decided to cut back on French fries and hamburgers. This followed his coronary bypass surgery.

   Which choice most effectively combines the underlined sentences?

   A) Jeremy decided to cut back on French fries and hamburgers, a decision he made that followed his coronary bypass surgery.

   B) Following his coronary bypass surgery, Jeremy decided to cut back on French fries and hamburgers.

   C) Jeremy decided to cut back on French fries and hamburgers, and this decision followed his coronary bypass surgery.

   D) Jeremy decided to cut back on French fries and hamburgers, which followed his coronary bypass surgery.

2. Bilingual children are more adept at solving mental puzzles than monolingual children. This finding was documented in a 2004 study by Ellen Bialystok and Michelle Martin-Rhee.

   Which choice most effectively combines the sentences at the underlined portion?

   A) monolingual children as documented

   B) monolingual children, and this finding was documented

   C) monolingual children, a finding that was documented

   D) monolingual children, findings documented

3. Evidence suggests that in a bilingual child's brain, both language systems are active even when the child is using only one language. In some instances, one language system may obstruct the other. This interference is not so much a handicap as a blessing, providing the child with a powerful cognitive workout.

   Which choice most effectively combines the sentences at the underlined portion?

   A) the other, so this interference

   B) the other: this interference

   C) the other, but this interference

   D) the other; moreover, this interference

4. Researchers have also discovered that bilingualism protects individuals against certain diseases of old age. These diseases include Alzheimer's and dementia.

   Which choice most effectively combines the underlined sentences?

   A) Researchers have also discovered that bilingualism protects individuals against certain diseases of old age, these diseases being Alzheimer's and dementia.

   B) Protection against certain diseases of old age, including Alzheimer's and dementia may also be provided by bilingualism it has been discovered by researchers.

   C) Researchers have also discovered that bilingualism protects individuals against certain diseases of old age, including Alzheimer's and dementia.

   D) Bilingualism protecting individuals against certain diseases of old age, including Alzheimer's and dementia, was found by researchers.

5. In 1962, labor activist Cesar Chavez organized the United Farmworkers Association. This union was dedicated to increasing the hourly wages and improving the living conditions of farm laborers across the United States.

Which choice most effectively combines the underlined sentences?

A) In 1962, labor activist Cesar Chavez organized the United Farmworkers Association, a union dedicated to increasing the hourly wages and improving the living conditions of farm laborers across the United States.

B) Dedicated to increasing the hourly wages and improving the living conditions of farm laborers across the United States, the United Farmworkers Association was organized by labor activist Cesar Chavez in 1962 to advocate for the rights of farm workers.

C) In 1962, labor activist Cesar Chavez organized the United Farmworkers Association, a union created by Chavez that was dedicated to increasing the hourly wages of farm laborers as well as improving the living conditions of farm laborers across the United States.

D) Increasing the hourly wages and improving the living conditions of farm laborers across the United States was the dedicated task of the United Farmworkers Association, which was organized by labor activist Cesar Chavez in 1962.

6. In addition to increasing the risk of wildfires in the American West, rising global temperatures are expected to raise sea levels. Raised sea levels will cause coastal flooding on the Eastern seaboard, especially in Florida.

Which choice most effectively combines the underlined sentences?

A) In addition to increasing the risk of wildfires in the American West, rising global temperatures are expected to raise sea levels: the result being an increase in coastal flooding on the Eastern seaboard, especially in Florida.

B) In addition to increasing the risk of wildfires in the American West, rising global temperatures are expected to raise sea levels, which will lead to coastal flooding on the Eastern seaboard, especially in Florida.

C) In addition to increasing the risk of wildfires in the American West, rising global temperatures are expected to raise sea levels, and raised sea levels caused by high global temperatures will lead to coastal flooding on the Eastern seaboard, especially in Florida.

D) In addition to increasing the risk of wildfires in the American West, rising global temperatures are expected to raise sea levels; the raised sea levels caused by high global temperatures will lead to coastal flooding on the Eastern seaboard, especially in Florida.

7. After much deliberation, Henry made his decision. He would ask Julia to marry him.

Which choice most effectively combines the underlined sentences?

A) After much deliberation, Henry made his decision: he decided that he would ask Julia to marry him.

B) After much deliberation, Henry made his decision, and he decided that he would ask Julia to marry him.

C) After much deliberation, Henry made his decision, his decision being that he would ask Julia to marry him.

D) After much deliberation, Henry made his decision: he would ask Julia to marry him.

8 | Following the Second World War, the United States and the Soviet Union entered into a "Cold War." <u>By 1946, the Soviets had occupied much of Central and Eastern Europe. Establishing a sphere of influence in Central and Eastern Europe which they had no intention of relinquishing.</u>

Which choice most effectively combines the underlined sentences?

A) By 1946, the Soviets had occupied much of Central and Eastern Europe, and they established a sphere of influence in this territory which they had no intention of relinquishing.

B) By 1946, the Soviets had occupied much of Central and Eastern Europe, establishing a sphere of influence which they had no intention of relinquishing.

C) By 1946, the Soviet Union had established a sphere of influence in Central and Eastern Europe which territory they had occupied and had no intention of relinquishing.

D) Establishing a sphere of influence, the Soviet Union had occupied much of Central and Eastern Europe by 1946 and had no intention of relinquishing their sphere of influence.

9 | The United States was eager to stem the tide of communism. <u>It bolstered the economies of Western Europe through the Marshall Plan and provided financial and military aid to both Greece and Turkey in 1947.</u>

Which choice most effectively combines the underlined sentences?

A) The United States bolstered the economies of Western Europe through the Marshall Plan and was eager to stem the tide of communism and provided financial and military aid to both Greece and Turkey in 1947.

B) Eager to stem the tide of communism, the United States bolstered the economies of Western Europe through the Marshall Plan and provided financial and military aid to both Greece and Turkey in 1947.

C) Bolstering the economies of Western Europe through the Marshall Plan, the United States was eager to stem the tide of communism and provided financial and military aid to both Greece and Turkey in 1947.

D) The United States was eager to stem the tide of communism, which bolstered the economies of Western Europe through the Marshall Plan and provided financial and military aid to both Greece and Turkey in 1947.

Figure-Based Questions

You will also encounter questions that ask you to extrapolate or identify basic information from graphs, charts, or other types of figures in relation to the passage. These questions will usually ask you to use the data in the figure to revise an underlined portion of the text. For these questions, try to understand the general trends in the figure and the relationship between the points being made in the passage and the information in the figure. Oftentimes, some of the answer choices are inaccurate based on what is in the figure; however, some answers may be accurate but not relevant to the point being made, so be sure to consider the context of the passage in answering.

Figure-Based Questions — Try It!

Studios continue to push to make more and more big-budget "event" movies. While it may certainly be true that these franchise movies make money for studios and enable them to produce small-budget films, the overall attendance at the movies **1** has decreased significantly each year since 1980. Thus, studios should reconsider their heavy investment in franchise properties.

1

Which choice best illustrates the information in the figure and makes the point of the sentence clear?

A) NO CHANGE

B) has steadily declined since 2000.

C) has gone up nearly 300 million since 1980.

D) has fluctuated wildly over the past 35 years.

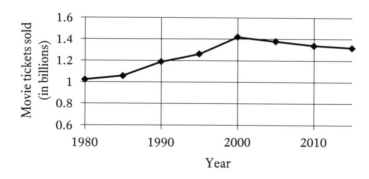

Figure-Based Questions Practice Set

Montgomery County Population Density Zones				
Zone	Definition	Est. Pop.	Pop. %	Sq. Mileage
Rural	<1000/sq. mi.	121,392	11.38	302.2
Suburban	1000-2000/sq. mi.	90,547	8.49	45.2
Urban	2000-3000/sq. mi.	87,251	8.18	32.49
Metropolitan	3000+/sq. mi.	767,627	71.95	127.68

Because of the close proximity of very different types of geographical locations, from vast stretches of undevelopable land to super-densely populated regions, population data are frequently misleading, as is illustrated by population data for Maryland's Montgomery County. For the entire county, the population density is just over 2,000 people per square mile, **1** which classifies the county as a whole as "urban." However, **2** almost a third of the area of the county is actually classified as "rural," but this land accounts for only about one ninth of the total population. Thus, the county is both more rural and more metropolitan than the density of the county as a whole suggests.

1

Based on the table, which of the following accurately characterizes the density of the county as a whole?

A) NO CHANGE

B) which makes the county predominantly a "rural" region.

C) indicating that the county is a "metropolitan" area.

D) which makes all of the county seem to be a "suburban" region.

2

Which choice best supports the point of the paragraph and accurately reflects the data in the table?

A) NO CHANGE

B) over half of the county's total square mileage is classified as "suburban,"

C) the vast majority of the county is considered "urban,"

D) more than half of the county's area is classified as "rural,"

TRAINING PROCESS

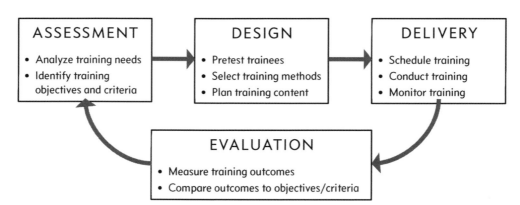

According to Jimenez and Alexander, businesses should develop a training process that is recursive, **3** starting by designing training and then checking how well it works. **4**

3

Which choice most accurately reflects the information in the figure and completes the idea of the sentence?

A) NO CHANGE

B) moving through a rigid procedure that starts with assessment, moves to design and delivery, then concludes with evaluation.

C) starting by assessing their needs, then designing and delivering training, and then evaluating the entire process in order to repeat it with additional training.

D) starting by evaluating the effectiveness of a training, then designing and delivering the training, and finally assessing the needs met by the training before beginning the process over again.

4

Which of the following is most accurate about the process described in the figure?

A) It can begin and end anywhere.

B) It can go forward or backward.

C) It is a process that is intended to be started and finished at the same point.

D) It is a process that is intended to be repeated indefinitely.

Standard English Conventions

Glossary of Grammatical Terms

In order to succeed on the SAT Writing and Language Test, you may need to refresh your memory (or learn for the first time!) about some basic terms and definitions for English grammar. While these terms are not directly tested on the test, knowing them can help you to understand the rules that follow.

Parts of Speech

Noun   a person, place, or thing

Stephen took his sisters to the library to check out a set of books.

Singular noun   refers to just one: **book, building, child, Stephen, library**

Plural noun   refers to more than one: **books, sisters, buildings, children**

Collective noun   a singular word that refers to a group: **flock, family, set, team, organization, class**

Pronoun   a word that replaces a noun, called the pronoun's antecedent

Sally woke up early so she would not be late for the interview.

Subject (nominative) pronoun   replaces the subject of a sentence, the noun doing the action

She is on the varsity team.

Object (objective) pronoun   replaces the object of a sentence, the noun receiving the action

Siobhan passed the ball to him.

Verb   a word indicating an action or suggesting a state of being, paired with a subject or subjects in a sentence

Before Sahim runs outside each morning, he is barely awake.

Adjective   a word that modifies a noun

The mangy, scrappy dog likes to run around the tall, stately oak tree.

Adverb   a word that modifies a verb, adjective, or other adverb

Though he had performed extremely well on the test, Ian sheepishly raised his hand.

Preposition   a word that precedes a noun or pronoun, called its object, and relates it to the rest of the sentence

In the summer, Lisa and Gisi hike along a piece of the Appalachian trail with their friends, Lou and Aditya.

Conjunction   a connecting word that joins two parts of a sentence

After you and Pooja join, our team will have five players, but we are still looking for more people.

Coordinating conjunction   used to join together two grammatically equal elements in a sentence, such as two nouns, two phrases, or two independent clauses. There are seven coordinating conjunctions: **for, and, nor, but, or, yet**, and **so** (a.k.a. FANBOYS). These are the *only* coordinating conjunctions!

I grew up in Denmark, and I still have many friends and relatives there.

Subordinating conjunction   used to join an independent and dependent clause. These include **after, although, as, because, before, if, since, so that, though, unless, until, when, whenever** and many more.

I will speak with my friend when I get back from my vacation so that we can spend time together.

Parts of a Sentence

Subject   the noun or pronoun that is doing the action of the sentence, the noun the sentence is about.

> <u>Jane</u> recently decided <u>she</u> would spend her junior year studying in Paris.

Verb   the word or group of words that expresses the action of the sentence. Always paired with a subject, the verb indicates what the subject is doing or what is being done to the subject. Not all "action words" are the **verb** of a clause!

> The barking dog <u>runs</u> around the park.

> The scurrying mouse <u>was chased</u> by the cat.

Clause   a group of words that contains a subject and a verb. Every sentence must contain at least one independent clause, but many sentences in the passages that make up the Writing and Language Test have multiple clauses.

Independent clause   a clause that can be a sentence on its own. Independent clauses can be joined to a dependent clause or another independent clause.

> Though Nick was running late for his flight, <u>he stopped for breakfast anyway</u>.

> <u>I often relax after dinner and consider the importance of proper use of em-dashes</u>.

Subordinate/dependent clause   part of a sentence that contains a subject and verb but is not capable of being a sentence in its own right. These can come before or after an independent clause, or they even can be inserted into the middle of another clause, enclosed by paired **commas** or **dashes**.

> <u>Because it's nice out</u>, my roommate and I are having dinner on the roof.

> Mondays, <u>which are the days I usually have physics tests</u>, are my least favorite.

Phrase   a group of words without a subject or a verb. There are many different types of phrases in the English grammatical system, but there are two types that are essential to know for the purpose of the SAT.

Prepositional phrase   a group of words that begins with a preposition and ends with a noun.

> <u>In my opinion</u>, summer vacation is best spent relaxing <u>on the beach</u> or hiking <u>in the mountains</u>.

Appositive phrase   a noun phrase that does not contain a verb and renames or explains another noun. Like some dependent clauses, a nonessential appositive can be inserted into an independent clause by placing a pair of commas or dashes around it.

> Wednesdays—<u>often the busiest day of the week</u>—have been very quiet lately.

> Henry, <u>my older brother's oldest child</u>, is an exceptionally precocious boy.

Sentence Structure and Punctuation

The SAT Writing and Language Test has more questions about sentence structure than any other aspect of grammar. Often, these questions appear to be about punctuation, but the best way to get them correct consistently is not to memorize a list of rules about punctuation, but to understand the structure of the sentence. There are two essential errors regarding sentence structure tested on the SAT:

1   **Fragment**   any group of words that does not contain an independent clause but is punctuated as a complete sentence. Questions dealing with fragments on the SAT often do not involve punctuation, so they can be tricky to recognize. Consider the following example:

Example 1   The people <u>not minding much because</u> they were anxious to leave before the storm started anyway.

    A) NO CHANGE
    B) didn't mind much because
    C) not minding as much since
    D) not minding too much as

    This question is tricky, because most of the changes in the answer choices are irrelevant distractions. Only (B) is correct, because only (B) makes the first part of the sentence an independent clause, and thus makes the sentence *not* a fragment. To catch this error on the test, *always* read at least to the end of the sentence: you will almost always be able to "hear" that it is not a complete sentence.

2   **Run-on sentence (comma splice)**   a sentence with more than one **independent clause** combined with only a comma. This error can be corrected in several different ways, and the SAT will often make you recognize each of these in the course of a test, though you will never have to choose between them, because they are all correct! Consider these examples of comma splices:

Incorrect   We know how good we <u>are, we are</u> sure to win.
        There are many surprising people in the <u>world, some of them live</u> right under our noses.

These comma splices can be corrected any of the following ways:

2.1 IC [, FANBOYS] IC.

This is probably the most commonly used way to combine independent clauses. Coordinating conjunctions are *only* the words **for, and, nor, but, or, yet,** and **so,** and so you can memorize them as FANBOYS. Note that a **comma** is the *only* punctuation mark to use with a **coordinating conjunction,** and that the part both before and after the conjunction *must* both be independent clauses.

Correct   We know how good we <u>are, so we are</u> sure to win.
        There are many surprising people in the <u>world, and some of them live</u> right under our noses.

Incorrect   We know how good we <u>are, thus we are</u> sure to win.
        There are many surprising people in the <u>world; so some of them live</u> right under our noses.

2.2 IC [;] IC. Often in the form IC [; *conjunctive adverb*,] IC.

A semicolon functions just like a period and a capital letter between clauses, so if you can read what is before and after the semicolon as a sensible complete sentence, then the semicolon is correct. Often, semicolons are used with **conjunctive adverbs**, such as **thus**, **therefore**, **however**, and many more, which come directly after the semicolon and are followed by a comma.

Correct   We know how good we <u>are; thus, we are</u> sure to win.

There are many surprising people in the <u>world; some of them live</u> right under our noses.

NOTE: Conjunctive adverbs do *not* necessarily have to be preceded by a semi-colon; therefore, if the conjunctive adverb is *not* between two independent clauses, simply punctuate with a comma both before and after.

Correct   We <u>know, however,</u> how good we are, and we <u>are, thus,</u> sure to win.

Incorrect   We <u>know; however,</u> how good we are, and we <u>are; thus,</u> sure to win.

2.3 IC [:] IC.

The use of a colon between two independent clauses is not very common, but it comes up often on the SAT, so be sure to know it. Usually, the colon can only be used when the two clauses are very closely related, such as the second explaining or providing an example of the first.

However, you will *not* be asked to judge whether the colon is appropriate based on the relationship between the two clauses, because that decision is somewhat subjective.

Correct   We know how good we <u>are: we are</u> sure to win.

2.4 IC [—] IC.

The dash can be used between independent clauses when there is a strong break between the ideas of the two clauses or whenever a colon could be used. Again, you will never be asked to judge whether the dash is appropriate based on the relationship between the two clauses.

Correct   There are many surprising people in the <u>world—some of them live</u> right under our noses.

2.5 IC [.] IC.

Any two independent clauses can also be split into two complete sentences.

Correct   We know how good we <u>are. We are</u> sure to win.

2.6 IC.

Another way the SAT will frequently correct a comma splice is to turn the original two independent clauses into a single clause by combining the verbs. When combining two verbs or two subjects, rather than two clauses, with the word **and**, no comma is needed.

Correct   We know how good we <u>are and are</u> sure to win.

Incorrect   We know how good we <u>are, and are</u> sure to win.

2.7 IC, DC.

The SAT also often corrects comma splices by turning the second clause into a dependent clause, which makes the comma correct.

Correct   We know how good we <u>are, which makes us</u> sure to win.

There are many surprising people in the <u>world, some of whom live</u> right under our noses.

3   **Complex sentences** are those that contain at least one independent clause and one dependent clause. A sentence that starts with a dependent clause and ends with an independent clause always has a **comma** (and no other punctuation) between the two clauses. Some questions on the SAT will make you choose the correct punctuation in this instance, while others will make you change part of the sentence to make existing punctuation correct; therefore, always be sure to read all the way through the sentence!

Correct   As I grow <u>older, I</u> begin to see things rather differently.

                <u>Because he was</u> the best goalie we had, Stephen was chosen to start that fateful day.

Incorrect   As I grow <u>older: I</u> begin to see things rather differently.

                <u>He was</u> the best goalie we had, Stephen was chosen to start that fateful day.

Sentence Structure and Punctuation—Try It!

Correct all errors in the underlined portions of the following sentences:

1. Although he was not previously known to be a great <u>speaker; Jonathan</u> impressed the audience with his witty stories.

2. Jonah ran a mile in six minutes <u>and then he</u> swam a mile in ten minutes.

3. However, <u>out</u> of control her personal life may <u>be—Crighton</u> never lets it interfere with her professional life.

4. Dalby is gifted at <u>Math, however,</u> he has a hard time learning vocabulary.

5. In their desire to win the contract, the firms bid the price too low, thereby <u>they made</u> the project unviable.

6. Roger won the <u>match, hence,</u> he gets the <u>trophy, it</u> matters little that his opponent was injured.

7. <u>Because I grew</u> up watching my brothers play basketball; thus, I decided to try out for the high school team.

8. That I understood the <u>game, did</u> not mean I could <u>play, I</u> spent most of the season on the bench.

9. Both the <u>people and</u> their dogs were severely <u>traumatized; because</u> the fire at the dog show started so <u>unexpectedly, and</u> spread so quickly.

10. People have a few different complaints about the use of wind power, the most common <u>of them</u> is that wind turbines are unsightly.

Sentence Structure Practice Set

Choose the best answer for each of the following sentences.

1. Runners can decrease their likelihood of injury by stretching their <u>legs, they</u> can improve their times by controlling their pace and breathing.

   A) NO CHANGE
   B) legs and
   C) legs; and they
   D) legs, and also

2. Though Jethro Tull continues to play <u>tours in which the band has</u> never quite been able to recapture the brilliance of their seminal work in the early 70s.

   A) NO CHANGE
   B) tours, despite which the band have
   C) tours; however, the band has
   D) tours, the band has

3. The invention of the modern printing press in Europe is attributed to Johannes Gutenburg, a fifteenth-century <u>publisher. Developing</u> the technology of moveable type in his workshop.

   A) NO CHANGE
   B) publisher, he developed
   C) publisher developed
   D) publisher who developed

4. Fossil fuel combustion contributes to atmospheric levels of nitrogen oxides, some <u>of them</u> cause smog and acid rain.

   A) NO CHANGE
   B) nitrogen oxides
   C) of which
   D) DELETE the underlined portion

5. That the store is currently having a sale on gardening tools <u>which</u> makes now the best time to purchase.

   A) NO CHANGE
   B) that
   C) and
   D) DELETE the underlined portion

6. Temperate grasslands, which cover huge areas, are found in both temperate and tropical <u>regions, they</u> are characterized by low total annual rainfall.

   A) NO CHANGE
   B) regions and
   C) regions; and
   D) regions they

7. Because I am a fan of Bill <u>Murray I am going to see the special showing of his best movie,</u> *Groundhog Day*, at the independent theater down the street.

   A) NO CHANGE
   B) Murray; I am going to see the special showing of his best movie,
   C) Murray, I am going to see the special showing of his best movie
   D) Murray, I am going to see the special showing of his best movie,

8 Recently, many people seeking a career in business find that their writing skills are essential to their success.

A) NO CHANGE
B) people seek a career in business
C) people sought a career in business
D) people, seeking a career in business

9 Heart rate, blood pressure, and overall physical fitness, not to mention intangible aspects like personal fulfillment, all of which have been shown to be negatively correlated with stress levels.

A) NO CHANGE
B) they all
C) all
D) each of which

10 A government taxation plan that benefits those with the greatest means in order to enable them to grow wealth that will "trickle down" and benefit those with less means; "Trickle-down economics" has been a part of the economic discussion in the United States for almost 100 years.

A) NO CHANGE
B) less means—
C) less means,
D) less means

11 The damage was more extensive than Martinez had imagined: upon receiving the news of the blackouts, she immediately sprang into action.

A) NO CHANGE
B) blackouts and immediately springing into action.
C) blackouts, and immediately sprang into action.
D) blackouts. She immediately sprang into action.

12 It is not hard to understand why many Americans feel the need to drive their own cars rather than use public transit—because many people live a great distance from their places of work, many jobs require people to go to multiple locations during the course of their work day, and some public transit systems in the US are not very dependable.

A) NO CHANGE
B) transit: many people
C) transit, many people
D) transit; since many people

13 Many people did not realize what the impact of the decision would be, but some being more forward thinking and immediately recognized the likely effects and acted accordingly.

A) NO CHANGE
B) some
C) some of them
D) some were

14 To improve the gas economy of their <u>vehicles;</u> most car companies have turned to hybrid automobiles.

A) NO CHANGE
B) vehicles,
C) vehicles:
D) vehicles—

15 The Velvet Underground's last record evinces less experimentation than any of their earlier <u>albums, however, it</u> was the most radio-friendly and produced several of Lou Reed's most memorable tunes.

A) NO CHANGE
B) albums, but it
C) albums, nonetheless, it
D) albums; but it

16 In fact, recent studies <u>indicate that, more</u> people spend more time working now than at any previous time in history.

A) NO CHANGE
B) indicate, that more
C) indicate that more
D) indicate that, "more

17 Therefore, many studios desire to create not only franchises but also "shared cinematic <u>universes," they allow</u> multiple movies each year to cross over with each other in terms of plot and character, creating a constant flood of marketing for each new film.

A) NO CHANGE
B) universes;" of which they allow
C) universes," these allow
D) universes," which allow

18 Charlie Chaplin, an impressive all-around <u>entertainer, who</u> found the transition from silent film to "talkies" surprisingly difficult.

A) NO CHANGE
B) entertainer,
C) entertainer, he found
D) entertainer; he found

19 However, the <u>brothers found that</u> their unique blend of atmosphere and cuisine was not easily mass-produced, a development that they were unprepared for after their initial successes.

A) NO CHANGE
B) brothers, finding that
C) brothers, having found
D) brothers found, and that

20 Caesar's writing in *The Gallic Wars*, though it may not have been high <u>art; it</u> has been a boon for the study of both Latin and history.

A) NO CHANGE
B) art, it
C) art,
D) art. It

Punctuation: Essential and Nonessential Elements

A second aspect of punctuation tested on the SAT is punctuating essential and nonessential elements. Nonessential elements require punctuation, while essential ones require none. In order to distinguish between essential and nonessential elements of a sentence—whether a single word, a phrase, or an entire clause—ask yourself the following question:

> *"If I leave out the element, does the essential meaning of the sentence change?"*

If yes, the element is essential; if no, it is nonessential!

Sometimes, determining whether an element is essential or nonessential may appear subjective: if it is truly ambiguous whether an element is nonessential, the test will *never* give a correctly punctuated essential and nonessential version in the answer choices. Often, simply recognizing where the element in question begins and ends is enough to rule out *all* incorrect answers.

Here are a few basic rules regarding punctuation of essential and non-essential elements:

1 **Essential elements** should *not* be set off by commas.

   Correct   The movie that makes the most money each year is rarely the year's best movie.

   In this sentence the dependent clause "that makes the most money" is essential. The clause is essential because it is needed for the sentence to be logical. Thus, no punctuation is used to set the clause apart.

2 **Nonessential elements** are surrounded by a pair of commas or dashes if they appear in the middle of a clause. If the nonessential element is at the beginning of the sentence, it will be followed by a single comma, and if it is at the end of the sentence, it will be preceded by a single comma.

   Correct   *Rogue One*, which made the most money last year, was not the year's best movie.

   In contrast to the example in 1, the dependent clause "which made the most money last year" is nonessential, despite being very similar to the previous example. Because the sentence has already identified the specific movie, the clause is not essential to understand the sentence. Thus, the clause must be set apart from the rest of the sentence.

   NOTE: Nonessential phrases and clauses can also be set off by parentheses. When parentheses are used, they are always a pair, and all other punctuation remains as it would be if the parentheses and what is within them were not present.

   Correct   His favorite movie (though not one he recommends to many) is *Dogma*.

   Incorrect His favorite movie, (though not one he recommends to many), is *Dogma*.

3 **That** introduces an essential clause, which does not need to be set off by commas, whereas **which** usually introduces a clause that is non-essential, which requires commas. The words **who, whom,** and **whose** can also be used to introduce clauses, but these clauses can be essential or non-essential.

   Correct   Jokes that are made at the expense of others are not amusing.

   Those comments, which hurt Jake more than he is willing to say, should never have been made.

   I love someone who is not in love with me, but he loves Jenny, who is in love with him.

4 **Participial** (verb form used as an adjective) **phrases** require commas if they are nonessential. Typically, participles identifying which person or thing is referred to are essential.

   Correct   Middle management, seeking to save money, laid off 10 percent of the workforce.

   The barista making lattes on the machine used to babysit for my kids.

5   **Appositive** phrases require commas if they are nonessential but should not have commas if they are essential. Typically, appositives that follow a specific named person or thing are non-essential.

   Correct   My <u>mother, Marian</u>, called my <u>friend Anya</u> to say that she would be late.

Essential and Nonessential Elements Exercises—Try It!

Correct all errors with commas and dashes in the underlined portions of the sentences.

1. The <u>dog, that bit my child should never</u> have been off her leash.

2. Your mother, a genuinely <u>kind woman gave</u> me a beautiful gift.

3. She is a member of Habitat For <u>Humanity—which receives</u> donations from the general public.

4. Beethoven, who <u>was musically gifted composed</u> 32 piano sonatas.

5. Removing <u>her socks she walked</u> into the ocean.

6. Those running for the <u>presidency who must be at least 35 campaign</u> for months on end.

7. <u>Teasing, that turns into bullying, has</u> become a major issue in schools.

8. The famous <u>musician—Michael</u> Jackson put out numerous instant hit songs.

9. <u>Children, interested in helping others, are</u> more likely to become compassionate adults.

10. Carrying heavy <u>packages—the mailman, tripped</u> on the porch stoop.

11. <u>My sister, Lily coaches</u> a basketball team with three <u>players, who are injured</u>.

12. My favorite pencil <u>sharpener, which I bought online broke</u> down earlier this morning.

Essential and Nonessential Elements Practice Set

Choose the best answer for each of the following.

1. Elvis ordered the peanut butter and banana sandwich; an item that is served at his favorite restaurant.

    A) NO CHANGE
    B) sandwich, an item that is served
    C) sandwich; an item served
    D) sandwich, an item served,

2. The Olympic gymnast Lilia Podkopayeva, who trained for up to eight hours a day, won the all-around medal which is given for the highest overall score in the competition.

    A) NO CHANGE
    B) medal
    C) medal; which is given
    D) medal, which is given,

3. Although it has been removed from many banned book lists, *The Catcher in the Rye*, Salinger's famous novel, remains a controversial work for many.

    A) NO CHANGE
    B) *The Catcher in the Rye* Salinger's famous novel
    C) *The Catcher in the Rye*, Salinger's famous novel
    D) *The Catcher in the Rye*, Salinger's famous novel—

4. Consider the *Harry Potter* film series, for example, after completing films of the original seven novels, the studio announced not a new film but a new series set in the same universe.

    A) NO CHANGE
    B) series—for example—
    C) series, for example;
    D) series; for example—

5. The court's published opinions—satirized in a series of political essays by Hans Dertz— became known as "The Petty Papers."

    A) NO CHANGE
    B) by Hans Dertz,
    C) by Hans Dertz:
    D) by Hans Dertz

6. The best choice to lead the team was clearly visionary artist Teddy Earner whose work had inspired the project in the first place.

    A) NO CHANGE
    B) artist, Teddy Earner whose
    C) artist, Teddy Earner, whose
    D) artist Teddy Earner, whose

7. Except for Leonardo himself, none of the crew knew how to update, or even how to maintain any of the highly advanced machinery they worked with every day.

    A) NO CHANGE
    B) update, or even how to maintain, any
    C) update or, even, how to maintain, any
    D) update—or even how to maintain, any

8. Surprisingly, people who were most successful in the original experiment achieved <u>new scores. That were well</u> above those of subjects who participated only in the second experiment.

A) NO CHANGE
B) new scores and they were well
C) new scores, that were well
D) new scores that were well

9. In the <u>1590s Elizabeth I's status as the "Virgin Queen"</u> was both a patriotic ideal and a practical problem.

A) NO CHANGE
B) 1590s Elizabeth I's status, as the "Virgin Queen,"
C) 1590s, Elizabeth I's status as the "Virgin Queen"
D) 1590s, Elizabeth I's status as the "Virgin Queen,"

10. Nonetheless, though undeniably <u>popular, earning nearly 1 billion dollars worldwide,</u> the film was seen as humorless, cluttered, and even difficult to follow.

A) NO CHANGE
B) popular (earning nearly 1 billion dollars worldwide),
C) popular: earning nearly 1 billion dollars worldwide,
D) popular—earning nearly 1 billion dollars worldwide,

11. Surprisingly, the players typically thought of as the best of the <u>80s;</u> Larry Bird, Julius Erving, and Magic Johnson, just to name a few—did not play on the US Olympic team in the 1980s, but Michael Jordan did.

A) NO CHANGE
B) 80s,
C) 80s
D) 80s—

12. Jeff Tweedy's original band, Uncle Tupelo—which was hailed as St. Louis' 4th <u>best country band in 1993,</u> was much less experimental than Wilco.

A) NO CHANGE
B) best country band, in 1993—
C) best country band in 1993—
D) best country band, in 1993,

Punctuation: Other Uses

While many questions deal with punctuation on the SAT, it is concerned with only a relatively small set of rules, focused on commas, semicolons, colons and dashes. The rules for each regarding sentence structure and essential elements are in the preceding pages, but there are also a few rules based on other uses of each punctuation mark, which are covered here.

Commas

The **comma** (,) is used in many different ways. The following guidelines help in understanding when to use commas.

1   Use commas to separate items in a **list** of three or more items.

    Correct   My friends had gathered from places as far away as <u>Denmark, England, Singapore,</u> and South Africa.

The comma before the word **and** is called a serial comma (also known as an Oxford comma). Its use is debated, and it will therefore not be tested on the SAT. However, the SAT seems to prefer its use, so it should not be considered an error when it appears.

  1.1   Use a comma between adjectives that each describe the same noun and are not joined by **and** (but could be).

      Correct   My friends and I followed the <u>narrow, winding path</u> up to the <u>ancient, deserted castle</u>.

If you can put **and** between the adjectives, there should be a comma between them because each of the adjectives modifies the noun separately. NOTE: You should *never* place a comma between the *last adjective* and the *noun* itself, so you can often check for a comma there first and eliminate several answer choices.

  1.2   Do *not* use a comma between **cumulative** adjectives, which build on each other. If you cannot place "and" between two adjectives, you should *not* put a comma between them.

      Correct   At the party we ate a <u>delicious red velvet layer</u> cake.

There are no commas in the list of adjectives above because **layer** describes **cake**, **red velvet** describes the **layer cake**, and **delicious** describes the **red velvet layer cake**. You cannot insert **and** between any of the adjectives and have the phrase make sense, so there should be no commas.

2   Do *not* over-punctuate. The SAT sometimes adds extraneous commas—often where you can "hear" a pause—to sentences in order to confuse you. More commas are not always better, so ask yourself: "Why would I *need* a comma here?"

Consider the following sample question.

Example 2   The best thing to do in many <u>situations, is often the difficult, but</u> still correct thing to do.

    A) NO CHANGE

    B) situations is often the difficult, but

    C) situations, is often the difficult but

    D) situations is often the difficult but

This sentence should not have any commas in it, so while we may be tempted by the apparent pauses in answer choices (A), (B), and (C), the correct answer is (D).

Commas—Try It!

Correct any errors in comma use in the underlined portions of each sentence.

[1] Bilbao is a <u>fascinating, Spanish town, but</u> we were too tired to enjoy it.

[2] <u>Intense, daily, aerobic</u> exercise helps in <u>blood circulation, heart-health and,</u> blood pressure control.

[3] Shaun laughed all the <u>way, to the friendly, neighborhood,</u> Capital Plaza Bank.

[4] Dan climbed into his <u>dark, blue Corvette, and</u> sank into the <u>new, black, leather</u> seats.

[5] Most of us can cook <u>well, but</u> the problem is we don't have the time to cook healthy, <u>unique appetizing,</u> <u>dishes,</u> that would sustain <u>us, and</u> appeal to our sophisticated palates.

Semicolons, Colons, and Dashes

1. The **semicolon** (;) is used to separate major sentence elements that hold equal grammatical rank. For the purposes of the test, the only rule you need to know about the semi-colon is covered in the sentence structure section. When choosing answers, remember that a semicolon is exactly the same as a period and a capital letter: if you see both options in answer choices and nothing else is different, BOTH are WRONG!

2. The **colon** (:) is used to call attention to the words following it. In addition to its use between two independent clauses, you can use a colon after an independent clause to set off a **list**, **definition**, **example**, or a **quotation**. Remember: you cannot use a colon if there is not a complete independent clause to introduce the element that follows the colon.

    Correct   As I approached the farm stand, I noticed the delicious smells wafting <u>my way:</u> peaches, apples, pears, to name but a few.

    He was almost ready to do what he had always <u>wanted:</u> marry the girl of his dreams.

    Incorrect   My friends sat around discussing our favorite opera, which is: *The Marriage of Figaro.*

    In order to bake my grandmother's favorite cookies tonight, I need to buy items such as: flour, baking soda, eggs, and chocolate chips.

3. The **dash** (—), also known as the **em-dash**, can be used in the place of a **colon**. As noted in punctuating nonessential elements, a pair of dashes can be used to set of a nonessential word, phrase, or clause, but dashes *cannot* be used in place of a comma for any other use.

    Correct   I invited all my friends to the <u>party</u>—Jack, Jill, Hansel, and Gretel.

    That traitorous <u>rat</u>—Stephen Bartleby—is now afraid to show his face in Chicago.

    Incorrect   When people realize that there is nothing <u>wrong</u>—they will change their minds.

    Many people choose cars as a reflection of their <u>personality</u>—a proof of their status, and an indication of their values.

Semicolons, Colons, and Dashes—Try It!

Correct any errors in semicolon, colon, or dash use in the underlined portions of each sentence.

☐1   Anthony played the teak wood <u>guitar—as if</u> his life depended upon it.

☐2   Tinit descended the wooden <u>steps; opened the creaky old door;</u> and stepped into a musty hallway.

☐3   Katie plans to stay in Chicago because she loves so much about <u>the city; the beach—the architecture—the</u> parks, and the people.

☐4   There are many reasons teens drink too much <u>soda, such as:</u> advertising, lack of oversight, <u>peer pressure—</u> and more.

☐5   Washington, DC, the nation's capital, is well known for its <u>monuments; however,</u> some critics bemoan the lack of originality in its <u>architecture; especially</u> when compared to that of <u>cities like:</u> Paris, <u>Vienna—and</u> even New York City in America.

End Marks and Quotation Marks

On rare occasions, the SAT tests other types of punctuation, such as end marks and quotation marks, so it is useful to know some basic rules regarding each.

1   Most questions that include end marks (periods especially) can be treated as sentence structure questions, as discussed in the section on punctuation and sentence structure. However, occasionally, questions will require you to choose between different end marks, such as a question mark or period. Only use a question mark if a sentence directly asks a specific question.

    Incorrect   Many people wondered whether the advent of computers would eradicate the need for typewriters?

    Correct   Many people wondered: would the advent of computers eradicate the need for typewriters?

2   Quotation marks are a particularly difficult type of punctuation for many students, and the rules regarding punctuating quotes are many and confusing. However, there are only a few rules you need to know in order to get these questions correct on the test:

    2.1   Quotation marks *must* be used in pairs, so if an answer option uses a quotation mark and there is not another quotation mark to open or close the quote, then *no* quotation mark is needed. The test *does not* expect you to know whether something is a quote, so simply use the presence or absence of a pair to decide whether to use quotation marks.

    Incorrect   No one really wanted to question his authority, so he ruled <u>"as an almost uncontested tyrant.</u>

    Correct   No one really wanted to question his authority, so he ruled <u>"as an almost uncontested tyrant."</u>

    No one really wanted to question his authority, so he ruled <u>as an almost uncontested tyrant.</u>

2.2 Quotes do *not* have to be preceded by punctuation unless the sentence would require punctuation without the presence of quotation marks or the quoted material is a full sentence beginning with a capital letter.

Incorrect   In the end, most students felt <u>that, "grades</u> were less important than learning."

Researchers have found that, perhaps <u>unsurprisingly "more</u> income does not equal more savings."

Correct   In the end, most students felt <u>that "grades</u> were less important than learning."

Researchers have found that, perhaps <u>unsurprisingly, "more</u> income does not equal more savings."

2.3 In certain instances, a full sentence quote can be preceded by a comma, while in others it should be preceded by a colon. The test will *not* make you decide which is correct in a given sentence, so either is acceptable for the purpose of the test.

Correct   *The New York Times* <u>has made such an argument:</u> "Nobody knew the scale of the problem until it was too late."

The New York Times <u>commented,</u> "Nobody knew the scale of the problem until it was too late."

End Marks and Quotations Marks — Try It!

Correct any errors in the underlined

☐1 Celony didn't realize <u>that, "nobody</u> used dot matrix printers anymore, but how could he have <u>known.</u>

☐2 Steve's ma <u>declared "The</u> important question is whether you have treated each other <u>with respect?"</u>

Punctuation: Other Uses Practice Set

1. As the films progressed, so did the stylized nature of the action: film critic Blan Doss suggests <u>that, "the</u> fight scenes were as elaborately choreographed as a ballet, and they took on an aspect of musicality."

   A) NO CHANGE
   B) that "the
   C) that: "the
   D) that—"the

2. The entire gym was <u>decorated with festive, billowing, colorful, streamers,</u> put up by the homecoming committee.

   A) A) NO CHANGE
   B) decorated with festive, billowing colorful, streamers
   C) decorated, with festive, billowing, colorful streamers,
   D) decorated with festive, billowing, colorful streamers

3. Throughout their educational careers, students are required to take notes <u>at classes; lectures; and</u> other academic events.

   A) NO CHANGE
   B) at: classes, lectures, and
   C) at classes, lectures, and
   D) at: classes, lectures, and,

4. There are many uses for "junk <u>mail," such as: kindling for a fire,</u> identity theft, and paper airplanes.

   A) NO CHANGE
   B) mail;" such as, kindling for a fire
   C) mail," such as kindling for a fire,
   D) mail:" such as: kindling for a fire

5. The group believed they had all the necessary <u>players: a visionary leader, a masterful administrator, an economic guru, an engineering genius, and sixteen hardworking salespeople.</u>

   A) NO CHANGE
   B) players; a visionary leader, a masterful administrator, an economic guru, an engineering genius, and sixteen hardworking salespeople.
   C) players—a visionary leader, a masterful administrator, an economic guru, an engineering genius—and sixteen hardworking salespeople.
   D) players: a visionary leader—a masterful administrator—an economic guru—an engineering genius, and sixteen hardworking salespeople.

6. The theoretical physicist and cosmologist George Gamov was a developer of a modern explanation for the origin of the <u>universe; the</u> Big-Bang Theory.

   A) NO CHANGE
   B) universe; which is
   C) universe:
   D) universe: being

7 At least since the time of Robert Malthus, critics have asked if the world can reasonably sustain the growth <u>of humanity's total population, and collective consumption.</u>

A) NO CHANGE
B) of humanity's total population and collective consumption?
C) of humanity's total population and collective consumption.
D) of humanity's total population, and collective consumption?

8 By working together early in their careers as script supervisors on a soap <u>opera, script doctors on several major motion pictures, and show runners on a popular television show—</u> the two developed a cohesive and seamless style that shows in their later work when they had gained full creative control.

A) NO CHANGE
B) opera; script doctors on several major motion pictures; and show runners on a popular television show;
C) opera, script doctors on several major motion pictures, and show runners on a popular television show;
D) opera, script doctors on several major motion pictures, and show runners on a popular television show,

9 The aristocracy, the merchant <u>class, and even the poorest</u> members of the social order benefited from the change, but the power of the monarch was clearly in decline.

A) NO CHANGE
B) class, and, even the poorest
C) class, and even the poorest,
D) class—even the poorest,

10 There was only one problem left to <u>solve: how should the powers gained be exercised without returning to tyranny.</u>

A) NO CHANGE
B) solve—how should the powers gained be exercised—without returning to tyranny?
C) solve: how should the powers gained be exercised without returning to tyranny?
D) solve—how should the powers gained be exercised without returning to tyranny.

11 When he headed into the woods that night, the contents of his backpack made plain his unpreparedness for the harsh realities of a life lived in the <u>wild; three granola bars, an iPod (with a solar charger),</u> a bottle of water, two magazines, and a Superman sleeping bag.

A) NO CHANGE
B) wild—three granola bars, an iPod—with a solar charger;
C) wild. Three granola bars, an iPod (with a solar charger),
D) wild: three granola bars, an iPod (with a solar charger),

12 They took only the necessities with them for the long trip on the <u>bus, such as: snacks,</u> drinks, and access to Netflix on their phones.

A) NO CHANGE
B) bus, such as snacks,
C) bus: such as, snacks,
D) bus: snacks;

13 | At the school's fall festival, families could compete as a team in multiple events—apple bobbing, pumpkin carving and painting, relay sack racing, and face painting.

A) NO CHANGE

B) apple bobbing, pumpkin carving, and painting, relay sack, racing and face painting.

C) apple, bobbing, pumpkin, carving and painting, relay sack, racing, and face, painting.

D) apple bobbing, pumpkin carving and painting; relay sack racing, and face painting.

14 | Those at scene described the smoke as, "billowing from the windows as well as holes that had burned through the roof."

A) NO CHANGE

B) as

C) as:

D) as—

15 | Jack Kirby became known for his highly stylized, over-muscled, blocky, figures, surrounded by cluttered geometric shapes, all rendered in primary colors.

A) NO CHANGE

B) highly, stylized, over-muscled, blocky figures surrounded by cluttered geometric shapes; all

C) highly stylized, over-muscled, blocky figures surrounded by cluttered geometric shapes, all

D) highly stylized, over-muscled, blocky, figures surrounded by cluttered, geometric shapes, all

Verb Usage

Verbs that are paired with subjects are called "finite" verbs, or main verbs, because they change their form based on the subject, tense, and mood of the sentence. You can usually recognize a question on verb usage by seeing various forms of a verb in the answer options.

Subject-Verb Agreement

In present tense verbs and all tenses of the verb *to be*, the verb must agree with the subject in *number* (singular or plural). Singular forms of regular verbs end in *-s*, and plurals have no extra ending. To check for subject-verb agreement, follow these steps:

1. In any sentence, first locate the verb.
2. Then find the subject for that verb.
3. Place the subject right before the verb and read it out loud. Does it sound correct?

Subject-Verb Agreement Rules

1. Compound subjects combined with **and** are always plural, and compound subjects combined with **or** or **nor** follow the noun closest to the verb.

   Correct   Danger <u>and adventure await</u> all those who take on the challenge.

   Either Rogers or his <u>co-stars are</u> responsible for the initial success of the program.

   Incorrect   Neither you <u>nor I are</u> able to understand what that must have felt like to people in 1650.

   Both Yancey <u>and Billips was</u> able to reach the goal.

2. Many indefinite pronouns that logically seem to be plural are actually singular. **Either, neither, everyone, everybody, anyone, any, anybody, no one, not one, someone, somebody, nobody** and **each** are singular. Don't overthink on these—most of them "sound" correct when they are!

   Correct   <u>Every one</u> of the many contestants <u>sees</u> himself as capable of winning.

   <u>Not one</u> of the players on my baseball team <u>was</u> capable of individual glory, but as a team, we were unbeatable.

   <u>Each</u> of my friends <u>loves</u> ice cream.

   Incorrect   <u>They each brings</u> many things to the table.

   <u>Everyone</u> in the entire class of 700 students <u>were</u> surprised by the graduation speaker.

3. **None, some** and **all** can be singular or plural depending upon the context implied by the prepositional phrase that accompanies it.

   Correct   <u>Some of the players</u> on the team <u>run</u> fast.

   <u>None of the food is</u> any good.

   <u>Some of the cake remains</u> uneaten.

   Incorrect   All of the pieces of cake tastes the same.

   None of our salt are kosher salt.

4   In an **inverted sentence** (a sentence where the verb comes before the subject), place the subject before the verb, and then verify subject-verb agreement. **There** is often used to introduce an inverted sentence, so be sure to find the subject later in the sentence for a sentence that starts "There is/are/was/were…"

    Correct   In his desk <u>are</u> a very old, worn <u>dictionary and a box</u> of worms.

                   There <u>were no clear answers</u> to the problem of its pollutants, however.

    Incorrect   Far beyond the farthest pale <u>lives Aimless the wanderer and her sister Blab</u>.

                   To solve this kind of issue, there <u>is</u> more than two effective, and often equally inexpensive, <u>methods</u>.

5   **Collective** nouns (nouns that describe a group of people or things as one unit—family, team, group, organization, etc.) are always *singular*, unless the name is explicitly plural or the collective noun is made plural to refer to a group of groups.

    Correct   The <u>team</u> really <u>pulls</u> together when it needs to.

                 The <u>Banshees</u> <u>are</u> really an underrated band.

    Incorrect   The largest <u>pride of lions, with its numbers dwindling all the time, are</u> rarely seen anymore.

                   The five <u>families, each more depraved than the last, was</u> gathered for the meeting.

Verb Tense/Mood Rules

1   Verbs vary their form based on *when* an action takes place. Verb tense is indicated by other verbs in the paragraph or by key words such as "within ten years" or "in 1870."

    Correct   Some experts <u>are</u> confident that the changes <u>will be</u> widely noticeable in just a few years. Others feel that the effects <u>may never be felt</u> by the average person.

                 <u>In the 19th century,</u> what we <u>take</u> as commonplace today <u>would have been considered</u> fantasy.

    Incorrect   Some experts <u>will be</u> confident that the changes <u>will be</u> widely noticeable in just a few years. Others feel that the effects <u>are never felt</u> by the average person.

                 <u>In the 19th century,</u> what we <u>took</u> as commonplace today <u>was considered</u> fantasy.

2   **Perfect tenses** (those using forms of **have**) and **modals** (helping verbs, such as **could, would, may**, etc.) are often used in answer choices to create confusion. Often, you can eliminate answers using subject-verb agreement, as the complexities of when to use perfect tenses and other modals are rarely the only way to choose the correct answer, but here is a quick explanation of when to use them:

2.1 **Perfect tenses** are used to indicate completed actions or actions whose time is relative to another verb in the sentence. They always use forms of **have**, never **of**. Most verbs use the simple past form when the perfect tense is used, but certain verbs have irregular forms, most of which can be recognized by "ear."

Present Perfect verbs indicate actions that started in the past and are complete in the present. These verbs use **have** for third-person plural subjects and **has** for third-person singular subjects.

Past Perfect verbs indicate actions that *began* and *were completed* in the past. These verbs use **had** for both plural and singular subjects. The past perfect tense is used to indicate that actions precede other past tense actions or to imply that a past completed action is no longer true.

Correct	After working for 45 years, Michael, together with two other men in his precinct, has finally retired from law enforcement.
	The players had tried to keep up through the first half but by the third quarter were listless.
Incorrect	The years—especially this year in which so much turmoil had erupted—has not been kind to James.
	They had became a larger problem for the community as a whole, and the community haven't sang their praises in response.

2.2 **Modals** are often used to qualify the meaning of a verb. Subjunctive modals (**could, would, should**) are used to indicate past actions that either did not happen or are unlikely to have happened and future actions that might happen. Modals such as **can, may**, and **might** are used to indicate future actions that may happen and either current or past actions that are uncertain. Notice that there is some possible crossover in their use: the SAT will never make you decide based on the subtle differences between the uses of these helping verbs, and often other aspects of the answer choices can be used to eliminate answers.

Correct	Johnson could have left then, but he chose to persevere instead.
	The industry may end up having to be strictly controlled by governments if it cannot self-regulate effectively.
Incorrect	Stevedores can have led a strike, but by that time it would of done little good.
	Nobody should have did it, but everybody does.

Verb Usage—Try It!

Correct any errors with verbs in the underlined portions of each sentence

1. Lacey, unlike her brothers and sisters, <u>write</u> well.

2. Each of the twenty-seven desks <u>has a book</u> on it, and students <u>must chose</u> a desk based on their preferred book.

3. My brother or I <u>rakes</u> the leaves when our parents <u>told</u> us to do so, as they do every fall weekend.

4. Though it is an independent project, they each <u>having</u> to check in with the professor before <u>having started</u> the assignment.

5. Under the banyan tree, there <u>is</u> a tangle of desiccated roots and an ascetic's bowl; within the roots <u>lives</u> a fully grown rat and an albino squirrel, both of whom are territorial.

6. The report issued by the collective offices of the Board of Rectors, the Alumni Commission and the Board of Directors, which <u>should of corrected</u> many school-wide problems, <u>were</u> widely unpopular among the student body.

7. The average English person <u>cannot had any</u> idea how enormous the changes to world history <u>will be</u> when William the Conqueror succeeded in his conquest of England in 1066.

8. Although we won the case, if the judge <u>had find</u> my client guilty, we <u>will appeal</u> to the High Court.

Verb Usage Practice Set

1 The civilian speaker argued that the most important people in the room were those in the audience <u>who had served</u> in the military.

A) NO CHANGE
B) who has served
C) who was serving
D) whose serving

2 In so far as <u>team sports teaching us</u> not a particular skill but the discipline and teamwork required to work hard toward a common goal, they offer long-term tools for academic and professional achievement.

A) NO CHANGE
B) team sports has taught us
C) team sports teach us
D) team sports taught us

3 On the quantitative section of the Graduate Management Admissions test (GMAT), a test taken by students applying to graduate school in business and management, students with a strong quantitative curriculum in <u>college has traditionally</u> done very well and still do.

A) NO CHANGE
B) colleges have traditionally
C) colleges had traditionally
D) college have traditionally

4 If excess fecal matter is introduced into the ecosystem, it can pollute waterways, <u>depleting the oxygen content</u> of streams and rivers as it decomposes.

A) NO CHANGE
B) and depletes the oxygen content
C) and deplete the oxygen content
D) which deplete the oxygen content

5 The now-defunct string trio had been the brainchild of former Irish Studies Professor Sean O'Steamy, <u>wanting</u> to explore further both the musical talents and the Celtic heritage of himself and his colleagues.

A) NO CHANGE
B) who wants
C) who wanted
D) he wanted

6 While I <u>await</u> for the doctor's attention, I finished two cups of coffee and read all the magazines in the office.

A) NO CHANGE
B) awaiting
C) waited
D) awaited

7 As we see in several countries, persistent and severe income inequality are correlated with declines in overall productivity, and, over time, with deep recessions.

A) NO CHANGE
B) is
C) is being
D) has been

8 The Newport Apples, widely considered the first bluegrass players to come to the United States from Australia, was unique for its incorporation of a uniquely Australian aboriginal instrument called the Didgeridoo.

A) NO CHANGE
B) were unique for their
C) was unique for their
D) were unique for its

9 According to the US Environmental Protection Agency, the presence of coal and fossil fuel industry professionals in the scientific bodies meant to regulate those industries have no negative impact upon the environment.

A) NO CHANGE
B) having
C) have had
D) has

10 Proponents of gun safety make the argument that there was numerous reasons for background checks, including keeping guns from violent criminals and people with mental illness.

A) NO CHANGE
B) there is
C) there are
D) there has been

11 For many decades, dogs have guarded the Turner place, protecting it from the angry neighbors who could damage the property, not to mention scared the children of the residence.

A) NO CHANGE
B) scaring
C) scare
D) have scared

12 Some patients do not respond to the new therapy as well as others did, and some even respond adversely.

A) NO CHANGE
B) do,
C) have,
D) will,

13 The centerpiece of the work is dominated by images of cats with various anthropomorphic expressions and <u>including</u> a repeated motif of a large grinning Cheshire on an opulent sofa, an image to symbolize decadence.

A) NO CHANGE
B) included
C) includes
D) had included

14 There <u>were</u> a number of steps you can take to determine whether hunting is the right field for your dog and, if it is, to prepare yourself and your canine for such a career.

A) NO CHANGE
B) has been
C) had been
D) are

15 Not all research into regional varieties of the Arkansas swamp dialect <u>requires</u> such time, effort, and resources, however.

A) NO CHANGE
B) are requiring
C) have required
D) require

Pronouns

You can usually identify questions dealing with pronouns by noticing that the forms of a single pronoun are used in answer choices or by various pronouns being used in the answer choices.

Pronouns and Antecedents

Most pronoun questions on the SAT deal with the relationship between a pronoun and its antecedent, which is the noun that the pronoun refers to. Pronouns must have clear antecedents, and they must agree with their antecedents in number and type.

A pronoun must have a **clear antecedent**.

> In some questions, the underlined pronoun may have multiple possible antecedents or the antecedent may be entirely ambiguous. In such cases, choose the version that makes clear the intended meaning of the sentence.

> **Incorrect** The coach told the quarterbacks to show up early for practice so that <u>they could record some film.</u>

> **Correct** The coach told the quarterbacks to show up early for practice so that <u>he could record some film of them.</u>

> **Incorrect** Abe attended all the Redskins games with his <u>roommates; they</u> were always entertaining.

> **Correct** Abe attended all the Redskins games with his <u>roommates, who</u> were always entertaining.

A pronoun must agree with its **antecedent** in **number** and **type**.

> Find the antecedent (the noun that the pronoun is replacing) for each pronoun, and check to see if the antecedent is singular or plural. Remember that a singular antecedent requires a singular pronoun. Also remember that **who** (together with its other forms) refers to people, and **which** refers to things, while **that** can be used for people or things.

> **Incorrect** The University of North Carolina, <u>who</u> is a top academic school in the state, has one of the most famous basketball teams in the NCAA; as of 2017, <u>they</u> have won six NCAA championships.

> **Correct** The University of North Carolina, <u>which</u> is a top academic school in the state, has one of the most famous basketball teams in the NCAA; as of 2017, <u>it</u> has won six NCAA championships.

> **Incorrect** Every <u>student</u> must ensure that <u>they</u> bring <u>their</u> books to class.

> **Correct** All <u>students</u> must ensure that <u>they</u> bring <u>their</u> books to class.

Pronoun Person

Pronouns must stay *consistent* in **person** throughout each sentence; i.e. if a paragraph uses third person pronouns to refer to an indefinite antecedent, you *cannot* switch to 1st or 2nd person pronouns.

Person	1st (the self)	2nd (person spoken to)	3rd (person spoken about)
Pronouns Used	**I, me, we, us**, etc.	**you, your**, etc.	**she, her, they, them, everyone**, etc.

> **Incorrect** <u>One</u> must always wash <u>his</u> hands if <u>you</u> do not wish to get sick.
>
> <u>I</u> love to swim because <u>one</u> feels so weightless in the water.

> **Correct** <u>You</u> must always wash <u>your</u> hands if <u>you</u> do not wish to get sick.
>
> <u>I</u> love to swim because <u>I</u> feel so weightless in the water.

Pronoun Case

Pronouns also have different forms based on how they are used in sentences, an attribute called **case**. The two important cases to know for the test are **nominative** (in place of subject nouns) and **objective** (in place of object nouns).

Case	Forms	Uses
Nominative	**I, we, you, he, she, it, they, who**	subjects; comparisons; complements of linking verbs (e.g. forms of "be")
Objective	**me, us, you, him, her, it, them, whom**	direct objects; indirect object; objects of prepositions

Incorrect   Joanna picked her over I.

Correct   Joanna picked her over me.

The most commonly tested case-based pronoun questions deal with choosing **who** or **whom**. As indicated above, **who** is a nominative form and **whom** is an objective form. In order to check which is correct, it is often helpful to replace **who/whom** in the sentence with **he/him** or **they/them**. Consider this sentence:

The leader, who/whom was just elected, didn't know who/whom to trust.

Ask yourself, would you say "he was just elected" or "him was just elected;" "to trust they" or "to trust them"? Since it would be "**he** was just elected" and "to trust **them**," you should choose **who** and **whom**, respectively.

Pronoun Usage

A final note on pronouns: certain forms of pronouns sound the same but are written differently. These are also covered in Usage (see page 108) but here is a summary for pronouns:

it's = it is	you're = you are	they're = they are	who's = who is
its = it possesses	your = you possess	their = they possess	whose = who possesses

Pronouns—Try It!

Correct all errors in the underlined portions of the following sentences.

1. Germany's growth slowed in the late nineteen nineties, the economist argued, because <u>of their problems</u> with high unemployment.

2. I don't know <u>whom the robbers</u> were, but I do know that <u>he or she</u> took all my possessions.

3. The one who is responsible for the theft shall soon be arrested, but <u>they</u> are not sure where <u>they are</u>.

4. I always go to bed early before a big test because <u>you really need sleep</u> to perform well.

5. <u>Who</u> do you fear?

6. When the School Board, <u>who are</u> responsible for the school's reputation, saw that internal assessment grades were rising while standardized test scores were declining, <u>it decided</u> to ask teachers to toughen grading standards.

Pronouns Practice Set

[1] Light pollution makes it difficult to see Jupiter and Saturn, obscuring its brightness among the artificial lights of the city.

A) NO CHANGE
B) there
C) their
D) it's

[2] Since the players are expected to master many positions—some of which are unfamiliar—during the course of his four years at the school, studying teammates' strengths is strongly encouraged.

A) NO CHANGE
B) his or her
C) one's
D) their

[3] The memorization of too many formulas can be detrimental to the educational progress of students, which often fail to learn the concepts behind the formulas they are taught.

A) NO CHANGE
B) that
C) who
D) they

[4] People who choose the cheapest package for that truck often find themselves regretting the decision.

A) NO CHANGE
B) oneself
C) their selves
D) they were

[5] Before "Nowhere Man," all Lennon-McCartney compositions that appeared as singles or on an album were known for their basic themes of young love and broken hearts.

A) NO CHANGE
B) was known for its
C) were known for its
D) was known for their

[6] Though controversial in some Wall Street circles, "Fearless Girl" has brought much acclaim to sculptor Kristen Visbal, whom was previously best known for her sculptures of famous football coaches.

A) NO CHANGE
B) who is
C) she was
D) who was

[7] The Nissan Leaf, the Chevy Bolt EV, and the Tesla Model S all made strong statements about the future of the automobile engine, yet none of them dominates the car market in the way that Ford's Model T did in the 1910s and 20s. Still, it might have paved the way for Tesla's Model 3 to become the first cool and affordable fully electric car.

A) NO CHANGE
B) those
C) that one
D) the Bolt EV

8　One of the side effects of the success that marketers have had in selling processed food is that people have come to believe that monitoring the nutritional value of the food <u>eaten by them</u> is someone else's responsibility.

A)　NO CHANGE
B)　they eat
C)　eaten by him or her
D)　you eat

9　Because of last night's 16-inning game, Miami doesn't have three of its eight relievers available for the remainder of today's game, and they've already used four <u>of them</u> in the last two innings.

A)　NO CHANGE
B)　of those
C)　of the other five
D)　of the rest of those

10　Nostalgia for comic books contributes to the enthusiasm for superhero movies among those <u>which watch it.</u>

A)　NO CHANGE
B)　who watch it.
C)　whom watch them.
D)　who watch them.

Parallelism and Comparisons

Although the answer choices for parallelism questions frequently include slight variations in the forms of words, parallelism and comparison questions can be difficult to recognize. A key way to recognize both issues is to look for lists and comparisons in the sentence as a whole—the form of the items in the list or comparison determine the form of the correct answer for the underlined section.

Lists

When a sentence includes a list, the items listed need to be in the same grammatical form, e.g. all prepositional phrases or all infinitives, rather than a mixture of different grammatical structures.

Incorrect   My classmate Alexander has vacationed in Mexico, Italy, and in India.

Major time wasters on the job include watching sports clips, playing computer games, and to discuss politics.

Major time wasters on the job include watching sports clips, playing computer games, and political discussions.

Correct   My classmate Alexander has vacationed in Mexico, Italy and India.

My classmate Alexander has vacationed in Mexico, in Italy and in India.

Major time wasters on the job include watching sports clips, playing computer games, and discussing politics.

Comparisons

When a sentence includes a comparison, the items being compared must be not only grammatically parallel but also logically parallel—you must compare like to like. For example, you cannot compare the cost of one medicine with another medicine, you can only compare the cost of one medicine with *that of* another.

A second element tested on comparison questions is the pronoun used—comparisons of grammatically singular things use "that of" while those of grammatically plural things use "those of."

Incorrect   The value one gets from consistent use of a home gym compares favorably with a gym membership.

The value one gets from consistent use of a home gym compares favorably with those of a gym membership.

Correct   The value one gets from consistent use of a home gym compares favorably with that of a gym membership.

A final note on comparisons: adjectives have positive, comparative (using **more** or ending in **-er**) and superlative (using **most** or ending in **-est**) forms.

Positive	Comparative	Superlative
He is a good soccer player.	He has become a better soccer player this year.	He is the best soccer player in the entire school.
You are beautiful.	You are more beautiful than your sisters.	You are the most beautiful person I have ever seen.

Although this aspect is rarely tested, remember that comparative forms of adjectives are used to compare two nouns or to compare one noun to the rest of a group, and that superlative forms are limited to instances when more than two nouns are compared.

Incorrect   Most historians truly believe that he is the <u>better general of those who led the Americans</u>.

Correct   Most historians truly believe that he is the <u>better general of the two</u>.

Most historians truly believe that he is the <u>best general of those who led the Americans</u>.

Idiomatic Constructions for Lists and Comparisons

Watch out for the following idiomatic constructions:

"**Not so much**…" must always be accompanied by "**as**…".

"**Not only**…" must always be accompanied by "**but also**…".

In many constructions "**Just as**…" must be accompanied by "**so**…".

"**Neither** … **nor**" and "**either** … **or**" constructions must be followed by the same verb construction.

"**More**…" must always be accompanied by "**than**…"

These structures are always created using exactly these words, and the words/phrases coming *immediately after* them must be grammatically parallel.

Incorrect   After the game, he was not so much <u>tired but rather he was feeling depressed</u>.

Correct   After the game, he was not so much <u>tired as depressed</u>.

Incorrect   The Trailblazers are not only the best defensive team <u>but they are also true humanitarians, as well</u>.

Correct   The Trailblazers are not only the best defensive team <u>but also true humanitarians</u>.

Incorrect   I was not either happy for us nor was I sad for them when the series ended.

Correct   I was <u>neither happy for us nor sad for them</u> when the series ended.

Parallelism and Comparisons—Try It!

Correct any errors in the underlined sections.

1. I like snowboarding <u>better</u> than <u>to skate</u>.

2. Rick is either playing the <u>fool, or he is playing</u> video games.

3. Amanda has trouble with study skills, memory techniques, and <u>managing her time</u>.

4. I neither like football <u>nor do I</u> understand it, but I suppose it is, ironically, my <u>better sport</u>.

5. Most professionals prefer the benefits of working from home <u>to an office</u>.

6. I plan to enjoy the adventure of traveling this summer either in Europe <u>or Central America</u>, but either region seems more exciting than <u>that of travelling in the US</u>.

7. Ashley will <u>write the essay, proofread, and e-mail it</u> before tomorrow.

8. <u>Not only are they paying</u> for our daughter's wedding but also for the honeymoon.

Parallelism and Comparisons Practice Set

1 Appearing with an increase in gang culture, new graffiti popped up throughout the city, mostly on abandoned buildings, unused billboards, and <u>sprayed on</u> highway overpasses.

A) NO CHANGE
B) they were sprayed on
C) on
D) DELETE the underlined portion

2 Professional athletes must train year round: <u>lift weights,</u> running, and honing their skills.

A) NO CHANGE
B) lifting weights,
C) they lift weights,
D) to lift weights,

3 The settlers expected the climate of Virginia, with its latitude more southerly than <u>that of Rome, to be fairer than what Rome was like.</u>

A) NO CHANGE
B) Rome, to be fairer compared to Rome.
C) those of Rome, to be fairer than Rome.
D) that of Rome, to be fairer than the climate of Rome.

4 Despite negative public opinion, the congressman has improved the lives of citizens in his district by implementing free childcare, <u>lower unemployment,</u> and reforming labor laws.

A) NO CHANGE
B) low unemployment,
C) lowering unemployment,
D) for lower unemployment,

5 For the first time, prints of his works, so long legally prohibited from being mass produced, will be made available to the general public at prices similar to <u>other artists' works.</u>

A) NO CHANGE
B) that of prints of other artists' works.
C) that of other artists' works.
D) those of prints of other artists' works.

6 Outdated ideas, <u>old practices too,</u> and technologies are looked down upon as relics of the past.

A) NO CHANGE
B) also old practices
C) in addition to old practices
D) practices,

7   Thanksgiving is my favorite holiday: it is a time to spend with family, an excuse to overindulge in delicious food, and it reminds me to be thankful for all I have.

A) NO CHANGE
B) a reminder
C) I remember
D) remembering

8   The management of a home building project is similar to running to a business—you need to have effective coordination between many different people doing many different tasks.

A) NO CHANGE
B) as the running of a business:
C) to that of a business—
D) with running a business:

9   Not only was I exhausted by the end of the race, but also dehydrated due to the lack of water stations along the course.

A) NO CHANGE
B) but also dehydrating
C) also dehydrated
D) but I was also dehydrated

10   Ever since Mr. Smith became principal, his goal has been to improve school unity by stronger bonds between students, encouraging collaboration among teachers, and hosting school-wide barbeques.

A) NO CHANGE
B) strong bonds
C) strengthening bonds
D) build strong bonds

11   To the first test tube, the scientist added water and magnesium sulfate; to the other, she added water and sodium carbonate was added.

A) NO CHANGE
B) and sodium carbonate.
C) and also adding sodium carbonate.
D) as well as the addition of sodium carbonate.

12   Many people are shocked when they learn the ways in which key skills needed for an office setting are similar to those skills needed for martial arts and acrobatics.

A) NO CHANGE
B) that of the disciplines of
C) people mastering
D) DELETE the underlined portion

Apostrophes

Although questions dealing with apostrophes often cover more than one topic, they are easy to recognize—look for changes in apostrophe use! If you know these well, you can often eliminate answer choices with more complex errors in them.

The **apostrophe** is used to show *possession* (ownership) or indicate a *contraction*.

NOTE: Plural nouns *do not* use apostrophes unless they are also showing possession!

Possession

1   When a **singular** noun *does not* end in **-s**, add **'s** to show possession.

    Incorrect   The <u>girls</u> coat was hidden under the <u>familys'</u> blanket.

    Correct The <u>girl's</u> coat was hidden under the <u>family's</u> blanket.

2   When a **singular** noun *ends* in **-s**, add **'** or **'s** to show possession. You will *not* be tested on which of these two is correct for a given word, as *both* are acceptable for singular nouns ending in **-s**.

    Incorrect   The principal vetoed the senior <u>classes'</u> suggestion for a day off.

                    Many theologians do not understand <u>Jesus teaching's</u>.

    Correct   The principal vetoed the senior <u>class's</u> suggestion for a day off.

                    Many theologians do not understand <u>Jesus' teachings</u>.

3   When a **plural** noun *ends* in **-s**, add **'** to show possession.

    Incorrect   The debate team met for pizza to celebrate the <u>teams'</u> victory.

    Correct   The debate team met for pizza to celebrate the <u>students'</u> victory.

4   When a **plural** noun *does not* end in **-s**, add **'s** to show possession.

    Incorrect   The <u>childrens' toy's</u> were scattered about the playroom.

    Correct   The <u>children's toys</u> were scattered about the playroom.

5   To show **joint** possession, make only the last noun possessive. To show individual possession, make all nouns possessive.

    Incorrect   Are you attending <u>Stephanie's and Sandy's</u> party?

    Correct   Are you attending <u>Stephanie and Sandy's</u> party?

    Incorrect   <u>Stephanie and Sandy's</u> parties were different, but equally fun.

    Correct   <u>Stephanie's and Sandy's</u> parties were different, but equally fun.

Contractions

6   In **contractions**, use an apostrophe in *place of any omitted letters.*

    Correct   Suzanne <u>can't</u> believe that her school <u>isn't</u> allowing cell phones on campus anymore.

7   Be sure to know the difference between **possessive pronouns** (*that never take an apostrophe*) and **contracted pronouns** (*that do take an apostrophe*). To check if a contraction is correct, read it as two separate words. For example, *it's = it is, you're = you are, who's = who is,* and *they're = they are.* Remember that **its'** is ***not*** a word.

    Incorrect   <u>Their's</u> no doubt <u>you're</u> performance on ChoralSingers.com was incredible! <u>Its</u> evident that <u>your</u> deserving of all <u>you're</u> accolades as <u>you're</u> video is now on <u>it's</u> fifth day as the most watched on <u>they're</u> site.

    Correct   <u>There's</u> no doubt <u>your</u> performance on Choral Singers.com was incredible! <u>It's</u> evident that <u>you're</u> deserving of all <u>your</u> accolades as <u>your</u> video is now on <u>its</u> fifth day as the most watched on <u>their</u> site.

Apostrophes—Try It!

Correct any errors in the underlined portions of the following sentences.

1. <u>Its heart</u> had stopped beating, but the <u>amphibians tail</u> still quivered with life.

2. Sometimes when the <u>Smiths' friends dog</u> starts to howl, the friend howls in accord.

3. The <u>grassroots' bring-out-the vote</u> effort rejuvenated the community and increased <u>it's</u> involvement in social welfare.

4. "<u>Its</u> mid-day," mother exclaimed, "and <u>your</u> still in bed!"

5. "<u>Your</u> braver than any of them," Scarlet told Rhett, with admiration in <u>her eye's.</u>

6. These <u>books covers'</u> were torn before <u>they're</u> arrival here.

7. On <u>Los Angeles'</u> Rodeo Drive, most <u>shop's</u> are too expensive for me to even look at.

8. <u>Stephen's and Seth's</u> recently finished film is going to be shown at Sundance this year; they hope <u>it's</u> content will challenge <u>there audiences thinking.</u>

9. Jane <u>Austen's</u> *Emma* is both a love story and a detective novel.

10. My <u>dogs collar</u> is blue but both of my cousin <u>Joan's dogs collars'</u> are green; when our Chihuahuas play together we can only tell them apart by <u>there collar's.</u>

Apostrophe Practice Set

[1] The Washington Monument is again open to

the public after repairs on its elevator.

A) NO CHANGE
B) repairs on it's
C) repair's on its'
D) repairs' on its

[2] Tracking each students' grades throughout

high school helps the school board identify any

school-wide trends.

A) NO CHANGE
B) student's grades
C) students' grades
D) all student's grades

[3] Kansas' governor addressed the Kansas

Legislature in the annual "State of the State,"

in which he described his new budget proposal.

A) NO CHANGE
B) Kansas governor
C) The governor of Kansas'
D) Kansases governor

[4] Germany's population is declining while the

reverse is true for that of most more developed

country's, in which populations grow due to

longer lives more than compensating for fewer

births.

A) NO CHANGE
B) countrys'
C) countries,
D) countries'

[5] Most employers do not even look at a

perspective employees' references' until after

the interview process.

A) NO CHANGE
B) perspective employee's references
C) prospective employees' references
D) prospective employee's references

[6] Many of Disney's character's origins are more

unsettling than those characters' kid-friendly

films suggest.

A) NO CHANGE
B) Disneys' character origins
C) Disney character's origins
D) Disney's characters' origins

Modifiers

A **modifier** is a word or phrase that modifies or describes another word or phrase. A modifier *must* be placed immediately next to the word that it is modifying. When the modifier starts the sentence, it must modify the subject of the sentence. If a modifier is placed incorrectly, the meaning of the sentence can become unclear and even inadvertently humorous.

Most commonly, you can recognize a **modifier** question when a sentence has an introductory verbal phrase (called a misplaced or dangling participle) that is not underlined followed by an underlined group of words. These questions are tough to recognize, because they look like the wordiness of the choices is being tested, or perhaps that you are supposed to choose between active and passive forms of the main verb, but you must always choose the subject that is *doing* the **action** of the introductory phrase in order to get these questions correct.

Incorrect   Humming cheerfully, the boat was rowed by the oarsman into the choppy seas.

Engulfed in flames, the office workers escaped the building just in time.

Correct   Humming cheerfully, the oarsman rowed the boat into the choppy seas.

Engulfed in flames, the building was evacuated of all the office workers just in time.

In addition to introductory phrases, the SAT occasionally tests other types of modifying phrases and words. For clarity, modifiers must be placed as close as possible to the word that they modify, so choose the placement closest to the word the phrase logically should modify.

Incorrect   By a great stroke of luck, the detective saw the would-be assassin as he was about to pull the trigger with his binoculars.

By a great stroke of luck, the detective saw the would-be assassin with his binoculars as he was about to pull the trigger.

Correct   By a great stroke of luck, the detective saw with his binoculars the would-be assassin as he was about to pull the trigger.

Note that this sentence sounds "awkward," but is nonetheless the only correct option!

Modifiers—Try It!

Correct any errors in the underlined portions of the following sentences.

1 My cousin sold a house to a nice family with no hard wood floors.

2 On Halloween, we love the people who give brownies to the children wrapped in cellophane.

3 Waking up later than planned, the flight was missed by John.

4 Whistling as they worked, the job was found more manageable by the seven dwarves.

5 Having been abandoned decades before, the scientists were amazed to find the research center still had functioning punch card computers.

6 Never one to minimize the embarrassing aspects of a story, the description Steve gave of the projectile vomit striking his eyeball was both disgusting and hilarious.

Modifiers Practice Set

1 Running out of new ideas, <u>the blank computer screen stared at me.</u>

A) NO CHANGE
B) the computer screen was blank.
C) I stared at the blank computer screen.
D) staring at me was the blank computer screen.

2 Covered with rainbow sprinkles, <u>his mother admired Jonah's creativity in decorating the sugar cookies.</u>

A) NO CHANGE
B) Jonah's creativity was admired by his mother in decorating the sugar cookies.
C) the sugar cookies Jonah decorated led his mother to admire his creativity.
D) Jonah's creativity in decorating the sugar cookies was admired by his mother.

3 <u>The tourists on Segways blocked the path of the congressional staffers trying to get to work.</u>

A) NO CHANGE
B) The tourists blocked the path on Segways of the congressional staffers trying to get to work.
C) The tourists on Segways blocked the path, trying to get to work, of the congressional staffers.
D) Trying the get to work, the tourists on Segways blocked the path of the congressional staffers.

4 <u>She adopted a kitten for her brother named Princess Kitty.</u>

A) NO CHANGE
B) Named Princess Kitty, she adopted a kitten for her brother.
C) She adopted a kitten named Princess Kitty for her brother.
D) She adopted, named Princess Kitty, a kitten for her brother.

5 Tired of sleeping on her friend's couch, <u>Michelle's excitement rose when she found her own apartment.</u>

A) NO CHANGE
B) Michelle was excited to find her own apartment.
C) after finding her own apartment, Michelle's excitement rose.
D) finding her own apartment was exciting for Michelle.

6 Concerned citizens have questioned the plan, wondering whether the increase in spending <u>sufficiently and permanently will address</u> the housing needs of the neighborhood's poorest tenants.

A) NO CHANGE
B) will sufficiently and permanently address
C) sufficiently will permanently address
D) will address sufficiently permanently

7 Cleopatra <u>dies, bitten by venomous snakes wearing her royal gowns that symbolize Egyptian elegance.</u>

A) NO CHANGE
B) dies, wearing her royal gowns from venomous snakes that symbolize Egyptian elegance.
C) dies, bitten by venomous snakes while wearing her royal gowns that symbolize Egyptian elegance.
D) dies wearing her royal gowns that symbolize Egyptian elegance bitten by venomous snakes.

Idioms and Usage

Some of the most difficult questions to recognize what is being tested on the SAT are those that deal with usage and idioms. Often the changes between answer choices will be very small (such as a different preposition or even just a different letter in a word). Both of these topics can also be difficult because there are no rules to memorize in order to get the correct answer.

Idioms

Idioms are expressions that are determined by customary usage rather than any rule. For example, in English we say that we are "capable of using idioms properly" but not "capable to use idioms properly." Because there is no rule for idiom questions (*idiom* comes from Greek and Latin words meaning "peculiar, particular to oneself"), there is no principle or logic to which word or expression should be chosen in a given sentence, and no list could be memorized that would guarantee that you would be prepared for *every* idiom question that could come up on the test. While most idioms questions deal with prepositions, the test has also required students to choose between gerunds (**-ing** verb forms) and infinitives (**to** + verb), and certain idiomatic structures for comparisons and lists (see Parallelism and Comparisons on page 99) are commonly tested as well.

Instead of trying to memorize a list of idioms, be sure to notice when the answer choices vary their prepositions or the structuring of words, and read through the whole sentence and choose the one that sounds most natural. Idiom questions on the test often test other errors at the same time, so if you are not sure which word sounds best, make sure that there is no other error being tested in the answer choices.

Incorrect   He had difficulty staying <u>in topic</u>, but he was <u>capable to keep</u> his audiences engaged <u>about</u> his speeches anyway.

Correct   He had difficulty staying <u>on topic</u>, but he was <u>able to keep</u> his audiences engaged <u>in</u> his speeches anyway.

Usage

Usage questions test words that appear or sound very similar but mean different things, sometimes even belonging to different parts of speech. There is no complete list of all such terms, as words from **persecuted** and **prosecuted** and **expect** and **aspect** and many more can and have been tested, but here is a short list of commonly tested words that trip up many test takers.

1   **affect** (v.) and **effect** (n.)

Affect is most commonly a verb meaning to produce an effect. You can replace it in a sentence with verbs like <u>alter</u> to make sure that it fits in the sentence.

Effect is a noun that means the result of a cause, or something produced by a cause. You can replace it with nouns like **result** to make sure that it fits the sentence. Remember to link the **e** in result with **effect** and the **a** in alter with **affect**!

Correct   The <u>effect</u> of the disease on her lungs <u>affected</u> her ability to run.

2   **fewer** and **less**

Fewer refers to countable items while **less** refers to uncountable amounts.

Correct   I went to <u>fewer</u> practices than he; it is not surprising that I got <u>less</u> playing time in our game.

The distinction between **fewer** and **less** is the same as that between **many** and **much**—the SAT has tested these terms as well, and in "many more people" or "much more of the population."

3   than and **then**

Then refers to **time**, whereas **than** is used for **comparisons**. Remember to link the **a** and **e** in each pair to remember which is which. Because the letters that set them apart are buried in the middle of these short words, students will often fail to recognize this change in answer choices that also involve other changes. If you learn to recognize when these words are being tested, you will often be able to easily eliminate two answers on a **than/then** question.

Correct   Then, he knew for certain that he was less than ideally suited to be a lawyer.

First they were less prepared than other teams, but then later they caught up and surpassed all others.

4   it's and **its**
they're and **their** and **there**
you're and **your**,
who's and **whose**

A final element of usage commonly tested is the use of related pronoun forms. For more on the distinctions between these forms, see both Pronouns (page 95)and Apostrophes (page 103).

Finally, idioms and usage are often tested on a single question, and so it helps to identify the "parts" of the question and eliminate answers using one element at a time:

Example 3   Although the Russians had an advantage over the American team, the principle affect of their advantage was complacency.

A) NO CHANGE

B) the principal effect about

C) the principle affect about

D) the principal effect of

Many students are not confident about which to choose between **principle** and **principal**, which is the first element changed in the answer choices. However, if you start by isolating the changes and first eliminate based on aspects you are certain of, you can get this question correct without ever having to know the difference between **principle** and **principal**. Instead, start by eliminating all answer choices that have **affect** instead of **effect**, because we can replace the word with **result** but not with **alter**. Then, read the whole sentence with choice (B) and (D) in it, and you will choose (D) as the more "natural" sounding expression.

Idioms and Usage—Try It!

Correct all errors in the underlined portions of the sentences.

[1] Even today, a <u>personnel computer</u> is not <u>necessary to learning</u> new things; it is, however, very helpful for research.

[2] The headmistress claimed that each of her students has a much stronger work ethic but <u>less advantages of</u> home <u>then students</u> at the larger school nearby have.

[3] Your test scores are <u>inconsistent to your performance at</u> school, which is a <u>direct affect from</u> your school's emphases.

[4] A study can establish a connection <u>among too</u> variables but it cannot establish cause and <u>effect relationships affectively</u>.

[5] The socioeconomic divisions of Washington, DC, are very <u>different to</u> those <u>in Baltimore</u>.

[6] Although the police tried to prevent him <u>to leave</u> the country, he <u>alluded</u> pursuit for <u>much more years</u>.

Idioms and Usage Practice Set

1 Many technology companies are already experimenting with drones as a means <u>from</u> delivering packages.

A) NO CHANGE
B) through
C) of
D) DELETE the underlined portion.

2 To research the impact of social media on politics, I read a book <u>upon</u> the rise of "fake news."

A) NO CHANGE
B) for
C) with
D) about

3 Anyone with <u>excess to</u> a protractor, a tape measure, a screw, and some string can calculate the height of any building by constructing an astrolabe and using a little bit of basic trigonometry.

A) NO CHANGE
B) access of
C) access to
D) excess of

4 The coach pointed to the positive <u>affect of</u> senior leadership as the primary reason the team was undefeated.

A) NO CHANGE
B) affects on
C) effect to
D) effect of

5 I've travelled through Mexico, Arizona and Texas <u>in order to find</u> the best recipe for guacamole.

A) NO CHANGE
B) in order for finding
C) so to finding
D) so to find

6 The Governor went <u>so far</u> to blame the sluggish economy on the newspapers that were critical of his proposals.

A) NO CHANGE
B) so far as
C) as far
D) as far in

[7] Aerial photography showed that there had been <u>many less people at the ceremony then</u> at the march.

A) NO CHANGE
B) far fewer people at the ceremony then
C) far fewer people at the ceremony than
D) much less people at the ceremony than

[8] The journalists pointed their microphones <u>toward the actress who was the first to emerge of</u> the limo.

A) NO CHANGE
B) from the actress who was the first to emerge of
C) toward the actress who was the first to emerge from
D) from the actress who was the first to emerge toward

[9] Carbon-14 dating showed that the volcanic <u>explosion proceeded</u> the arrival of large predators to the area.

A) NO CHANGE
B) exposure proceeded
C) exposure preceded
D) explosion preceded

[10] The environmentalist <u>cited the decrease in crop yield near the site</u> of the explosion as evidence for the company's culpability.

A) NO CHANGE
B) sighted the decrease in crop yield near the sight
C) sited the decrease in crop yield near the cite
D) cited the decrease in crop yield near the sight

Table for Identifying SEC Questions

Use this table for quick reference to the information on Standard English Conventions tested on the SAT. Remember to start by noticing the changes in the answer choices to recognize what is being tested, and then ask the right questions to lead you to the correct answer every time.

Error Type	How to recognize it	What to ask	How to solve
Punctuation	Changes in punctuation (type and/or location) and minor word changes are the *only* differences in answer choices.	For all types of punctuation questions, compare answers, crossing out the incorrect punctuation marks in each wrong answer, and choose the one left.	
		Is the punctuation based on	
		… sentence structure?	For sentence structure, be sure to *read* the *whole* sentence and determine its clause structure.
		… nonessential elements?	Look for *pairs* of commas or dashes, and make sure whatever is between them could sensibly be dropped out of the sentence.
		… or lists?	Make sure commas separate any list of 3 or more items, and make sure that there is *no* comma between the last adjective in a list and the word it modifies.
Verbs	Changes in *form* of the verb are the primary differences between the answer choices.	Does the verb need to be conjugated?	Choose the correct conjugation for the subject!
		What is the subject of the underlined verb?	Read the subject and verb together and make sure they "sound" correct.
		What tense should the verb be in?	Choose the tense that matches the context.
Pronouns	Changes in pronoun form are the primary difference between the answer choices.	What is the antecedent of the pronoun? Is it clear?	Make sure that pronoun matches its antecedent in number and gender. Choose a specific noun instead of a pronoun if the antecedent is unclear.
		Is the pronoun a subject or an object?	For **who/whom**, read the sentence with **he or they** in place of **who**, and **him** or **them** in place of **whom**.

Error Type	How to recognize it	What to ask	How to solve
Parallelism and Comparisons	Different forms of related words and/or slight rearrangements of words within answer choices are the main difference between answer choices. These can be difficult to recognize due to kinds of differences that are possible in answer choices.	What is the structure of the other elements in the list or comparison?	Choose the answer choice that matches the rest of the list.
		What specific word or words are being compared?	Choose the answer choice that creates a logical and correct comparison.
Idioms and Usage	Changes in the preposition used or very similar-looking words are notable in answers. These are often combined with other error types.	Which preposition or form sounds best in the sentence?	Read the sentence or phrase with each option and choose the one that sounds best.
		Which word is intended?	Identify the meaning of each form, and choose the best for the context.
Apostrophes	Changes in the location and presence of apostrophes are notable in answer choices. These are often combined with other error types.	Is the word with the apostrophe possessive? Is it plural?	Check each answer's use of apostrophes: 's =singular possession, s' =plural possession *Never* choose 's or s' if the noun is *plural* but **not** *possessive*.
		Is the apostrophe intended to convey a contraction?	Read the contraction as the words it is made up of and see if it makes sense.
Modifiers	Usually the underlined section comes after an introductory phrase, and the answer choices vary the subject of the sentence. For most students, these are the toughest to recognize because they look like EOI questions.	What word is the phrase or word intended to modify?	Choose the answer that places the modifier and the word modified as close together as possible. For introductory phrases, make sure to choose the subject that the phrase modifies.

Mathematics Test Manual

There are two SAT Mathematics Tests. They are the third and fourth tests in your SAT sitting:

Math Test—No Calculator has 20 questions over 25 minutes. The first 15 questions have multiple choices, and the last 5 ask for student-produced responses.

Math Test—Calculator has 38 questions over 55 minutes. The first 30 questions have multiple choices, and the last 8 ask for student-produced repsonses.

Overview and Strategies

If there's one good thing about standardized tests, it is that they are predictable. In order for test scores to be consistent, the SAT uses the same *type* of questions from test to test. So, in order to do well, all you need to do is the following:

1. Know each type of question, *and*
2. Learn the strategies (quick ways) to solve each type of question accurately.

We've structured this workbook with the most frequently used strategies first. Next, we tackle the four major categories of questions that come up on the SAT.

- Heart of Algebra, which includes translating, solving, and interpreting linear equations and functions
- Passport to Advanced Math, which includes algebraic changes of form as well as higher level functions
- Problem Solving and Data Analysis, which emphasizes the interpretation of tables and graphs as well as statistical measurements and probability
- Additional Math Topics, which can include topics in geometry, trigonometry, and complex numbers

About 90% of all questions on any SAT come from the first three categories above, and those are split approximately even. It's also useful to note that questions from the Problem Solving and Data Analysis category only appear in the calculator-permitted section and constitute nearly half of that section's questions.

Strategies

A strategy is just a quick way to solve a problem accurately. Often you can come up with your own quick ways. The trick is to pause for a moment before you start solving and think about the easy way to solve the question. If you're like most students, though, during a timed test like the SAT, you won't even think about pausing.

The people who write the SAT Math realize that all of us have certain patterned ways of solving questions—the ways we learn in school. In high-pressure situations, we tend to fall back upon these ways that we know so well. Because test-makers want to reward the ability to think creatively under pressure, they devise questions that can seem difficult if you try to solve them in the most obvious way—the way you've learned in school.

One way you can prepare for these questions is to practice alternative strategies as much as you practice textbook methods in high school. If you become very familiar with the quick way, it's likely that you'll remember it during the SAT.

Back Solving

On the SAT, of the 58 Mathematics questions, 45 provide you with answer choices. Because the answer to the question is right there in front of you, you can often simply *try the various answers* until you see which one works.

There are some questions for which it is easiest to start with simple answer choices: 0 and 1, for example, are very quick to plug in and check, and for this reason they are often the best place to start if they are available.

For other questions, you can use the fact that the answer choices are usually in increasing or decreasing order. This is most helpful in cases like the following:

Example 1   For two consecutive even integers, the result of adding the smaller integer to three times the larger integer is 62. What are the two integers?

A) 14, 16

B) 16, 18

C) 18, 20

D) 20, 22

It is simplest to begin with a middle answer choice, i.e. 18 and 20. Adding the smaller number to three times the larger yields $18 + 3 \times 20 = 78$. This is clearly greater than the 62 you are looking for, so you know that choice (C) is incorrect. However, choice (D) is *also* incorrect because it will give you something *even larger* than choice (C) did.

You can try choice (B) next, i.e. 16 and 18. Adding the smaller number to three times the larger yields $16 + 3 \times 18 = 70$, which is still too big. You are now actually *done* because you have eliminated *all* answer choices except one, which is (A).

If you wanted to be extra careful, you could test that answer choice (A) does indeed give you the correct answer: Using 14 and 16 gives you $14 + 3 \times 16 = 62$, which is indeed the answer you are looking for.

Extraneous Solutions

Many problems, particularly involving fractions or radicals, can yield extraneous solutions because of the restrictions associated with the domains of such functions. Such a solution is found through the ordinary course of doing correct algebra but does not actually make the equation work. That is, you can do everything correctly and still arrive at an answer, or a solution set, that is not accurate. Of course if you are back solving the choices (whether they be single solutions or solution sets), you don't have to worry about this.

Example 2   The equation $\sqrt{x} + 3 = 1$ can be solved, using correct algebra, by first subtracting 3 and then squaring both sides of the equation. This will generate the solution $x = 4$, and yet if you plug 4 into the original equation, it clearly does not work. If an equation like this is part of a multiple-choice problem, there is no reason to do the algebra and run the risk of selecting an extraneous solution. Just back solve from the beginning.

Back Solving Problem Set

On the following problem set, focus on back solving by using your answer choices.

 1 If $(x-3)^2 = (2x-1)(x+3)$, which of the following could equal x?

 A) -2

 B) 0

 C) 1

 D) 2

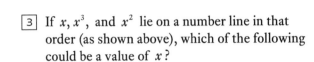

       Note: Figure not drawn to scale

 3 If x, x^3, and x^2 lie on a number line in that order (as shown above), which of the following could be a value of x?

 A) 2

 B) $-\dfrac{1}{3}$

 C) $\dfrac{3}{4}$

 D) 1

4 If $\dfrac{x^3}{y}$ is an integer but $\dfrac{x}{y}$ is not an integer, which of the following could be the values of x and y?

 A) $x=2, y=1$

 B) $x=3, y=9$

 C) $x=4, y=2$

 D) $x=3, y=2$

2 When each side of a given square is decreased by 2 inches, the area is decreased by 20 square inches. What is the length, in inches, of a side of the original square?

 A) 3

 B) 4

 C) 5

 D) 6

x	$f(x)$
-2	8
0	4
1	5
3	13
4	20

5 Which of the following functions is represented in the table above?

A) $3x+4$

B) $2x+3$

C) x^3-7

D) x^2+4

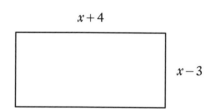

$x+4$

$x-3$

6 If the area of the rectangle above is 60, what is the value of x?

A) 5

B) 6

C) 7

D) 8

7 What is the solution set for

$$\frac{x}{x-2}-\frac{8}{x+3}=\frac{10}{x^2+x-6}?$$

A) $\{2, 3\}$

B) $\{-3, 2\}$

C) $\{2\}$

D) $\{3\}$

$$4x^2 < (4x)^2$$

8 For what value of x is the statement above false?

A) -4

B) 0

C) $\dfrac{1}{4}$

D) 1

$$1 \le x^2 \le 9$$

9 Which of the following represents all values of x that satisfy the above inequality?

A)

$\xleftarrow{\quad} \bullet \; | \; | \; | \; | \; | \; \bullet \xrightarrow{\quad}$
$-4 \;\; -3 \;\; -2 \;\; -1 \;\; 0 \;\; 1 \;\; 2 \;\; 3 \;\; 4$

B)

$\xleftarrow{\quad} | \; \bullet\!-\!\bullet \; | \; | \; \bullet\!-\!\bullet \; | \xrightarrow{\quad}$
$-4 \;\; -3 \;\; -2 \;\; -1 \;\; 0 \;\; 1 \;\; 2 \;\; 3 \;\; 4$

C)

$\xleftarrow{\quad} | \; | \; | \; | \; | \; \bullet\!-\!\bullet \; | \xrightarrow{\quad}$
$-4 \;\; -3 \;\; -2 \;\; -1 \;\; 0 \;\; 1 \;\; 2 \;\; 3 \;\; 4$

D)

$\xleftarrow{\quad} | \; \bullet\!-\!\!-\!\!-\!\!-\!\!-\!\bullet \; | \xrightarrow{\quad}$
$-4 \;\; -3 \;\; -2 \;\; -1 \;\; 0 \;\; 1 \;\; 2 \;\; 3 \;\; 4$

10 If $5^{k-4} \times 5^k + 16 = 41$, what is the value of k?

A) 0

B) 1

C) 2

D) 3

11 For which of the following functions is
    $f(-2) = f(2)$ true?

    A) $f(x) = x^2 + x$

    B) $f(x) = x^2 + 1$

    C) $f(x) = x + 2$

    D) $f(x) = x^3 + x$

14 What is the solution set for the equation
    $5 + \sqrt{x+1} = x + 4$?

    A) $\{0\}$

    B) $\{0, 3\}$

    C) $\{-1, 1\}$

    D) $\{3\}$

12 Warren is worth \$25.6 billion and Bill is worth
    \$23.04 billion. What percent of his net worth
    would Warren have to donate to Bill so that
    each is worth the same amount?

    A) 5%

    B) 8%

    C) 23%

    D) 89%

15 If $\dfrac{1}{5} + \dfrac{1}{6} + \dfrac{1}{7} > \dfrac{1}{5} + \dfrac{1}{6} + \dfrac{1}{x}$, then x could be which
    of the following?

    A) 5

    B) 6

    C) 7

    D) 8

13 What is the solution set for the equation
    $14 + \sqrt{x+2} = 11$?

    A) $\{7\}$

    B) $\{7, -11\}$

    C) $\{1\}$

    D) No solution

Plugging in Numbers

Plugging in Numbers is a useful strategy when a question has variables that maintain a constant relationship. By substituting real numbers for variables, you can solve questions arithmetically instead of algebraically.

There are three main steps to Plugging in Numbers.

1. Choose which number(s) to plug in and write it/them down.
    1.1. If there is an equation, plug in on the side where there is more action.
    1.2. Avoid choosing **0** or **1** as the number you plug in; these will often yield the same result for different choices. For the same reason, try not to use **30°**, **45°**, **60°** or **90°** for angles.
    1.3. Smaller numbers tend to work well in most cases, e.g. **2**, **3**, **4**, or **5**.
    1.4. Plug in different numbers for different variables.
    1.5. For percent problems use **100**.
    1.6. Solve for other variables in equations.
2. Write down and BOX your answer.
3. Plug the number(s) you've chosen into the same variables in the answer choices if necessary. (Note that you *must* try ALL the answer choices)
    3.1. Which one(s) matches your answer?
    3.2. If multiple answer choices work, try different numbers and repeat steps 1 to 3, though any choice you've eliminated is gone for good.

Example 1   If w is the first of three consecutive odd integers, what is the sum of the two even integers between the smallest and greatest odd integer, in terms of w ?

A) $3w$

B) $2w+4$

C) $w+10$

D) $3w+3$

Notice the complicated wording in the question. Many students will be confused by the time they get to the part about the even integers. So don't let yourself even get to that part without first plugging in a number.

1. Choose a number, specifically an odd integer, to plug in for w like, for example, **3**.
2. If $w=3$, then the consecutive odd integers are **3**, **5**, and **7**, and the even integers that are between those are **4** and **6**. The sum of **4** and **6** is **10**, so that is the number the correct choice ought to come out to when **3** is plugged in for w.
3. Plugging in **3** for w in all four choices shows that (A) works out to 9, (B) works out to 10, (C) works out to 13, and (D) works out to 12. The answer must be (B). Notice, had you plugged **1** in for w instead of **3**, choices (B) and (D) would have worked. Such a thing can happen with any number but is more common with special numbers like 1 and 0.

Plugging in Numbers Problem Set 1

1. If $y = 3^x + 3^x + 3^x$, then what is y in terms of x?

   A) 3^{3x}

   B) 9^x

   C) 3^{x^3}

   D) 3^{x+1}

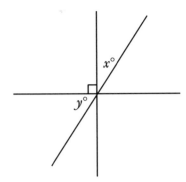

4. In the figure above, which of the following is equal to x?

   A) y

   B) $90 - x$

   C) $90 - y$

   D) $180 - y$

2. If $r, s,$ and t are consecutive odd integers, what is the difference between r and t?

   A) 1

   B) 2

   C) 3

   D) 4

5. If $\dfrac{1}{x} = \dfrac{x}{y}$, which of the following equals xy?

   A) $4x$

   B) $3x^2$

   C) x^3

   D) x

3. If $-1 < x < 0 < y < 1$, which of the following is the greatest?

   A) xy

   B) $-y$

   C) $-(y^2)$

   D) x^2

6   Andrew caught three times as many lobsters as crabs. Half of the lobsters he caught were female. If Andrew randomly chooses a shellfish from his bin, what is the likelihood that he picks a male lobster?

A) $\dfrac{3}{10}$

B) $\dfrac{3}{8}$

C) $\dfrac{5}{12}$

D) $\dfrac{6}{11}$

7   If x and y are positive consecutive integers, where $y > x$, which of the following is equal to xy?

A) $3x$

B) $4x$

C) $x^2 + y$

D) $x^2 + x$

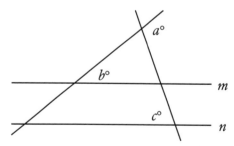

Note: Figure not drawn to scale

8   In the above figure, lines m and n are parallel. What is the value of c in terms of a and b?

A) $180 - (a + b)$

B) $180 + a - b$

C) $a + b - 180$

D) $a - b$

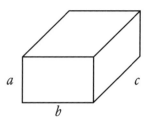

Note: Figure not drawn to scale

9   In the rectangular prism above, $b = 2a$ and $2c = 3b$. What is the volume of the box?

A) $6a^2$

B) b^3

C) $2b^2c$

D) $6a^3$

10   Ricky had d dollars in the bank. He withdrew $3/4$ of d to buy a plane ticket to Paris. He then spent $1/3$ of what was left on his lodging for the week. What fraction of the original amount remained in his account?

A) $\dfrac{1}{12}$

B) $\dfrac{1}{6}$

C) $\dfrac{1}{4}$

D) $\dfrac{1}{3}$

11   If J, K, and L are digits in the positive three-digit integer JKL, what is the decimal equivalent of $JKL \times 10^{-4}$?

A) $0.0JKL$

B) $0.JKL$

C) $JK,L00$

D) $J,KL0,000$

12. 30 percent of x is equal to y percent of 50. What is x in terms of y?

A) $\frac{1}{2}y$

B) $\frac{3}{5}y$

C) $\frac{5}{3}y$

D) $\frac{10}{3}y$

14. If k divided by 7 yields a remainder of 5, which of the following, when divided by 7, yields no remainder?

A) $3k$

B) $k^2 + 3$

C) $k + 3$

D) $k - 3$

13. Yu is taking a test. There are S number of sections, each containing A number of questions. If Yu answers one question, on average, in T minutes, how long will it take her, in hours, to complete the test?

A) $\frac{ST}{60A}$

B) $\frac{SAT}{60}$

C) $\frac{SA}{T}$

D) SAT

15. If $2a = \frac{3b^2}{c}$, what happens to the value of a when b and c are halved?

A) a is halved.

B) a is doubled.

C) a is not changed.

D) a is multiplied by 4.

Plugging in Numbers Problem Set 2

1. Chris, Mark, and Trevor are brothers. The average age of Chris and Mark is x. The average age of Mark and Trevor is y. If Chris is 26 years old, how old is Trevor in terms of x and y?

A) $\dfrac{x+y}{3}$

B) $13+y-x$

C) $26+2y-2x$

D) $\dfrac{2x+2y}{3}$

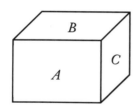

2. If $A, B,$ and C are the areas of the three faces of the rectangular prism (as shown above), in terms of $A, B,$ and C, what is the volume of the prism?

A) $\sqrt{ABC}$

B) $A^2B^2C^2$

C) $\dfrac{A^2B^2}{C^2}$

D) $\sqrt{\dfrac{AB}{C}}$

3. Jan bought 7 CDs for d dollars each. She gave the cashier t ten dollar bills. How many dollars change should Jan receive in terms of d and t?

A) $10t-7d$

B) $t-7d$

C) $10-d$

D) $t-7$

4. The sum of two numbers that differ by 2 is s. In terms of s, what is the value of the greater of the two numbers?

A) $\dfrac{s-2}{2}$

B) $\dfrac{s+1}{2}$

C) $\dfrac{2s+2}{2}$

D) $\dfrac{s+2}{2}$

5. If the average (arithmetic mean) of $a, b,$ and c is z, which of the following is the average $a, b, c,$ and d?

A) $\dfrac{3z+d}{4}$

B) $\dfrac{3z+d}{3}$

C) $\dfrac{z+d}{4}$

D) $\dfrac{z+d}{3}$

$$a+b=x$$
$$ab=y$$

6 Given that the equations above are true, what is $\frac{1}{a}+\frac{1}{b}$ in terms of x and y?

A) $x+y$

B) $\dfrac{x}{y}$

C) $\dfrac{y}{x}$

D) $\dfrac{1}{xy}$

7 If x and y are positive consecutive even integers where $y>x,$ which of the following is equal to y^2-x^2?

A) $4x$

B) $2x+2$

C) $4x+2$

D) $4x+4$

8 If the height of a cylinder is increased by 50% and the radius of its base is decreased by 50%, what is the ratio of the old volume to the new volume?

A) $4:9$

B) $8:3$

C) $2:1$

D) $8:1$

9 If the sum of the integers from −6 to an odd integer $x,$ inclusive, is $y,$ where $x>-6,$ which of the following shows the relationship between x and y?

A) $y=-5x$

B) $(x+6)=2y$

C) $x(x+1)=2(y+21)$

D) $-6+x=y$

10 If m is $\dfrac{3}{4}$ of $n,$ and n is $\dfrac{4}{5}$ of $p,$ what is the value of $\dfrac{m}{p}$?

A) $\dfrac{2}{3}$

B) $\dfrac{3}{5}$

C) $\dfrac{4}{9}$

D) $\dfrac{7}{9}$

11 The price of a television was first put on sale for 25 percent off and then, after the sale, the new price was increased by 30 percent. The final price was what percent of the initial price?

A) 95

B) 97.5

C) 100

D) 105

12 Before starting school, Jennie, Chrisi, and Kim went shopping. Jennie spent $35 more than Chrisi and $15 more than Kim. If Jennie spent $$j$, how much were their total purchases, in dollars, in terms of j ?

A) $j+50$

B) $3j-50$

C) $j+150$

D) $\dfrac{j+150}{3}$

14 If $a=b^4$ for any positive integer b, and $c=a+a^3$, what is c in terms of b ?

A) $b+b^3$

B) $b^{12}+b^4$

C) b^7+b^3

D) b^5+b^3

13 If c percent of $a+b$ is equal to $4b$, what is the value of $\dfrac{a}{b}$ in terms of c ?

A) $\dfrac{c}{25}-1$

B) $\dfrac{400}{c}-1$

C) $\dfrac{100}{c}$

D) $\dfrac{300}{c}$

15 In a high rise apartment building there is one washing machine for every 6 residents, one dryer for every 5 residents, and a parking space for every 4 residents. If there are x total washers, dryers, and parking spaces, then how many residents, in terms of x, live in the high rise building?

A) $\dfrac{37}{60}x$

B) $\dfrac{60}{37}x$

C) $120x$

D) $60x$

Calculators

Since questions in the Heart of Algebra, Passport to Advanced Math, and Additional Math Topics categories can come up both in the Calculator and No Calculator SAT sections, you should be sure to know how to answer all such questions in this manual without a calculator unless you see the icon to the right. Still, knowing how to use your calculator's operations and shortcuts is valuable for many questions.

The following guide references TI-84 calculators that have been upgraded to improve graphics. Many, though not all, of the functions listed below can be found on TI-83 calculators. Other graphing calculators have similar functions. Always check your owner's manual to see what operations your calculator will perform.

The Basics

- The number keys are white. These include both the decimal point $\boxed{.}$ and the negative sign $\boxed{(-)}$. Be sure not to confuse the negative sign with the subtraction symbol.
- Using the up or down arrows, you can select previous answers or entries and insert them into your current line by pressing $\boxed{\text{ENTER}}$. You can use the ENTRY button, $\boxed{\text{2ND}} \rightarrow \boxed{\text{ENTER}}$, to recall previous entries as well.
- Caret ($\boxed{\wedge}$) is used to raise to a power and is found above the four basic operations.
- $\boxed{x^2}$ can be used to both square or, with $\boxed{\text{2ND}}$, square root.
- The comma $\boxed{,}$ is used within other functions discussed later
- Parentheses should be used when operating with negative numbers or fractions, especially when not using n/d fraction mode (discussed later), to assure the order of operations, PEMDAS, is properly applied.

The $\boxed{\text{MATH}}$ button (left column, third from top) $\boxed{\text{MATH}} \rightarrow$ MATH NUM CPX PRB

- Under $\boxed{\text{MATH}} \rightarrow$ MATH you will find the following useful functions:
  - 1:▷Frac: to change a rational decimal to a fraction in lowest terms
  - 4:$\sqrt[3]{}$: to take the cube root of a number
  - 5:$\sqrt[x]{}$: to take any root of a number (put root before symbol)
- Under $\boxed{\text{MATH}} \rightarrow$ NUM you will find these useful functions:
  - 1:abs(: to initiate absolute value
  - 8:lcm(: to find the least common multiple of two numbers separated by a comma
  - 9:gcd(: to find the greatest common divisor (factor) of two numbers separated by a comma
  - D:n/d: to use a horizontal dividing line; you will see ⊟ on the screen and be able to enter calculations on top and bottom

Graphing

- $\boxed{\text{Y=}}$ to input functions where y has been isolated
- $\boxed{\text{WINDOW}}$ to adjust horizontal and vertical minima and maxima of graph screen and set scale for how frequently axes hash marks are shown
- $\boxed{\text{ZOOM}}$ to adjust the view
    - 1: ZBox: to create, with the cursor, a rectangle whose interior will be enlarged
    - 6: ZStandard: to return to basic window from –10 to 10 in each direction
    - 0: ZFit: to adjust window to show as much of inputted graph(s) as possible
    - A: ZQuadrant1: to show only the first quadrant
- $\boxed{\text{TRACE}}$ to have the cursor follow graph(s) in graph screen as the x and y values are reported at the bottom (use up and down arrows to toggle through multiple graphs)
- $\boxed{\text{TABLE}}$ ($\boxed{\text{2ND}} \to \boxed{\text{GRAPH}}$) to view a list of x and y coordinates for inputted functions
    - $\boxed{\text{TBLSET}}$ ($\boxed{\text{2ND}} \to \boxed{\text{WINDOW}}$)to adjust table information like where x should start and what the x interval should be
- $\boxed{\text{CALC}}$ ($\boxed{\text{2ND}} \to \boxed{\text{TRACE}}$) : use the following functions to calculate:
    - 2: zero: an x-intercept (or root); you will need to use the cursor to set left and right boundaries for the root you're looking for
    - 3: minimum and
    - 4: maximum: a turning point (again, between left and right boundaries)
    - 5: intersect: the intersection point between two curves nearest where the cursor selects the curves (toggle using up and down arrows to select the curves)
    - *Note*: It is often easier to graph a polynomial function and calculate its roots, turning points or transformations than to use algebraic methods like factoring or formulas.

Trick for listing factors

- If you want to see a list of factors of a number, divide that number by x in the $\boxed{\text{Y=}}$ screen and then view the table.

Trigonometric Functions

- $\boxed{\text{SIN}}$, $\boxed{\text{COS}}$, and $\boxed{\text{TAN}}$ operate on angles to find trig ratios
- $\boxed{\text{2ND}} \to \overset{\text{SIN}^{-1}}{\boxed{\text{SIN}}}$, $\overset{\text{COS}^{-1}}{\boxed{\text{COS}}}$, and $\overset{\text{TAN}^{-1}}{\boxed{\text{TAN}}}$ operate on trig ratios to find angles

Miscellaneous

- CATALOG ($\boxed{\text{2ND}} \to \overset{\text{CATALOG}}{\boxed{\text{0}}}$) lists functions alphabetically (jump using green letters)
- F1 ($\boxed{\text{ALPHA}} \to \overset{\text{F1}}{\boxed{\text{Y=}}}$) shortcuts to fraction modes
- F2 ($\boxed{\text{ALPHA}} \to \overset{\text{F2}}{\boxed{\text{WINDOW}}}$) shortcuts to operations like abs(

Calculator Problem Set

Utilize the functions of the calculator to help you answer the questions in the following set.

1. If $a = \frac{37}{11}b$ and $b = \frac{13}{17}c$, what is a in terms of c?

   A) $\frac{25}{14}c$

   B) $\frac{5}{2}c$

   C) $\frac{481}{187}c$

   D) $\frac{629}{143}c$

2. What is the value of $\frac{3xy^2 - 17}{5\sqrt{z}}$ when $x = -4, y = -3,$ and $z = 625$?

   A) $-\frac{1279}{125}$

   B) -1

   C) 1

   D) $\frac{1279}{125}$

3. In the function $y = \left| x^2 - 4 \right|$, for how many values of x does $y = 3$?

   A) None

   B) Two

   C) Three

   D) Four

4. What is the value of $\left| -4 \right| - \left| 20 - 33 \right|$?

   A) -17

   B) -9

   C) 17

   D) 57

5. The expression $\dfrac{3 + \frac{3}{5}}{2 + \frac{1}{10}}$ is equal to?

   A) $\frac{12}{7}$

   B) $\frac{9}{5}$

   C) $\frac{22}{7}$

   D) $\frac{22}{5}$

6 | Which of the following is an equivalent form of $f(x)=(x-8)(x+4)$ so that the x- and y-coordinates of the vertex appear as constants?

A) $f(x)=x^2+4x-32$

B) $f(x)=(x-2)^2-36$

C) $f(x)=(x-2)^2-32$

D) $f(x)=(x-4)^2-28$

9 | In the xy-plane, the graph of which of the following functions has x-intercepts of 2, 4, and 7?

A) $f(x)=(x+2)(x+4)(x+7)$

B) $f(x)=(x-2)(x-4)(x-7)$

C) $f(x)=x^3-56$

D) $f(x)=(x-8)(x-7)$

7 | The graphs of $y=-|x|$ and $y=\sqrt[3]{x}$ are *both* in which of the following quadrants?

A) I only

B) I and III

C) III only

D) III and IV

10 | If $\cos A=0.16$ and $0°<A<90°$, what is $\sin(90-A)°$?

A) 0.16

B) 0.4

C) 0.8

D) 0.84

8 | What are the equations of all the vertical asymptotes for the graph of the function $y=\dfrac{2x-4}{x^2-4}$?

A) $x=2$ and $x=-2$

B) $x=2$ only

C) $x=-2$ only

D) $x=0$, $x=2$ and $x=-2$

No Calculator Section

Section 3 of the SAT has 20 questions, 15 multiple-choice and 5 grid-in, for which you may not use your calculator. Almost all of these 20 questions are Heart of Algebra or Passport to Advanced Math questions. Two or three are from the Additional Math Topics category, and there are no Data Analysis questions in the no-calculator section.

The following suggestions can be used on any math problem but are especially handy when you don't have use of your calculator:

- Identify and underline all math words. Words like **sum, multiple** and **parallel**, and even simple math words like **odd** and **even,** can get lost or mistaken for a similar word when tackling a problem with many parts. Underlining them will burn them into your short-term memory and help you check for silly errors once you have your answer.

- Look for possible algebraic form changes. Many times the writers of SAT questions are just trying to see if you recognize that an expression can be written a different way. These form changes are not necessarily simplification steps, and you won't usually be told to apply them, but when something algebraic *can* be done, see what happens when you do it. Form changes include:
  - Applying EXPONENT rules
  - DISTRIBUTING or FOILing (double distributing)
  - FACTORING
  - Writing FRACTIONS in equivalent forms by looking for *common denominators*

- Sketch figures or graphs if none are provided. Often questions involving angle relationships or function types are simple once you have a visual aid. When sketching graphs, you will usually just need a pair of axes and an approximation of specific x and y values, slopes, intercepts, or turning points. Don't waste time making several hash marks or counting out every coordinate.

- Approximate calculations are usually good enough when you don't have a calculator. Non-calculator questions will not include grueling calculations, and when a moderate calculation is expected on a multiple-choice problem, the choices will usually be different enough so that you can use a simpler, approximate calculation. For example, if part of your work includes multiplying 37 by 104, it may be enough to just work out $40 \times 100 = 4000$ because there may only be one choice even in the same ballpark as 4000.

- Be on high alert when in ZONE F! This is a place where numbers don't behave as they should. ZONE F stands for: **Z**ero, **O**ne, **N**egatives, **E**xponents, and **F**ractions. These numbers and number types have properties that will not always follow the normal patterns. For example, there is a natural assumption that when you take numbers to powers, they should get larger, but watch what happens to these ZONE F numbers when they are raised to powers:

$$0^{12} = 0 \qquad 1^{53} = 1 \qquad (-2)^5 = -32 \qquad \left(\frac{1}{3}\right)^2 = \frac{1}{9}$$

In not one of these instances is the answer greater than the base!

Arithmetic Skills Problem Set

Do the following questions without a calculator to practice your basic arithmetic skills. Try to limit the amount of steps necessary to achieve a correct answer, but also pay attention to the order of operations, divisibility rules, fraction rules, and percent shortcuts.

☐1 Operate: $5 \times 12 - 3$

☐6 What is the product $\frac{3}{5} \times \frac{55}{27}$ in lowest terms?

☐2 Operate: $18 + 4 \cdot 6 - 1$

☐7 What is $\frac{2}{3}$ of $\frac{12}{13}$ of 26?

☐3 Operate: $4 + 2^3 - 21 \div 3$

☐8 What is $\frac{4}{15} \times \frac{5}{7} \times \frac{6}{16}$?

☐4 Operate: $\dfrac{5 \cdot 3 + 5 \cdot 2^2}{11 - 4}$

☐9 What is $\frac{35}{24} \div \frac{21}{40}$?

☐5 Operate: $54 \div 9 + 6^2 \div 3$

☐10 What is $\frac{12}{19} \times \frac{57}{28} \div \frac{15}{7}$?

[11] What is the result when 12,000 is divided by 10, multiplied by 3, and then divided by 900?

[16] Solve for x: $\dfrac{x}{9} = \dfrac{28}{36}$

[12] What is the result when 238 is subtracted from 738 and the difference is divided by 25?

[17] Solve for a: $\dfrac{6}{a} = \dfrac{42}{63}$

[13] What is the result when 76 is multiplied by $\dfrac{1}{4}$ and the result is subtracted from 20?

[18] Solve for n: $\dfrac{33}{110} = \dfrac{6}{n}$

[14] What is the result when 300 is divided by the sum of 68 and 7?

[19] Solve for c: $\dfrac{c}{c-4} = \dfrac{78}{52}$

[15] What is the result when 25 is divided by $\dfrac{1}{5}$ and the result is added to 65?

[20] Solve for v: $\dfrac{v}{36} = \dfrac{2v+1}{75}$

21 What is 30% of 45?

22 What is 15% of 120?

23 What is 250% of 40?

24 What is 0.5% of 1400?

25 16 is 20% of what number?

26 75% of what number is 66?

27 90 is 150% of what number?

28 What percent of 40 is 20?

29 19 is what percent of 95?

30 What percent of 80 is 100?

No Calculator Problem Set

This problem set consists of questions that you will see elsewhere in this book, in both the Heart of Algebra and Passport to Advanced Math chapters. These questions may be easier to do or check using strategies such as Back solving or Plugging in Numbers. Unfortunately you can't use those strategies as easily on the No Calculator section, so it is important to know how to apply the necessary algebraic techniques to answer and check these questions too.

You can try this problem set (without your calculator of course) before working your way through the Heart of Algebra and Passport to Advanced Math chapters, and then try it again once you've strengthened your algebraic skills in those chapters.

1. If $4(x-3)+8x=3(x+1)+9,$ what is the value of x?

   A) -3

   B) $\dfrac{7}{3}$

   C) $\dfrac{8}{3}$

   D) $\dfrac{13}{9}$

2. Don weighs 7 pounds less than twice as much as Megan weighs. If Megan weighs m pounds, then which of the following expressions represents Don's weight?

   A) $m-7$

   B) $2m-7$

   C) $2m+7$

   D) $7-2m$

$$3x+ y= 7$$
$$6x+2y=14$$

3. How many solutions are there to the system of equations shown above?

   A) None

   B) One

   C) Infinitely many

   D) Two

$$3x+ y= 7$$
$$6x+2y=10$$

4. How many solutions are there to the system of equations shown above?

   A) None

   B) One

   C) Infinitely many

   D) Two

5 $\dfrac{\left(x^2\right)^5 \cdot \left(x^4\right)^3}{x^2} =$

A) x^{12}

B) x^{20}

C) x^{60}

D) x^{118}

8 The formula for the surface area, S, of a rectangular solid is $S = 2lw + 2wh + 2lh$ where l is the length, w is the width, and h is the height. In terms of l, w, and S, what does h equal?

A) $S - 2lw - 2w - 2l$

B) $\dfrac{S - 2lw}{2}$

C) $\dfrac{S - 2lw}{2w + 2l}$

D) $\dfrac{S}{2lw + 2w + 2l}$

6 Which of the following is equal to $25^{\frac{5}{2}}$?

A) 62.5

B) $5^{\frac{5}{4}}$

C) 5^5

D) $\dfrac{1}{25^{\frac{2}{5}}}$

9 What is the range of the function $f(x) = |x| + 2$?

A) All real numbers

B) $f(x) \geq -2$

C) $f(x) \geq 2$

D) $-2 \leq f(x) \leq 2$

7 If $9x^2 - 4y^2 = a(3x + 2y)$, then what is the value of a in terms of x and y?

A) $x - y$

B) $x + 2y$

C) $3x - 2y$

D) $3x + 2y$

10 What are the solutions to $2x^2 + 12x + 8 = 0$?

A) $x = -3 \pm \sqrt{5}$

B) $x = -3 \pm 2\sqrt{10}$

C) $x = -6 \pm 2\sqrt{5}$

D) $x = -6 \pm \sqrt{10}$

11 For the equation $4x^2 + bx + 9 = 0$, which value of b gives the equation two distinct, real solutions?

A) -12

B) 0

C) 12

D) 15

12 If the graph of the function $f(x)$ has x-intercepts at -5, 5, and 7, which of the following could be $f(x)$?

A) $f(x) = (x-5)^2(x-7)$

B) $f(x) = (x-5)^2(x-7)^2$

C) $f(x) = (x+5)(x-5)(x-7)^2$

D) $f(x) = (x+5)^2(x-5)^2(x+7)^2$

13 If x and y are positive numbers and if $\sqrt{x} + \sqrt{y} = 10\sqrt{y}$, what is the value of x in terms of y?

A) $3y$

B) $9y$

C) $10y$

D) $81y$

14 Which of the following functions will have graphs with the same turning point?

I. $f(x) = -(x+3)^2 - 7$

II. $f(x) = (x-3)^2 - 7$

III. $f(x) = |x+3| - 7$

A) I and II only

B) I and III only

C) II and III only

D) I, II, and III

15 A marketer estimates that a website will increase its hits by 50% every 12 days. If the site got 200 hits today, which of the following functions estimates how many hits h the site will have d days from now?

A) $h(d) = 200(.5)^{12d}$

B) $h(d) = 200(.5)^{\frac{d}{12}}$

C) $h(d) = 200(1.5)^{12d}$

D) $h(d) = 200(1.5)^{\frac{d}{12}}$

Heart of Algebra

Algebra uses the language of mathematics to represent, relate, and solve for unknown quantities. It involves translating and organizing numbers, operations, and letters. Solving equations and inequalities that express linear relationships is a central skill upon which much of the remainder of algebra is based.

The College Board recognizes that the following are essential to succeed in a basic Algebra class:

- Translating word problems into algebraic expressions
- Solving linear equations and inequalities
- Understanding function notation
- Interpreting and graphing linear functions
- Solving and graphing systems of linear equations and inequalities

Algebraic Translation and Solving Linear Equations and Inequalities

Terminology

In order to translate word problems, you need to know the following definitions:

Variable   a letter that represents a number or set of numbers

Constant   a number that is unassociated with a variable

Coefficient   a number multiplied by a variable

Term   a constant or a product of a coefficient and variables (also known as a monomial)

Equation   a statement that two expressions have the same value

Inequality   a statement that expressions have a relationship using $<$, $>$, $\leq$, $\geq$, or $\neq$

Words and phrases associated with

Addition   sum, plus, increased by, added to, more than, greater than

Subtraction   difference, minus, decreased by, subtracted from, less than (be careful of the order)

Multiplication   product, times, multiplied by, for every, of (for fractions), twice (two times)

Division   quotient, ratio, divided by, over, rate

Inequalities   is less than, is greater than, no more than, no fewer than, at most, at least, between

Absolute Value

Used to represent the distance that one number is from another, the absolute value of an expression is always non-negative and is represented with vertical bars.

Example 1   To show the distance between the numbers 7 and 13 you can write $|7-13|$ or $|13-7|$, both of which equal the positive quantity 6.

Example 2   In order to express the inequality $10 < x < 20$, you can write $|x-15| < 5$, which translates as "x is always less than five away from 15."

Solving Linear Equations and Inequalities

In order to isolate a variable, you need to undo the operations that are applied to that variable. You must use opposite operations (e.g. subtraction for addition) to do this, and make sure that whatever you do to one side of the equal sign or inequality symbol, you also do to the other side.

Note: When both sides of an inequality are multiplied or divided by a negative number, you must *reverse the inequality symbol*.

Algebraic Translation Problem Set

[1] "27 less than the product of 6 and k is the same as k squared." Which of the following is equivalent to this statement?

A) $27 - 6k = k^2$

B) $6k - 27 = k^2$

C) $27 - 6 + k = k^2$

D) $6k - 27 = 2k$

[2] Which of the following equations is equivalent to the statement "the square root of a number x is equal to fourteen less than three times that number?"

A) $x^2 = 3x - 14$

B) $x^2 = 3x - 14$

C) $\sqrt{x} = 14 - 3x$

D) $\sqrt{x} = 3x - 14$

[3] Which of the following equations is equivalent to the statement "a number x multiplied by four greater than itself is equal to twice the square root of another number y?"

A) $x(x-4) = \sqrt{2y}$

B) $x(x-4) = 2\sqrt{y}$

C) $x(x+4) = 2\sqrt{y}$

D) $x(x+4) = \sqrt{2y}$

$$k^3 - h = 3k$$

[4] The equation above is equivalent to which of the following statements?

A) A number k squared is h greater than the product of three and k.

B) A number k cubed is h greater than the product of three and k.

C) Three times a number k is h greater than the number k squared.

D) Three times a number k is h greater than the number k cubed.

$$f(x) = x(x-2)$$

[5] The equation above describes which of the following situations?

A) A function f of a number x is equal to two less than twice that number.

B) A function f of a number x is equal to a number x multiplied by two less than that number.

C) A function f of a number x is equal to a number x multiplied by two greater than that number.

D) None of the above

$$y = kx^3 - x$$

6 The equation above describes which of the following situations?

A) A number y is equal to the product of a constant k multiplied by the cube root of a number x subtracted from the number x.

B) A number y is equal to a number x subtracted from the product of a constant k multiplied by the cube root of the number x.

C) A number y is equal to the product of a constant k multiplied by the cube of a number x subtracted from the number x.

D) A number y is equal to a number x subtracted from the product of a constant k multiplied by the cube of the number x.

7 Don weighs 7 pounds less than twice as much as Megan weighs. If Megan weighs m pounds, then which of the following expressions represents Don's weight?

A) $m - 7$

B) $2m - 7$

C) $2m + 7$

D) $7 - 2m$

8 Michael and Sylvia are comparing their CD collections, and Michael notices that he has precisely sixteen more than half as many CDs as Sylvia. If Sylvia has s CDs, how many does Michael have?

A) $\frac{1}{2}s + 16$

B) $\frac{1}{2}s - 16$

C) $2s + 16$

D) $16 - \frac{1}{2}s$

9 Eric is four years younger than Margaret and five years older than Lindsey. Which of the following is an expression for Lindsey's age in years in terms of Margaret's age m?

A) $m + 4$

B) $m - 5$

C) $m - 4$

D) $m - 9$

10 A cobbler is paid \$22 for every pair of shoes, s, he repairs and \$18.50 for every pair of boots, b, he repairs. What equation could be used to determine how much money in dollars, m, the cobbler earns?

A) $m = 18.50b + 22s$

B) $m = 22b + 18.50s$

C) $m = (18.50s)(22b)$

D) $m = 40.50bs$

11 George has a large number of quarters (q), dimes (d), and nickels (n). Which of the following equations represents the value, v, of all of the coins, <u>in cents</u>?

A) $0.05n + 0.1d + 0.25q = v$

B) $n + d + q = v$

C) $5n + 10d + 25q = v$

D) $(25 + 10 + 5)ndq = v$

12. Bat can read between 70 and 100 pages of a certain novel per hour. Based on this information, which of the following models how long in hours, h, it could take Bat to read 700 pages of this novel?

A) $7 \le h \le 10$

B) $70 \le h \le 100$

C) $10 \le h \le 17$

D) $h = \dfrac{700}{85}$

13. On Friday, Arian sent at least p e-mail messages each hour for 6 hours and Michael sent q e-mail messages each hour for 4 hours. Which of the following inequalities represents the total number of messages, t, sent by Arian and Michael on Friday?

A) $t \le (4+6)qp$

B) $t \ge 4p + 6q$

C) $t \ge 4q + 6p$

D) $t \ge q + p$

14. In the figure above, what is the value of $|c - d|$?

A) e

B) b

C) c

D) d

15. A soda company advertises that their bottles hold b fluid ounces of soda. Their goal is that every bottle will have a volume within 0.4 fluid ounces of this number. If they've met their goal and an inspector checks a bottle of soda with x fluid ounces in it, which inequality can be used to represent the relationship between b and x.

A) $b + x \le 0.4$

B) $b - x \ge 0.4$

C) $-0.4 \le b - x \le 0.4$

D) $0.4x \le b$

16. Which of the following is a correct interpretation of the equation $|x - 7| = 5$?

A) The value of x is 5 units away from 7.

B) The value of x is 7 units away from 5.

C) The value of x is 7 units less than 5.

D) The value of x is 5 units less than 7.

17. Jeremy can either spend fewer than 4 hours studying for exams and then go to a party, or stay home and study for 8 hours straight. Which of the following most accurately models the number of hours, x, that Jeremy will study?

A) $x < 4$ or $x = 8$

B) $4 < x < 8$

C) $x < 4$ or $x > 8$

D) $x < 8$

[18] If $3 < x < 9$, which of the following is true for all possible values of x?

    A) $|x - 6| > 3$

    B) $|x - 6| < 3$

    C) $|x + 6| < 3$

    D) $|x + 3| < 9$

[20] The weight capacity of the elevator at Bryson's Department Store is 2600 pounds. A group of people with a total weight of 1750 pounds gets on the elevator in the lobby and goes up. If, on average, a number of people totaling 328 pounds get on the elevator at each floor (and nobody gets off), which of the following inequalities can be used to determine the set of floors, f, for which the weight of the elevator will be over capacity?

    A) $f \leq \dfrac{4350}{328}$

    B) $f \geq \dfrac{4350}{328}$

    C) $1750 + 328f \leq 2600$

    D) $1750 + 328f > 2600$

[19] If $|3x - 9| < 0$, which of the following is a possible value of x?

    A)   4

    B)   0

    C)   –2

    D)   No possible value

Solving Linear Equations and Inequalities Problem Set

1. If $3x+7=5+x$, what is the value of x?

　　A) -6
　　B) -1
　　C) 2
　　D) 6

2. If $38,000=1,000(3x+8)$, what is the value of x?

　　A) 1
　　B) 10
　　C) 100
　　D) $1,000$

3. If $7(x-11)=-17$, what is the value of x?

　　A) $-\dfrac{94}{7}$
　　B) $-\dfrac{24}{7}$
　　C) $-\dfrac{6}{7}$
　　D) $\dfrac{60}{7}$

4. If $\dfrac{5x}{2}+3=13$, what is the value of x?

　　A) -2
　　B) 3.5
　　C) 4
　　D) 6.4

5. If $4(x-3)+8x=3(x+1)+9$, what is the value of x?

　　A) -3
　　B) $\dfrac{7}{3}$
　　C) $\dfrac{8}{3}$
　　D) $\dfrac{13}{9}$

$4x-12+8x$
$12x-12=3x+3+9$
$9x=24$

6. What is the value of x if $\dfrac{1}{5}x+\dfrac{1}{3}x=8$?

　　A) 15
　　B) 32
　　C) 64
　　D) 120

$\dfrac{8}{15}x=8$
120

7. If $7+2x=31$, then $5x=$?

　　A) 12
　　B) 24
　　C) 60
　　D) 155

24

8. If $8x-2=4x+8$, what is the value of $3x$?

　　A) 2.5
　　B) 6
　　C) 7.5
　　D) 10

9 If $-5x - 3 = -6x + 9$, what is the value of $\frac{x}{8}$?

A) 3

B) 1.5

C) 1

D) -1.5

13 For what value of x is $|3x - 5| + 7$ equal to 5?

A) -1

B) 1

C) $\frac{17}{3}$

D) No possible value

10 If $\frac{6}{x+2} = \frac{6}{2x-2}$, what is the value of x?

A) -4

B) 0

C) 1

D) 4

14 If $0 < 5x - 3 < 2$, what is one possible value of x?

11 If $a + b < a - b$, which of the following statements <u>must</u> be true?

A) $a > b$

B) $a = b$

C) $a < 0$

D) $b < 0$

15 If $5000 < d + 2000 < 5500$ and d is an integer, what is the least possible value of d?

12 If $x + 3y < x$, which of the following <u>must</u> be true?

A) $x < 0$

B) $x < y$

C) $y < 0$

D) $y > \frac{1}{3}$

Functions

A function consists of a dependent and an independent variable such that for each value for the independent variable (input), there is only one value of the dependent variable (output). Functions are often named $f(x)$ or simply y, in which case y is the dependent variable and x is the independent variable.

Terminology

Domain   the set of all numbers that you can plug in to a function for x and produce a real value of y

Range   the set of all real y values that result from a function

Composite functions   written either as $f(g(x))$ or as $f \circ g(x)$. To get an output for a composite function, you first plug the x-value into the interior function ($g(x)$ above) and then plug the result of that into the outer function ($f(x)$ above).

Functions — Try It!

1. If $f(x) = 2x^3 + x$, then $f(2) = ?$

$$16 + 2 = 18$$

2. If $f(x) = 3x - 2$, what is the value of $f(6)$?

$$16$$

3. What is the x-value in the previous function for which $f(x) = 13$?

4. If $g(x) = 3x + 2$ and $g(b) = 26$, what is the value of b?

5. If $f(x) = 3x - 2$ and $g(x) = \dfrac{x}{2} + 4$, what value of x does $f(x) = g(x)$?

Questions 6–8 all refer to the following function:

$$f(x) = x^2 + 2$$

6. What is $f(a) = ?$

$$a^2 + 2$$

7. What is $f(2a) = ?$

$$2a^2 + 2$$

8. What is $f(2b + 2) = ?$

$$(2b + 2)^2 + 2$$

9. If $f(x) = 6x - 11$ and $g(x) = \dfrac{1}{2}x + 3$, what is $f(g(2))$?

$$\frac{1}{2}(1 + 3$$
$$\frac{1}{2} + 3 = 3.5$$

10. If $h(x) = x^3$ and $h(2a) = 64$, what is the value of a?

$$a = 2$$

Functions Problem Set

1. If $f(x) = mx - 13$ and $f(7) = 71$, what is m?

   A) 4

   B) 11

   C) 12

   D) 14

2. The functions f and g are defined by
$f(x) = 3x^3 + x^2 - 4x - 10$ and $g(x) = f(x+2)$.
What is $g(-1)$?

   A) -70

   B) -10

   C) 10

   D) 68

3. If $f(t) = \dfrac{1}{2}t$ and $g(t) = t + 12$, for what value
of t is $f(t) = g(t)$?

   A) -24

   B) -18

   C) -12

   D) 24

4. If the function $f(x) = x^2 + 3x$, which of the
following is equal to $f\big(f(x)\big)$?

   A) $x^4 + 9x^2$

   B) $x^4 + 6x^3 + 9x^2$

   C) $(x^2 + 3x)^2 + 3(x^2 + 3x)$

   D) $(x+3)^4 + 3(x+3)^2$

5. If $f(3) = 7$, $f(6) = 5$, $g(5) = 12$, and
$g(6) = 10$, what is $g\big(f(6)\big)$?

   A) 10

   B) 12

   C) 22

   D) 50

x	$f(x)$	$h(x)$
0	−5	2
1	−2	10
2	0	3
3	1	9
4	3	4
5	6	8
6	10	5
7	15	7
8	21	6

6 The table above shows some values for functions $f(x)$ and $h(x)$. For which value of x is $h(x) = f(2x)$?

A) 1

B) 2

C) 3

D) 4

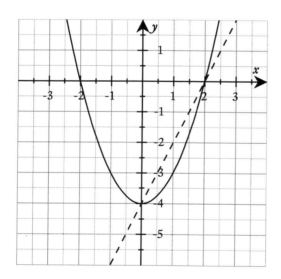

7 For the graphs of the functions $f(x)$ (solid line) and $g(x)$ (dotted line) above, what are all values of x for which $g(x) > f(x)$?

A) $-4 < x < 0$

B) $-2 < x < 0$

C) $0 < x < 2$

D) $x > 2$

8 The equation $g(x) = a \cdot f(x) + 4$ shows how the function g is defined in terms of the function f for all values of x, where a is a constant. If n is a number for which $g(n) = 40$, and $f(n) = 6$, what does a equal?

A) 4

B) 5

C) 6

D) 7

9 If $g(x) = 3x - 4$ and $f(x) = 2x + 3$, , what is the value of $f(3) - g(3)$?

4

10 The function $f(x)$ is defined by the equation $f(x) = 10x - 2$. If $f(3a) = 88$, then $a = ?$

Linear Functions

Linear functions have the property that as x increases, $f(x)$ (or y) increases or decreases by a constant amount. This constant amount is called the *slope*, and it is represented by m in the two most common forms of a linear function:

- $y = mx + b$, where b represents the y-intercept

- $y - y_1 = m(x - x_1)$, where (x_1, y_1) is a known set of coordinates that satisfy the function

A slope can also be found by dividing the change in y values by the change in x values. This is easily remembered by the formula:

- $\dfrac{\text{rise}}{\text{run}}$ or $\dfrac{y_2 - y_1}{x_2 - x_1}$

Linear functions graph as lines whose steepness is dependent on their slopes. Positive sloped lines run uphill (from left to right), negative sloped lines run downhill, and zero sloped lines are strictly horizontal. Note that a vertical line has no slope since there is no "run."

Parallel lines   lines that have the same slope but different y-intercepts

Perpendicular lines   lines which meet at a 90° angle and whose slopes are negative reciprocals of each other.

Interpreting Linear Formulas

Any formula which attempts to model a real-world scenario using a linear formula has two important components:

- A linear coefficient of the independent variable which represents the change in the dependent variable every time the independent variable increases by 1
- A constant term which represents a starting or ending point

Linear Functions — Try It!

The total cost in dollars, d, of renting a bicycle in Washington, D.C. can be modeled by the equation $d = 10h + 15$, where h is the length of the rental in hours.

Try it 1 What is the meaning of the number 10 in the formula above?

    A) It is the minimum number of hours a bicycle must be rented.

    B) It is the amount charged per hour, after an initial fee, to rent a bicycle.

    C) It is the initial charge to rent the bicycle.

    D) It is the maximum number of bicycles that can be rented per hour.

Try it 2 In the formula above, what is the meaning of the number 15?

    A) It is the minimum number of hours a bicycle must be rented.

    B) It is the amount charged per hour, after an initial fee, to rent a bicycle.

    C) It is the initial charge to rent the bicycle.

    D) It is the maximum number of bicycles that can be rented per hour.

Linear Functions Problem Set

1. If t is a linear function, $t(1)=7$ and $t(-1)=9$, what is the slope of t?

   A) –2
   B) –1
   C) 2
   D) 3

2. A line in the xy-plane passes through the point $(0, 5)$ and has a slope of $\frac{3}{4}$. Which of the following points lies on the line?

   A) $(3,9)$
   B) $(9,3)$
   C) $(4,8)$
   D) $(8,4)$

3. A line in the xy-plane has a positive slope and contains points in the second quadrant. Which quadrant will this line never pass through?

   A) Quadrant I
   B) Quadrant III
   C) Quadrant IV
   D) It will pass through all four quadrants

4. The line k in the xy-coordinate plane is given by the equation $5x+2y=10$. Line j has a slope that is twice the slope of line k and a y-intercept that is three times the y-intercept of line k. What is the equation of line j?

   A) $y=10x+30$
   B) $y=5x-15$
   C) $y=5x+15$
   D) $y=-5x+15$

   $y=\frac{-5}{2}x+5$

5. The line in the xy-plane that represents the graph of the function $y=3x+5$ is parallel to line k. If line k goes through the points $(0,-5)$ and $(a,1)$, what is the value of a?

   A) –11
   B) 2
   C) 8
   D) 21

   $\frac{1+5}{a-0}=3$

   $\frac{6}{k}=\frac{3}{?}$

6. In the xy-coordinate plane, line l contains the points $(3,5)$ and $(5,8)$ and line m contains the points $(3,1)$ and $(0,k)$. If lines l and m are perpendicular, what is k?

   A) –3
   B) –1
   C) 3
   D) 5

   $\frac{8-5}{5-3}=\frac{3}{2}$

   $-\frac{2}{3}=\frac{k-1}{-3}$

7. In the function $g(x) = 4x + k$, k is a constant. If $g(-3) = 1$, what is the value of $g(1)$?

A) -3

B) 5

$1 = -12 + k$

C) 13

D) 17

8. A line that passes through the points $(3, n)$ and $(n, 19)$ in the xy-plane also passes through the point $(1, 1)$. What is the value of n?

A) 7

B) 13

C) 15

D) 16

$\dfrac{19-1}{v-n} = \dfrac{n-1}{3-1}$

$\dfrac{18}{1-n} = \dfrac{n-1}{2}$

$36 =$

9. The graph of line m in the xy-plane has a slope of 3 and goes through the point $(-1, 2)$. A second line, n, goes through the points $(3, 2)$ and $(4, -1)$. If m and n intersect at the point (a, b), then what is the value of $a + b$?

A) 1

B) 6

C) 8

D) 9

10. In the function $H(t) = 120 + 12t$, H is the altitude of a balloon in feet, and t is the number of minutes after liftoff. Which of the following scenarios is described by the above equation?

A) The balloon starts at an altitude of 12 feet, and travels upwards at a velocity of 120 feet per minute.

B) The balloon starts at an altitude of 120 feet, and travels upwards at a velocity of 12 miles an hour.

C) The balloon starts at an altitude of 0 feet and travels upwards at a velocity of 120 feet per minute.

D) The balloon starts at an altitude of 120 feet, and travels upwards at a velocity of 12 feet per minute.

11. For the function $P(t) = 200 + 100t$, P represents the population size of a colony of bacteria, and t represents the number of hours after the beginning of an experiment. Which of the following is modeled by the aforementioned function?

A) The colony started out with 200 bacteria, and increased by 100 every hour.

B) The colony started out with 200 bacteria, and doubled every hour.

C) The colony started out with no bacteria, and increased by 100 bacteria every hour.

D) The colony started out with 100 bacteria, and increased by 200 every hour.

12 At Jones Auto Rental, it costs $120 to secure a luxury rental car, and an additional $40 per day to use the car. The total cost of renting a luxury car can be represented by the equation $c = 40d + 120$. If Ryan decides to rent a car with additional insurance coverage per day, I, which of the following equations could he use to calculate his total cost?

A) $c = 40d + 120 + I$

B) $c = 40Id + 120$

C) $c = 40d + 120I$

D) $c = (40 + I)d + 120$

13 A farmer uses the equation $c = 4x + 15.3$ to estimate the circumference, c, of a cantaloupe, in centimeters, after x weeks. Based on this model, what is the estimated per-week increase, in centimeters, of a cantaloupe's circumference?

A) 4

B) 11.3

C) 15.3

D) 19.3

Questions 14 and 15 refer to the following information.

A moving company is able to estimate the price of a job, p, in dollars, using the equation $p = 80 + 45nh$, where n is the number of movers and h is the number of hours the job will take using n movers.

14 Which of the following best interprets the meaning of 45 in the equation?

A) It is the number of person-hours required to complete a job.

B) It is the amount charged per person-hour of labor.

C) It is the amount charged regardless of the time spent working on the job.

D) It means that the job is billed out in 45-minute intervals.

15 Which of the following best interprets the meaning of 80 in the equation?

A) It is the number of person-hours required to complete a job.

B) It is the amount charged per person-hour of labor.

C) It is the initial amount charged regardless of the time spent working on the job.

D) It means that the job is billed out in 80-minute intervals.

Questions 16 and 17 refer to the following information.

Jacob is a Major League Baseball pitcher who is recovering from surgery. His manager has put a limit on the amount of pitches he can throw in games this year. Throughout the year, the amount of pitches, p, Jacob can still throw can be estimated by the inequality $p \leq 2250 - 15x$, where x represents the number of innings Jacob has already pitched.

16 What is the meaning of the value 2250 in the inequality?

   A) It is the minimum number of pitches Jacob throws in an inning.

   B) It is the amount of pitches Jacob has already thrown.

   C) It is the maximum number of pitches Jacob can throw for the year.

   D) It is the number of games Jacob has played.

17 What is the meaning of the value 15 in the inequality?

   A) It is the average number of pitches Jacob throws each inning.

   B) It is the average number of pitches Jacob throws each game.

   C) It is the number innings Jacob pitches each game.

   D) It is the number of games Jacob pitches each year.

18 Hose A takes 3 hours to fill an 80-gallon pool and Hose B takes 7 hours to fill the same pool. The following equation can be used to figure out how many hours it would take the two hoses, running simultaneously, to fill the pool: $\frac{80}{3}x + \frac{80}{7}x = 80$. Which of the following describes what $\frac{80}{7}x$ represents in the equation?

   A) The time it takes the faster hose to fill the pool

   B) The time it takes the slower hose to fill the pool

   C) The portion of the pool filled by the faster hose

   D) The portion of the pool filled by the slower hose

19 If $m(x) = 30x + c$ where c is a constant and $m(3.5) = 123$, what is the value of c?

20 If $f(x) = mx - 11$ and $f(10) = 19$, what is m?

Systems of Equations and Inequalities

A system of linear equations in two variables consists of two equations and can be written in the following form, where $A, B, C, D, E,$ and F are constants:

$$Ax + By = C$$
$$Dx + Ey = F$$

A **solution** to a linear system like this is an ordered pair (x, y) that satisfies both equations.

Infinite Solutions

When one equation is just a multiple of the other, there will be infinitely many solutions. You can tell that this is the case if $\dfrac{A}{D} = \dfrac{B}{E} = \dfrac{C}{F}$.

No Solutions

When the left side of one equation is a multiple of the left side of the other, but the right sides don't have the same relationship, there are no solutions. This will happen if $\dfrac{A}{D} = \dfrac{B}{E} \neq \dfrac{C}{F}$.

One Solution

If neither of the scenarios above is true, that is if $\dfrac{A}{D} \neq \dfrac{B}{E}$, then there is a single solution (x, y).

Graphing Method

Graph both equations by first isolating y. The point of intersection, if one exists, is the solution.

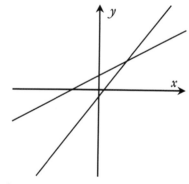

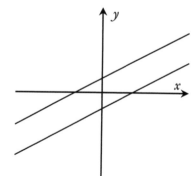

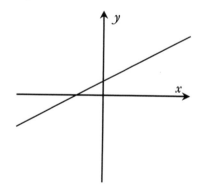

One solution
- Two intersecting lines
- Different slopes

No solutions
- Parallel lines
- Same slope
- Different y-intercept

Infinitely Many Solutions
- Both lines are the same graph
- Same slope
- Same y-intercept

Substitution Method

1. Solve one equation for one of its variables.
2. Substitute the expression from step 1 into the other equation and solve for the other variable.
3. Substitute the value obtained in step 2 into the equation from step 1 and solve.

Example 1   Follow the steps to solve the linear system below.

$$-3x + 2y = 4$$
$$4x + y = -9$$

Step 1	Step 2	Step 3
$4x + y = -9$	$-3x + 2y = 4$	$y = -4x - 9$
$y = -4x - 9$	$-3x + 2(-4x - 9) = 4$	$y = -4(-2) - 9$
	$-3x - 8x - 18 = 4$	$y = 8 - 9 = -1$
	$-11x = 22$	The solution is $(-2, -1)$.
	$x = -2$	

In the second step, if you get an equation that is never true, like $16 = 6$, there is no solution. If you get an equation that is always true, like $12 = 12$, there are infinitely many solutions.

Elimination Method

1. Multiply one or both equations by a constant so the coefficients of one variable are opposites.
2. Add the equations from step 1 to eliminate a variable, and solve for the remaining variable.
3. Substitute the value obtained in step 2 into one of the original equations and solve.

Example 2   Follow the steps to solve the linear system below.

$$2x + 3y = 11$$
$$5x - 2y = -20$$

Step 1	Step 2	Step 3
$2(2x + 3y = 11)$	$4x + 6y = 22$	$2x + 3y = 11$
$3(5x - 2y = -20)$	$15x - 6y = -60$	$2(-2) + 3y = 11$
	$19x = -38$	$3y = 15$
	$x = -2$	$y = 5$
		The solution is $(-2, 5)$.

Word Problems

The SAT often has at least one word problem that can be solved by writing and solving a system of linear equations. For this you have to first define your variables.

Example 3   A test has nineteen questions and is worth fifty points. The test consists of true/false questions worth 2 points each and multiple-choice questions worth 3 points each. How many true/false questions are on the test?

Let x = Number of true/false questions.

Let y = Number of multiple-choice questions.

You can now set up the equations:

$x + y = 19$

$2x + 3y = 50$

This can be solved by any of the three methods (elimination is exemplified below).

$$-2(x + y = 19) \rightarrow -2x - 2y = -38 \qquad x + y = 19$$
$$2x + 3y = 50 \rightarrow \underline{\quad 2x + 3y = 50 \quad} \qquad x + 12 = 19$$
$$y = 12 \qquad\qquad x = 7$$

So there are 7 true/false questions and 12 multiple-choice questions.

Systems of Linear Inequalities

These should be graphed so that you can see the region of solutions in the intersection of the two shaded solution sets. Solid lines are used for $\leq$ or $\geq$, and dashed lines are used for $<$ or $>$. Shade in the direction of any test point that works in the inequality.

Example 4 $y > -x - 1$

$$y \leq \frac{2}{3}x + 3$$

Graphing the system of inequalities above shows that though points like $(2,8)$ and $(0,-4)$ will only satisfy one of the inequalities, points like $(5,3)$ are in the solution set for the entire system.

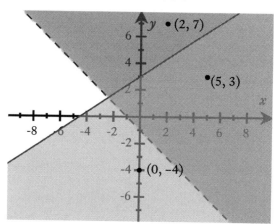

Systems of Equations and Inequalities Problem Set

$$3x + 2y = 7$$
$$2x + 3y = 7$$

1 Which of the following is a solution to the system shown above?

A) $(1,1)$

B) $(2,1)$

C) $\left(\dfrac{8}{5}, \dfrac{8}{5}\right)$

D) $\left(\dfrac{7}{5}, \dfrac{7}{5}\right)$

$$3x + 2y = 7$$
$$6x + 2y = 10$$

4 How many solutions are there to the system of equations shown above?

A) None

B) One

C) Infinitely many

D) The answer cannot be determined

$$3x + y = 7$$
$$6x + 2y = 14$$

2 How many solutions are there to the system of equations shown above?

A) None

B) One

C) Infinitely many

D) Two

$$2x + 6y = 18$$
$$5x + 15y = 45$$

5 What is the solution to the system of equations shown above?

A) $(3, 2)$ only

B) $(2, 6)$ only

C) There are infinitely many solutions

D) $(3, 2)$ and $(2, 6)$

$$3x + y = 7$$
$$6x + 2y = 10$$

3 How many solutions are there to the system of equations shown above?

A) None

B) One

C) Infinitely many

D) Two

6 A school math club is selling boxes of two types of cookies to raise money: chocolate chip for $4 a box and peanut butter for $6 a box. If $856 was raised and 169 boxes were sold, which of the following can be used to find how many boxes of each type were sold?

A) $x + y = 856$
    $4x + 6y = 169$

B) $4x + y = 169$
    $6x + 4y = 856$

C) $x - y = 169$
    $6x + 4y = 856$

D) $x + y = 169$
    $4x + 6y = 856$

$$ax + by = 16$$
$$3x + 6y = 24$$

7 If the system of equations shown above has an infinite number of solutions, what is the value of ab?

A) 2
B) 6
C) 8
D) 9

8 Fred and Bill go to the store. Fred buys 3 chocolate bars and 2 packs of gum for $4.75. Bill buys 3 chocolate bars and 1 pack of gum for $4.25. How much does one chocolate bar cost?

A) $0.75
B) $1.00
C) $1.25
D) $1.50

9 Fred and Bill go back to the store. This time, Fred buys 2 packs of cookies and 1 pack of donuts for $3.25. Bill buys 4 packs of cookies and 2 packs of donuts for $6.50. How much does 1 pack of donuts cost?

A) $0.75
B) $1.25
C) $1.75
D) The answer cannot be determined.

10 Jerry has \$3.06 in pennies, nickels, dimes, and quarters. The number of nickels is the same as the number of dimes, there are 6 pennies, and there are 25 coins in all. How many quarters are there?

A) 5

B) 7

C) 9

D) 11

11 A farmer has cows and chickens. Between all the animals, there are 134 legs. There are 37 animals. Which system below represents this situation?

A) $4x + 2y = 134$
    $x + y = 37$

B) $4x + 2y = 37$
    $x + y = 134$

C) $4x + 4y = 37$
    $x + y = 134$

D) $x + y = 37$
    $2x + y = 134$

12 The Fairfield High School History Club held a car wash to raise funds for a field trip to a museum. They charged \$5 to wash a car and \$7 to wash a truck. If they earned a total of \$275 by washing a total of 43 vehicles, how many cars were washed?

A) 13

B) 17

C) 19

D) 21

13 Ralph is gambling on the throw of a die. For every time he guesses the number on the die correctly, he wins \$7, and for every time he guesses incorrectly, he loses \$3. After 10 throws, Ralph has neither won nor lost any money. How many times did he guess correctly?

A) 3

B) 5

C) 7

D) 9

14 At George's elementary school, the children have bicycles and tricycles. The number of bicycles is 7 less than twice the number tricycles, and altogether there are 70 wheels. How many bicycles are there?

A) 17

B) 20

C) 23

D) 30

$$y + 2x < -1$$
$$y - 3x > 4$$

15 For how many positive values of x is there a solution to the system of inequalities shown above?

A) Infinitely many

B) One

C) Two

D) None

$$y < -20x + 3k$$
$$y > 30x + 4m$$

16   If $(0, 0)$ is a solution to the system of inequalities above, which of the following relationships between k and m must exist?

A) $k > m$

B) $m > k$

C) $m = k$

D)   The relationship cannot be determined.

$$15x - 6y = 48$$
$$mx - ny = 18$$

17   In the system of equations shown above, m and n are constants. If the system has an infinite number of solutions, what is the value of $\dfrac{m}{n}$?

18   Given that $2x + 4y + 6z = 12$ and $x + 3y + 5z = 3$, what is the value of $x + y + z$?

$$\frac{2}{3}x + \frac{3}{4}y = 12$$
$$\frac{10}{12}x + \frac{4}{8}y = 15$$

19   What is the x coordinate of the solution to the system of equations shown above?

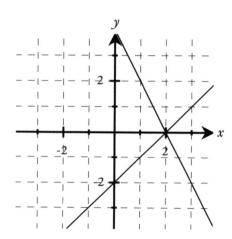

20   What is the x-value for the solution to the system of equations given by the lines shown in the figure above?

Passport to Advanced Math

The College Board emphasizes two key components of what must be mastered to succeed in an Algebra 2 or even a Pre-calculus class: Form Changes and Higher-Level Functions.

Form Changes

Form Changes are the ways in which you can make a quantity or mathematical expression look different in order to operate. A form change does not necessarily imply a simplification. Form changes include:

- Applying exponent rules
- Distributing and FOILing
- Factoring
- Operating with radicals and fractional exponents
- Altering fractions to utilize common denominators
- Using algebra to move expressions around an equal sign (solving literal equations)

Higher-Level Functions

These are functions whose relationships are more complicated than strict linear trends. You should know the characteristics associated with such functions as well as how they can be graphed and how those graphs can be transformed. They include:

- Quadratic functions
- Polynomial functions of degree greater than 2
- Exponential functions
- Absolute value functions
- Rational functions
- Radical functions

Exponents

The following problems highlight the rules of exponents.

$a^0 = 1$ $a^{-x} = \dfrac{1}{a^x}$

$a^x a^y = a^{x+y}$ $\dfrac{a^x}{a^y} = a^{x-y}$

$\left(a^x\right)^y = a^{xy}$ $a^x \bullet b^x = (ab)^x$

Try It!

If you want to test your understanding of the rules above, do not use a calculator:

| 1 | $5^3 \bullet 5^6 = 5^x$ | 2 | $\dfrac{7^5}{7^3} = 7^x$ |

| 3 | $2^{-4} = x$ | 4 | $\left(\left(2^2\right)^2\right)^2 = 2^x$ |

| 5 | $3^{-2} \bullet 4^{-2} = x^{-2}$ | 6 | $3 \bullet 3^2 \bullet 3^{-1} = 3^x$ |

When two different bases are used, see if you can change the base of one expression into the base of the other (usually change to the smaller base). Consider the following example:

Example 1 $\quad \left(8^2\right)^3 = 2^x$

First use that $8 = 2^3$, so $\left(8^2\right)^3 = \left(\left(2^3\right)^2\right)^3$.

Then use the rules for exponents to get that $\left(2^6\right)^3 = 2^{18}$, so $2^{18} = 2^x$; thus $x = 18$.

Try It!

| 1 | $\dfrac{9^9}{9^{-9}} = 3^x$ | 2 | $4 \bullet 8 \bullet 16 = 2^x$ |

Exponents Problem Set

1 $\dfrac{\left(x^2\right)^5 \cdot \left(x^4\right)^3}{x^2} =$

   A) x^{12}

   B) x^{20}

   C) x^{60}

   D) x^{118}

2 $\dfrac{x \cdot 10^6}{y \cdot 10^{-1}} =$

   A) $xy \cdot 10^{-6}$

   B) $xy^{-1} \cdot 10^7$

   C) $xy \cdot 10^7$

   D) $xy^{-1} \cdot 10^5$

3   If $3^x = 5$, then $3^{3x} = ?$

   A)   5

   B)   10

   C)   25

   D)   125

4 $\dfrac{\left(3^x \cdot 3\right)^3}{9^x} =$

   A) 3^{6x}

   B) 3^{3-x}

   C) 3^{4x}

   D) 3^{x+3}

5 $6x^6 12x^6$ is equivalent to:

   A) $18x^{12}$

   B) $18x^{36}$

   C) $72x^{12}$

   D) $72x^{36}$

6   If $4^x = 100$, then which of the following must be true?

   A) $1 < x < 2$

   B) $2 < x < 3$

   C) $3 < x < 4$

   D) $x = 25$

7   Which of the following is equivalent to $(2x^3)^6$?

   A) $2x^9$

   B) $2x^{18}$

   C) $64x^9$

   D) $64x^{18}$

8   Which of the following is equivalent to $(y^5)^{10}(y^{10})^5$?

   A) y^{30}

   B) $2(y^{50})$

   C) y^{100}

   D) y^{2500}

9. If $a^x = 2$ and $a^y = 8$, what does a^{x-y} equal?

A) -6

B) $\dfrac{1}{4}$

C) 4

D) 16

10. If $(w^2 \cdot w^4)^x = w^{72}$ and $(w^y)^y = w^{49}$, where $w > 1$ and $y > 1$, what is the product of x and y?

A) 19

B) 63

C) 84

D) 124

11. Which of the following values of x satisfies the equation $(4)(2^x) = 8^4$?

A) 4

B) 6

C) 8

D) 10

12. Which of the following has the greatest value?

A) 2^{400}

B) $\left(2 \cdot 2^3\right)^{300}$

C) 8^{300}

D) $\left(4 \cdot 2^2\right)^{200}$

13. If $\left(a^2\right)^3 \cdot a^3 = a^x$, what is x ?

14. If g, h and k are positive integers greater than 1 such that $gx^k = x^{k+1}$, what is $g - x$?

15. If $13^9 = 13 \cdot 13^a$, then $a = ?$

Distributing and Factoring

Distributing

Any term that is multiplied by an entire expression involving addition and/or subtraction may also be multiplied by each of the terms within the expression before the calculation is performed.

$$a(b+c-d) = ab+ac-ad.$$

FOIL

This term is an mnemonic device to help us to remember how to *double distribute* when multiplying two binomials:

$$(a+b)(c+d) = \underset{\text{Firsts}}{ac} + \underset{\text{Outers}}{ad} + \underset{\text{Inners}}{bc} + \underset{\text{Lasts}}{bd}$$

Some students learn to double distribute using a 2×2 box structure instead. Either way, and no matter the sizes of the polynomials being multiplied, you must be sure to multiply each term of one of the polynomials by each term of the other polynomial.

Factoring

Factoring means breaking an expression up into its component factors. One way to factor a polynomial is to pull out a common factor, which is like reversing the process of a single distribution.

Example 1 $6x^8 - 9x^3 + 12x^2 = 3x^2(2x^6 - 3x + 4)$

Factoring can also entail reversing the process of FOIL.

Example 2 $x^2 - 5x - 36 = (x-9)(x+4)$

It helps to remember a few formulas for perfect squares of binomials and for the difference of two squares:

$$\left.\begin{array}{l}(x+y)^2 = x^2 + 2xy + y^2 \\ (x-y)^2 = x^2 - 2xy + y^2\end{array}\right\}\text{The perfect square formulas}$$
$$x^2 - y^2 = (x+y)(x-y)\big\}\text{The difference of two squares}$$

Example 3   Consider the following polynomial: $2x^3 + 8x^2 + 8x$

The first step is to look for common factors:

In this case, $2x$ goes into each term, so you can factor that out:

$$2x^3 + 8x^2 + 8x = 2x\left(x^2 + 4x + 4\right)$$

The next step is to see if the problem fits a formula or if you can easily reverse FOIL.

This particular polynomial has a factor that is a perfect square of $(x+2)$ because

$$(x+2)^2 = x^2 + 4x + 4,$$

so the complete factoring of the polynomial can be written as

$$2x^3 + 8x^2 + 8x = 2x\left(x^2 + 4x + 4\right) = 2x(x+2)^2$$

Distributing Problem Set

[1] Which of the following expressions is equivalent to $-7x(2x^3 - 5x + 3)$?

   A) $-14x^3 + 35x - 21$

   B) $-14x^4 - 35x^2 + 21x$

   C) $-14x^4 + 35x^2 - 21x$

   D) $-5x^4 - 12x^2 - 4x$

[2] Which of the following expressions is equivalent to $(x-4)(3x+1)$?

   A) $3x^2 - 13x - 4$

   B) $3x^2 - 11x - 4$

   C) $3x^2 - 3x - 4$

   D) $3x^2 + 13x - 4$

[3] The expression $(5a - 7b^2)(5a + 7b^2)$ is equivalent to:

   A) $10a$

   B) $10a - 14b^2$

   C) $25a^2 - 49b^4$

   D) $25a^2 + 49b^4$

[4] For all x and y, $(3x + y)(x^2 - y) = ?$

   A) $3x^3 - y^2$

   B) $3x^3 - 3xy - y^2$

   C) $3x^3 - 4xy + x^2 y^2$

   D) $3x^3 - 3xy + x^2 y - y^2$

[5] The expression $m^4 n^3 (m + mn)$ is equivalent to:

   A) $2m^4 n^3$

   B) $m^4 n^3 + m^4 n^4$

   C) $m^5 n^3 + m^5 n^4$

   D) $m^5 + m^5 n^4$

[6] Which of the following is equivalent to $(5x - 3)^2$ for all values of x?

   A) $10x - 6$

   B) $25x^2 - 9$

   C) $25x^2 - 15x - 9$

   D) $25x^2 - 30x + 9$

[7] Which of the following is equivalent to $3a(2a - b)^2$?

   A) $7a^2 - 7ab + 4ab^2$

   B) $12a^3 - 12a^2 b + 3ab^2$

   C) $18a^3 - 9a^2 b$

   D) $36a^4 - 36a^3 b + 9a^2 b^2$

[8] If $x + y = 2$ and $c + d = 5$, what is the value of $xc + yd + xd + yc$?

   A) 7

   B) 10

   C) 14

   D) 20

[9] If $(a + b)^2 = 169$ and $(a - b)^2 = 25$, then $ab = ?$

[10] If $(4x^3 - 2x + 5) - 3(6x^2 - 5x + 10)$ is written in the form $ax^3 + bx^2 + cx + d$, where a, b, c, and d are constants, what is the value of c?

Factoring Problem Set

1. Which of the following is a factor of
$x^2 - 6x + 5$?

   A) $x - 1$
   B) $x - 2$
   C) $x - 6$
   D) $x + 5$

2. If $a^2 - b^2 = 45$ and $a - b = 5$, then $b = ?$

   A) $\dfrac{1}{3}$
   B) 2
   C) 5
   D) 7

3. Which of the following is equivalent to
$25m^2 - 81n^{10}$?

   A) $(5m - (3n)^4)(5m + n^6)$
   B) $(5m - 9n^5)(5m + 9n^2)$
   C) $(5m + 9n^5)(5m - 9n^5)$
   D) $(5m - 9n^5)(5m - 9n^5)$

4. $(7x + 10) - (4x - 8)$ is equivalent to

   A) $3(x + 6)$
   B) $3x + 2$
   C) $3(x + 2)$
   D) $3(x + 18)$

5. For $x^2 \neq 36$, $\dfrac{(x+6)^2}{x^2 - 36} = ?$

   A) $-\dfrac{1}{6}$
   B) $\dfrac{1}{x - 6}$
   C) $\dfrac{1}{x + 6}$
   D) $\dfrac{x + 6}{x - 6}$

6. If $a^2 = b^2 + 80$, which of the following expressions must equal 80?

   A) $2(a + b)$
   B) $a^2 + b^2$
   C) $(a - b)(a - b)$
   D) $(a + b)(a - b)$

7. Where $\dfrac{x + 3}{x^2 - 2x - 15}$ is defined, it is equivalent to which of the following expressions?

   A) $-\dfrac{3}{x - 15}$
   B) $\dfrac{1}{x - 5}$
   C) $\dfrac{3}{x + 5}$
   D) $\dfrac{1}{x + 5}$

8 Which of the following is <u>not</u> a factor of $x^5 - x^3$?

A) x^3

B) $x - 1$

C) $x^2 - 1$

D) $x^3 - 1$

9 If $x \neq 0,\ x \neq -1,\ x \neq 1,\ \dfrac{x-1}{x^4 - x^2}$ is equivalent to which of the following?

A) $\dfrac{-1}{x^3 - x}$

B) $\dfrac{1}{x^2(x-1)}$

C) $\dfrac{1}{x^2(x+1)}$

D) $\dfrac{x}{x^3 - 1}$

10 If $9x^2 - 4y^2 = a(3x + 2y)$, then what is the value of a, in terms of x and y ?

A) $x - y$

B) $x + 2y$

C) $3x - 2y$

D) $3x + 2y$

11 Which of the following is equivalent to $\dfrac{x^2 - 121}{11 - x}$, for $x \neq 11$?

A) $x + 11$

B) $-x + 11$

C) $-x - 11$

D) $x - 11$

12 If $pq = 11$ and $p - q = 3$, what is the value of $p^2 q - pq^2$?

A) 14

B) 22

C) 33

D) 88

13 If $x^4 - y^4 = 81$ and $x^2 + y^2 = 9$, then what is $x^2 - y^2$?

14 If $\dfrac{m^{x^2}}{m^{y^2}} = m^{10}$ and $x + y = 5$, what is the value of $x - y$?

15 If $a + b = c$ and $3a + 5c + 3b = 56$, what is the value of c ?

Radicals and Fractional Exponents

A radical, or root, is the opposite of a power. That is, if taking x to the nth power gives you y, then x is the nth root of y. This can be shown with a radical symbol as follows: $x^n = y$ means $x = \sqrt[n]{y}$

Square roots invert squaring, cube roots invert cubing, fourth roots invert taking a number to the fourth power, and so on.

You can also express roots using fractional exponents. For example, $\sqrt{x} = x^{\frac{1}{2}}$ and $\sqrt[3]{x} = x^{\frac{1}{3}}$.

Power-Over-Root Rule

When an exponent is expressed as a fraction, raise the base to the power of the numerator and turn the denominator into a root. You can do this in either order:

$$x^{\frac{a}{b}} = \sqrt[b]{x^a} = \left(\sqrt[b]{x}\right)^a$$

Example 1 $32^{\frac{3}{5}} = \left(\sqrt[5]{32}\right)^3 = 2^3 = 8$

When a radical is in an equation, isolate the radical, and then raise both sides to the appropriate power. If a variable is raised to a fractional exponent, take both sides to the reciprocal power. Always watch out for extraneous solutions, and keep in mind that $\sqrt{}$ means only the positive, or principal, square root.

Example 2 Solve for x: $\sqrt{x+14} - 2 = x - 8$

First, add 2 to both sides:

$$\sqrt{x+14} = x - 6$$

Then, square both sides:

$$\left(\sqrt{x+14}\right)^2 = (x-6)^2$$
$$x + 14 = x^2 - 12x + 36$$

Solve the resulting quadratic equation, and then check for extraneous solutions:

$$x^2 - 13x + 22 = 0$$
$$(x-11)(x-2) = 0$$
$$x = 11 \text{ and } x = 2$$

Check the solutions:

$$\sqrt{11+14} = 11 - 6$$
$$\sqrt{25} = 5 \text{ (good)}$$

$$\sqrt{2+14} = 2 - 6$$
$$\sqrt{16} = -4 \text{ (reject)}$$

The solution is therefore only $x = 11$.

Example 3 Solve for x: $2x^{\frac{3}{4}} - 5 = 11$

First add 5 to both sides:

$$2x^{\frac{3}{4}} = 16$$

Divide through by 2:

$$x^{\frac{3}{4}} = 8$$

Take both sides to the reciprocal power:

$$\left(x^{\frac{3}{4}}\right)^{\frac{4}{3}} = 8^{\frac{4}{3}}$$

Finally, apply the power-over-root rule:

$$8^{\frac{4}{3}} = \left(\sqrt[3]{8}\right)^4 = 2^4 = 16$$

The solution is therefore $x = 16$.

Radicals and Fractional Exponents Problem Set

☐1 The expression $x^{-3}y^{\frac{1}{3}}$ is equivalent to which of the following?

A) $\dfrac{\sqrt[3]{y}}{x^3}$

B) $\dfrac{1}{xy}$

C) $\dfrac{\sqrt[3]{x}}{y^3}$

D) $\dfrac{y\sqrt{y}}{x^3}$

☐2 Which of the following is equal to $25^{\frac{5}{2}}$?

A) 62.5

B) $5^{\frac{5}{4}}$

C) 5^5

D) $\dfrac{1}{25^{\frac{2}{5}}}$

☐3 $\left(64m^6n^3p^{12}\right)^{\frac{1}{3}} =$

A) $4m^2np^4$

B) $64m^6np^4$

C) $4m^6n^3p^{12}$

D) $4m^6np^4$

☐4 If a and b are both greater than 1, which of the following is equivalent to $\dfrac{a^{\frac{1}{5}}b^{-4}}{a^{-3}b^{\frac{1}{2}}}$?

A) $\dfrac{a^{\frac{3}{5}}}{b^2}$

B) $\dfrac{\sqrt[5]{a^3}}{b^2}$

C) $\dfrac{(a^3)\sqrt[5]{a}}{(b^4)\sqrt{b}}$

D) $\dfrac{\sqrt[5]{a^3}}{(b^4)\sqrt{b}}$

☐5 If $a^{\frac{1}{3}} = b^4$ and $b^{-2} = c^3$, what is a in terms of c?

A) c^{-18}

B) c^{27}

C) c^6

D) c^{-2}

☐6 $16^{\frac{1}{6}}$ is equivalent to all of the following except one. Which one?

A) $\sqrt[3]{4}$

B) $8^{\frac{2}{9}}$

C) $2^{\frac{2}{3}}$

D) $\sqrt[12]{32}$

[7] If x and y are positive numbers and if $\sqrt{x} + \sqrt{y} = 10\sqrt{y}$, what is the value of x in terms of y?

A) $3y$

B) $9y$

C) $10y$

D) $81y$

[9] What is the solution set for the equation $\sqrt[3]{x-5} = 2$?

A) $\{-3, 13\}$

B) $\{9\}$

C) $\{13\}$

D) No solution

[8] If $b > 0$ and $\left(b^2 + 51\right)^{\frac{1}{2}} = 10$, what is the value of b?

A) 3

B) 5

C) 7

D) 10

[10] If $x = \sqrt{3}$, $y = 2x$, and $4y = \sqrt{24z}$, what is the value of z?

Fractional Operations and Equations

Fractional expressions often require a change of form in order to operate. You can change the form of a fraction by reducing it or by multiplying the top and bottom by the same expression. Both of these actions constitute a form change, but not a value change, because you are technically multiplying or dividing by 1.

Reducing

Reducing is just dividing the top and bottom of a fraction by the same thing. Polynomials will often need to be factored before you can see what can be divided out.

Example 1 $\dfrac{x^2-5x+6}{x^3-2x^2} = \dfrac{(x-2)(x-3)}{x^2(x-2)} = \dfrac{x-3}{x^2}$

Adding and Subtracting

Fractions can be added or subtracted when they have common denominators, so you may have to multiply the top and bottom of one or both fractions by some expression in order to achieve this.

Example 2 $\dfrac{3}{x+2}-\dfrac{2}{x} = \dfrac{3}{x+2}\cdot\left(\dfrac{x}{x}\right)-\dfrac{2}{x}\cdot\left(\dfrac{x+2}{x+2}\right) = \dfrac{3x}{x(x+2)}-\dfrac{2(x+2)}{x(x+2)} = \dfrac{3x-2x-4}{x(x+2)} = \dfrac{x-4}{x^2+2x}$

Multiplying

Multiply fractions across—top with top and bottom with bottom. You may reduce before or after multiplying.

Example 3 $\dfrac{3}{x+2}\cdot\dfrac{x-2}{x} = \dfrac{3\cdot(x-2)}{(x+2)\cdot x} = \dfrac{3x-6}{x^2+2x}$

Dividing

In order to divide fractions you must first flip the second fraction to its reciprocal and then **multiply** across as usual. Some students use "keep-change-flip" to remember this. It means that you should **keep** the first fraction as it is, **change** the sign from division to multiplication, and then **flip** the second fracton upside down.

Example 4 $\dfrac{2x}{x+4}\div\dfrac{3x-2}{x^2-1} = \dfrac{2x}{x+4}\cdot\dfrac{x^2-1}{3x-2} = \dfrac{(2x)(x^2-1)}{(x+4)(3x-2)} = \dfrac{2x^3-2x}{3x^2-2x+12x-8} = \dfrac{2x^3-2x}{3x^2+10x-8}$

Complex Fractions

Complex fractions are fractions that contain other fractions within them. The most efficient way to simplify a complex fraction is to multiply every term by the Least Common Denominator (LCD) of all terms.

Example 5   Simplify $\dfrac{4-\dfrac{49}{x^2}}{2-\dfrac{7}{x}}$.

This has an LCD of x^2 : $\dfrac{4(x^2)-\dfrac{49}{x^2}(x^2)}{2(x^2)-\dfrac{7}{x}(x^2)} = \dfrac{4x^2-49}{2x^2-7x} = \dfrac{(2x+7)(2x-7)}{x(2x-7)} = \dfrac{2x+7}{x}$

Fractional Equations

You can add or subtract on either side of the equation, if applicable, using common denominators and then cross-multiply to solve, or you can multiply the entire equation through by the LCD.

Beware that some fractional equations have extraneous solutions if they make the bottom of one of the original fractions equal zero. In multiple-choice problems, you are better off back solving from the beginning to avoid being trapped by this.

Example 6   Solve for x if $\dfrac{1}{x+2}+\dfrac{2}{x}=\dfrac{-2}{x(x+2)}$.

Multiply through to get a common denominator: $\dfrac{1}{x+2}\left(\dfrac{x}{x}\right)+\dfrac{2}{x}\left(\dfrac{x+2}{x+2}\right)=\dfrac{-2}{x(x+2)}$

$\dfrac{x}{x(x+2)}+\dfrac{2(x+2)}{x(x+2)}=\dfrac{-2}{x(x+2)}$ $\Leftrightarrow$ $\dfrac{x+2x+4}{x(x+2)}=\dfrac{-2}{x(x+2)}$

Set the numerators equal to get $3x+4=-2$, so $3x=-6$ and $x=-2$.

But this is *not* a solution! The domain of our original equation did *not* include $x=-2$, so this equation actually has no solutions.

Fraction Decomposition

A fraction of algebraic expressions can be divided out to produce a quotient and, often, a remainder. Just like with numbers, the remainder must then go over the original denominator to produce a proper fraction.

Example 7 $\dfrac{6x+13}{3x+5} = \dfrac{6x+10+3}{3x+5} = \dfrac{6x+10}{3x+5}+\dfrac{3}{3x+5} = 2+\dfrac{3}{3x+5}$

These questions are usually easier to do by plugging in numbers or back solving the choices when you can.

Fractional Operations and Equations Problem Set

$\boxed{1}$ Where $x \neq 0$, express the sum $\dfrac{2x+5}{2x} + \dfrac{3x-4}{3x}$ in lowest terms.

A) $\dfrac{2x+1}{x}$

B) $12x-7$

C) $\dfrac{5x+1}{5x}$

D) $\dfrac{12x+7}{6x}$

$\boxed{2}$ Which of the following is equivalent to the product $\dfrac{a^2-49}{a^2+4a-21} \times \dfrac{a^2-9}{a-7}$?

A) $\dfrac{a(a^2-9)}{a^2+4a-21}$

B) $\dfrac{a+7}{a-3}$

C) $a-7$

D) $a+3$

$\boxed{3}$ When divided and reduced, $\dfrac{x^2+10x+25}{x^2-9} \div \dfrac{x^2-25}{x-3}$ equals

A) $\dfrac{10x-1}{x-3}$

B) $\dfrac{x+5}{x+3}$

C) $\dfrac{(x+3)(x+5)}{x+5}$

D) $\dfrac{x+5}{(x+3)(x-5)}$

$\boxed{4}$ If the expression $\dfrac{x^2}{x+5}$ is written in as $\dfrac{25}{x+5}+C$, what is C in terms of x?

A) $x+5$

B) $x-5$

C) x^2

D) x^2-25

$\boxed{5}$ For $x \neq 0$ and $y \neq 0$, which of the following is a simplified form of $\dfrac{\dfrac{x}{y}-\dfrac{y}{x}}{1+\dfrac{x}{y}}$?

A) $\dfrac{-y}{x}$

B) $\dfrac{x-y}{x}$

C) $\dfrac{y-x}{x}$

D) $-y$

6 For $x \neq 0$, which of the following is a simplified

form of $\dfrac{2 - \dfrac{2}{7x}}{x - \dfrac{1}{49x}}$?

A) $\dfrac{2}{x+1}$

B) $\dfrac{7}{x+1}$

C) $\dfrac{14}{7x+1}$

D) $\dfrac{2x-14}{x^2-1}$

9 If $x + y = 5$ and $xy = 20$ what is the value of

$\dfrac{1}{x} + \dfrac{1}{y}$?

7 Which of the following is equivalent to

$\dfrac{8x+11}{2x+5}$?

A) 3

B) $\dfrac{4x+11}{5}$

C) $4 - \dfrac{9}{2x+5}$

D) $4 - \dfrac{2}{2x+5}$

10 What is the negative of x in the equation

$\dfrac{3x+2}{x} = \dfrac{4x-2}{3x} + \dfrac{1}{3}$?

8 If $\dfrac{1}{3}a - \dfrac{1}{5}b = 4$, what is the value of $5a - 3b$?

Literal Equations Problem Set

Using the same rules of algebra you use when there is only one variable, solve for the stated variable in terms of the others.

1. If $ax + b = c$, which of the following expressions gives the value of x in terms of a, b, and c?

   A) $c - b - a$

   B) $\dfrac{c}{a} - b$

   C) $\dfrac{c + b}{a}$

   D) $\dfrac{c - b}{a}$

2. The formula for kinetic energy is $K = \dfrac{1}{2}mv^2$.

   Which of the following expressions gives the value of velocity, v, in terms of m and K?

   A) $\sqrt{\dfrac{2K}{m}}$

   B) $\sqrt{\dfrac{K}{2m}}$

   C) $\sqrt{\dfrac{m}{2K}}$

   D) $\sqrt{2mK}$

3. If $kx = -x^2$ for all values of x, what is the value of k?

   A) -2

   B) -1

   C) $-x$

   D) x

4. If $7a + k = 4a + 2$, what is k in terms of a?

   A) $2 - 3a$

   B) $3a - 2$

   C) $3a + 2$

   D) $11a + 2$

5. If $ar - f = b$ and $a \neq 0$, what does $r = $?

   A) $\dfrac{b + f}{a}$

   B) $\dfrac{b - f}{a}$

   C) $b + f - a$

   D) $b - f + a$

6. If the equation for the slope, m, of a line that goes through the point (x_1, y_1) is represented as $m = \dfrac{y - y_1}{x - x_1}$, which of the following equations expresses y properly?

   A) $y = m(x - x_1) - y_1$

   B) $y = m(x - x_1) + y_1$

   C) $y = \dfrac{m - y_1}{x - x_1}$

   D) $y = (m + y_1)(x - x_1)$

7 The weight in grams of a certain insect's larva can be modeled by the function $w = \frac{1}{12}t + 8$, where t equals time in hours after an initial measurement. Which of the following expresses the time after measurement in terms of the larval weight?

A) $12w - 8$

B) $\frac{1}{12}w - 8$

C) $\frac{1}{12}w + 8$

D) $12(w - 8)$

8 If $m = n^{-1}p^{-2}q$, which of the following expressions gives the value of n in terms of m, p, and q?

A) mp^2q

B) $\frac{mp^2}{q}$

C) $\frac{p^2}{mq}$

D) $\frac{q}{mp^2}$

9 If $a = b(c + d)$, which of the following expressions gives the value of d in terms of a, b, and c?

A) $c - b - a$

B) $a - b - c$

C) $\frac{a - bc}{b}$

D) $\frac{a}{bc}$

10 The formula used to convert degrees Celsius to degrees Fahrenheit is $F = \frac{9}{5}C + 32$. Which of the following formulas will convert degrees Fahrenheit to degrees Celsius?

A) $C = \frac{9}{5}F + 32$

B) $C = \frac{9}{5}F - 32$

C) $C = \frac{5}{9}F - 32$

D) $C = \frac{5}{9}(F - 32)$

11 If $a = \frac{b}{b+c}$, what is the value of b in terms of a and c?

A) $\frac{ac}{c - a}$

B) $\frac{c}{1 - a}$

C) $\frac{ac}{a - 1}$

D) $\frac{ac}{1 - a}$

12 The standard form of a quadratic function is $y = ax^2 + bx + c$. Which of the following gives b in terms of y, a, c, and x?

A) $y - ax^2 - x - c$

B) $\frac{y - ax^2 + c}{x}$

C) $y - c - ax$

D) $\frac{y - c}{x} - ax$

13. The formula for the surface area, S, of a rectangular solid is $S = 2lw + 2wh + 2lh$ where l is the length, w is the width, and h is the height. In terms of l, w, and S, what does h equal?

A) $S - 2lw - 2w - 2l$

B) $\dfrac{S - 2lw}{2}$

C) $\dfrac{S - 2lw}{2w + 2l}$

D) $\dfrac{S}{2lw + 2w + 2l}$

14. The formula for the surface area, S, of a right circular cylinder is $S = 2\pi r^2 + 2\pi rh$, where r is the radius of the base and h is the height. If the radius of the base of a right circular cylinder is x and the surface area is y, what is the height in terms of x and y?

A) $\dfrac{y - 2\pi x^2}{2\pi x}$

B) $\dfrac{y - 2\pi x}{2\pi}$

C) $y - x$

D) $y - 2\pi x$

$$h = \frac{\left(\dfrac{a}{23}\right)\left(\dfrac{b}{c}\right)^x}{35 - \left(\dfrac{12}{a}\right)^{x-1}} I$$

15. The formula shown above can be used to predict the height in inches, h, of a tree with initial height I when a, b, and c ounces of three different fertilizers are used and x months have passed. Which of the following expresses I in terms of h, a, b, c, and x?

A) $I = \dfrac{35 - \left(\dfrac{12}{a}\right)^{x-1}}{\left(\dfrac{a}{23}\right)\left(\dfrac{b}{c}\right)^x} h$

B) $I = \dfrac{\left(\dfrac{a}{23}\right)\left(\dfrac{b}{c}\right)^x}{35 - \left(\dfrac{12}{a}\right)^{x-1}} h$

C) $I = \dfrac{\left(\dfrac{12}{a}\right)}{\left(\dfrac{a}{23}\right)\left(\dfrac{b}{c}\right)^x} h + 35$

D) $I = \dfrac{\left(\dfrac{12}{a}\right)}{35 + \left(\dfrac{a}{23}\right)\left(\dfrac{b}{c}\right)} h$

Quadratic Functions

Quadratic functions graph as parabolas and can be written in three distinct forms: **standard form**, **vertex form**, and **factored form**. The parabola will have an **axis of symmetry** that goes through its **vertex**, or turning point. The lead coefficient, a, cannot equal 0. The parabola will smile when a is positive, making the vertex a **minimum**, and frown when a is negative, making the vertex a **maximum**. All quadratics have a y-intercept where $x = 0$ and **roots** where $f(x) = 0$. When the roots are real numbers, they are the x-intercepts of the parabola.

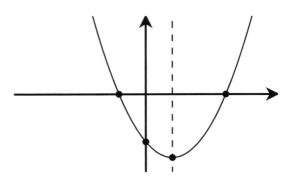

Standard Form

$$f(x) = ax^2 + bx + c$$

- Axis of symmetry: $x = \dfrac{-b}{2a}$

- y-intercept: $(0, c)$

- Roots: $x = \dfrac{-b \pm \sqrt{b^2 - 4ac}}{2a}$

  - Sum of the Roots: $\dfrac{-b}{a}$

  - Product of the Roots: $\dfrac{c}{a}$

- Discriminant: $D = b^2 - 4ac$
  - Real roots when D is positive
  - One double root when $D = 0$
  - Imaginary roots when D is negative

Vertex Form

$$f(x) = a(x - h)^2 + k$$

- This form can be constructed from standard form by **completing the square**.
- The vertex is (h, k) and the axis of symmetry is $x = h$.
- The SAT will often describe this form as one where "the coordinates of the vertex can be seen as constants."

Factored Form

$$f(x) = a(x - r_1)(x - r_2)$$

- This form can be constructed from standard form by factoring (when it is factorable).
- The SAT will often describe this form as one where "the x-intercepts can be seen as constants." Those x-intercepts, or roots, are r_1 and r_2.

- The axis of symmetry goes through the midpoint of the roots, so its equation is $x = \dfrac{r_1 + r_2}{2}$.

Quadratic Functions Problem Set

1. A ball is thrown up from a height of 4 feet. The equation describing the ball's height after t seconds is $h(t) = 4 + 10t - 16t^2$. What is the ball's height after 0.4 seconds?

   A) It will have hit the ground

   B) 1.6 feet

   C) 5.44 feet

   D) 10.56 feet

$$a(x) = x^2 + 1$$
$$b(x) = -x$$

2. Given the functions $a(x)$ and $b(x)$ defined above, for how many values of k is it true that $a(k) = b(k)$?

   A) None

   B) One

   C) Two

   D) Three

3. What are the solutions to $2x^2 + 12x + 8 = 0$?

   A) $x = -3 \pm \sqrt{5}$

   B) $x = -3 \pm 2\sqrt{10}$

   C) $x = -6 \pm 2\sqrt{5}$

   D) $x = -6 \pm \sqrt{10}$

4. What is the sum of the roots of the quadratic function $y = 3x^2 - 15x + 8$?

   A) -15

   B) -5

   C) 5

   D) 15

5. What is the product of the values of a that satisfy $a^2 - 12a + 9 = 0$?

   A) -9

   B) 9

   C) $-18\sqrt{3}$

   D) $18\sqrt{3}$

x	$f(x)$
0	-6
1	-6
2	-4
3	0

6. If $f(x)$ is a quadratic equation represented by the table of values shown above, which of the following could be $f(x)$?

   A) $f(x) = x^2 - 6$

   B) $f(x) = x^2 + 3x + 6$

   C) $f(x) = x^2 - x + 3$

   D) $f(x) = x^2 - x - 6$

7. For a certain quadratic equation
$ax^2 + bx + c = 0$, the 2 solutions are $x = -\dfrac{2}{3}$ and
$x = \dfrac{1}{2}$. Which of the following are factors of
$ax^2 + bx + c$?

A) $(3x+2)$ and $(2x-1)$

B) $(3x+1)$ and $(2x-3)$

C) $(3x-2)$ and $(2x+1)$

D) $(3x-2)$ and $(2x-1)$

8. For the function $f(x) = ax^2 + bx + c,$ where
$a = 3,\ b = 0,$ and c is a constant, if $f(-2) = 12,$
what is the value of $f(2)$?

A) –12

B) 4

C) 12

D) 36

9. The function $h(t) = -4.9t^2 + 70t$ can be used
to model the height of a projectile with an
initial velocity of 70 meters per second t
seconds after it is fired. Approximately how
many seconds after being fired will the
projectile hit the ground?

A) 4.9

B) 7.1

C) 14.3

D) 70

10. What is the distance between the two points
where the parabola with equation
$y = x^2 - 20x + 96$ intersects the line given by
the equation $y = 60$?

A) 4

B) 16

C) 18

D) 20

$$y = x^2 - x - 6$$
$$y = x^2 - 3x + 6$$

11. What is the x-value of the solution of the
system of equations shown above?

A) 2

B) 3

C) 6

D) No solution

12 A square-shaped piece of cardboard will have squares of side-length x cut from each corner. The resulting edges will be folded up, forming a box with no top. The side of the original cardboard square is y. What is the volume of this box?

A) $x(y-x)(y-x)$

B) $x(y-2x)(y-2x)$

C) $x^2 y$

D) $(x-y)^3$

15 If m is constant, what are the solutions of
$3x^2 = 2mx - m$?

A) $x = \dfrac{m}{3} \pm \dfrac{\sqrt{m^2 - 3m}}{3}$

B) $x = \dfrac{m}{3} \pm \dfrac{\sqrt{m^2 - 12m}}{3}$

C) $x = \dfrac{2m}{3} \pm \dfrac{\sqrt{m^2 - 3m}}{3}$

D) $x = m \pm \sqrt{m^2 - 3m}$

Questions 13 and 14 refer to the following information:

$$y = a(x-5)(x+1)$$

13 What is the x-coordinate of the vertex of the parabola that represents the quadratic equation above (when $a \neq 0$)?

A) 5

B) 2

C) –1

D) –2

16 Which of the following is the vertex form of the quadratic function $y = x^2 + 12x + 32$?

A) $y = (x+8)(x+4)$

B) $y = (x+6)(x-4)$

C) $y = (x+6)^2 - 4$

D) $y = (x-6)^2 - 4$

14 What is the y-coordinate, in terms of a, of the vertex of the parabola that represents the quadratic equation above (when $a \neq 0$)?

A) $-9a$

B) $-5a$

C) $-4a$

D) $4a$

17 If $x^2 + 2ax + a^2 = 16,$ what is one possible value of $x + a$?

A) 2

B) 4

C) 8

D) 16

$$(2x+3)(x+2) = (x+3)(x-3)$$

19 The above equation has how many real solutions?

20 If $x > 0$ and $x^2 - 10x - 24 = 0,$ what is the value of x?

18 For the equation $4x^2 + bx + 9 = 0,$ which value of b gives the equation two distinct, real solutions?

A) –12

B) 0

C) 12

D) 15

Polynomial Functions

Polynomial functions (ex. $f(x) = x^3 + 2x^2 - 6$) written in standard form $f(x) = ax^n + bx^{n-1} + cx^{n-2}...$ are identified by their degree, n, the highest exponent to which x is raised. *Linear* functions are polynomial functions with degree 1, and *quadratic* functions are polynomial functions with degree 2. Other examples of polynomial functions are *cubic* functions (degree 3) and *quartic* functions (degree 4).

Factored form $f(x) = a(x-r_1)(x-r_2)(x-r_3)...$ where r_k is a root of the polynomial. The relationship between a root, r, and a factor, $(x-r)$, is very important.

Roots   The number of roots of a polynomial is equivalent to its degree. When roots are real numbers, they are the x-intercepts of the polynomial's graph. The **multiplicity** of root r is the number of times $(x-r)$ is a factor of a polynomial. If a root has a multiplicity of 2, it is a double root, and the graph will appear to bounce off of that root on the x-axis. If a root has a multiplicity of 3, it is a triple root, and the graph will show inflection (a brief plateau) as it crosses the x-axis at that spot.

End behavior   Odd-degree polynomials will end in different directions. If a is positive, odd-degree polynomials will go to $-\infty$ as x goes to $-\infty$ and will go to ∞ as x goes to ∞. If a is negative, the reverse happens. Even-degree polynomials go to ∞ in both directions if a is positive and go to $-\infty$ in both directions if a is negative.

Example 1 $f(x) = x^3 - 3x^2 - 6x + 8$ *Example 2* $f(x) = -(x+1)^2(x-3)^2$ *Example 3* $f(x) = -(x+3)^2(x-1)^3$
$= (x+2)(x-1)(x-4)$

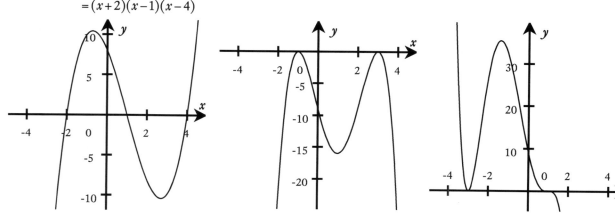

Remainders   When a polynomial function, $P(x)$, is divided by a binomial, $(x-c)$, the remainder will be equal to $P(c)$. If the remainder is 0, then $(x-c)$ is a factor of $P(x)$, and c is one of its roots.

Factoring by grouping   Some cubic and higher-degree functions can be factored by grouping terms two at a time and pulling out factors of each pair to reveal further factoring.

Example 4 $f(x) = x^3 + 3x^2 - 16x - 48 \ = \ (x^3 + 3x^2) + (-16x - 48)$

$= x^2(x+3) - 16(x+3) \ = \ (x+3)(x^2 - 16)$

$= (x+3)(x+4)(x-4)$

Polynomial Functions Problem Set

1. Which of the following is not a root of the function $y = 3(x+3)(x-5)(x+5)$?

   A) -5

   B) -3

   C) 3

   D) 5

2. If a polynomial function $p(x)$ has real roots of -6, 1 and 2, which of the following must be a factor of $p(x)$?

   A) $x-12$

   B) $x-6$

   C) $x-2$

   D) $x+2$

3. Which of the following functions has three real distinct roots?

   A) $y = (x-9)^2(x-3)^2(x+1)^2$

   B) $y = (x-9)^3$

   C) $y = (x-9)^2(x-3)$

   D) $y = (x-3)(x-3)(x+1)$

4. If the graph of the function $f(x)$ has x-intercepts at -5, 5, and 7, which of the following could be an expression for $f(x)$?

   A) $f(x) = (x-5)^2(x-7)$

   B) $f(x) = (x-5)^2(x-7)^2$

   C) $f(x) = (x+5)(x-5)(x-7)^2$

   D) $f(x) = (x+5)^2(x-5)^2(x+7)^2$

5. The graph of a polynomial $f(x)$ passes through the following points: $(-2, 3)$, $(0, 1)$, $(2, 0)$, and $(4, -4)$. Which of the following must be a factor of $f(x)$?

   A) $x-4$

   B) $x-2$

   C) $x-1$

   D) $x+2$

6. When the polynomial function $f(x)$ is divided by $x-8$, the remainder is 5. Which of the following must be true?

   A) $x-8$ is a factor of $f(x)$

   B) $x-3$ is a factor of $f(x)$

   C) $f(8) = 5$

   D) $f(5) = 8$

7. What are the roots of the function $y = 3x(4x^2-9) + 5(4x^2-9)$?

   A) -3, 0, and 2

   B) $-\dfrac{5}{3}$, $-\dfrac{3}{2}$, and $\dfrac{3}{2}$

   C) $-\dfrac{5}{3}$, $-\dfrac{3}{2}$, and $\dfrac{5}{3}$

   D) $-\dfrac{5}{3}$, $-\dfrac{2}{3}$, and $\dfrac{2}{3}$

8. When the polynomial function $f(x)$ is divided by $x+6$, the remainder is 0. Which of the following <u>must</u> be true?

    I. $x-6$ is a factor of $f(x)$
    II. $x+6$ is a factor of $f(x)$
    III. $f(6)=0$

A) I only
B) II only
C) I and III only
D) II and III only

9. Which of the following accurately describes the graph of the function $y=a(x+2)(x-3)^2$, where $a>0$?

A) After it crosses the x-axis at -2, all y-values are non-positive.
B) After it crosses the x-axis at -2, all y-values are non-negative.
C) After it crosses the x-axis at -2, all y-values are positive.
D) After it crosses the x-axis at -2, all y-values are negative.

10. Between which of the following x-values <u>must</u> the graph of the function $y=2x(x+5)(x-4)$ turn?

A) -5 and -4
B) 0 and 2
C) -5 and 0
D) 4 and 5

11. If $a(x)=x^3-5x^2+6x$ and $b(x)=x^2-5x+6$, which of the following polynomials will be divisible by $x+5$?

A) $a(x)+b(x)$
B) $a(x)+5b(x)$
C) $5a(x)+b(x)$
D) $5(a(x)+b(x))$

12. If $x>0$, what is one possible solution to the equation $x^5(x^2-13)=-36x^3$?

13. What is the only positive real solution to the equation $(25x^2-16)(9x^2+4)=0$?

14. For what real value of x is the equation $x^3-3x^2+7x-21=0$ true?

15. For what real value of x is the equation $6x^3-9x^2+2x-3=0$ true?

Exponential Functions

Exponential functions have the form $f(x) = a(b)^x$ where a is the y-intercept and b is the base, or common ratio. The base b should always be greater than zero and not equal to one. Otherwise, exponential functions can be grouped into two categories:

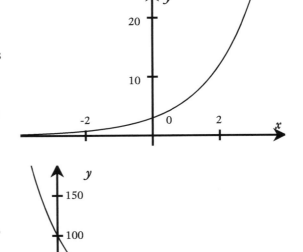

Exponential Growth

This occurs when $b > 1$ and has constantly increasing values as x increases. The graph is asymptotic to the x-axis as x gets smaller, and the rate of increase is dependent on the size of b.

The example to the right is the graph of $y = 3(2)^x$, which, for $x \geq 0$, models the act of starting at the number 3 and doubling every time x increases by one.

Exponential Decay

This occurs when $0 < b < 1$ and has constantly decreasing values as x increases. Therefore the graph is asymptotic to the x-axis as x gets larger.

The example to the right is the graph of $y = 100(.4)^x$.

Notice how, like in the growth example, the graph crosses the y-axis at $(0, a)$.

Applications

Exponential growth and decay functions are often used to model things that change as a percentage of themselves like populations, bank accounts, and masses of radioactive elements.

The compounding formula $A(t) = P(1 \pm r)^t$ can be used to analyze both exponential growth and exponential decay scenarios. In this formula, P represents the principal (initial) amount, r the rate of change (as a decimal), and t the number of times the rate is compounded.

Example 1 What function can be used to show the amount, $A(t)$, a house is worth after t years if the house was bought for $425,000 and its value increases steadily at 3.5% per year?

Since $P = 425,000$ and $r = 0.035$, you can use $A(t) = 425,000(1.035)^t$.

Example 5 What is the daily rate of decline of a population of bees if the formula $B(t) = 500(.83)^{7t}$ is used to estimate the bee colony's population t weeks after a certain pollutant was released near its hive?

The formula is already accounting for the daily rate since the exponent $7t$ represents the amount of days in t weeks. Since $1 \pm r = .83$, r must be a decrease of $.17$, which means a 17% daily decline.

Exponential Functions Problem Set

1. An exponential growth function, $A(t) = 5000(1.2)^t$, models the amount of money in a certain brokerage account, with a $5000 principal amount, t years after the principal is paid. If the return is calculated annually, what is the annual return rate on this account?

   A) 1.2%

   B) 2%

   C) 20%

   D) 120%

2. The value of a car depreciates (decreases) at an annual rate of 15 percent. If the initial value of the car is $22,000, which of the following functions models the value of the car, in dollars, after x years?

   A) $f(x) = 22,000(.15)^x$

   B) $f(x) = 22,000(.85)^x$

   C) $f(x) = .15(22,000)^x$

   D) $f(x) = .85(22,000)^x$

3. The population of bacteria on a cookie that has been recently dropped on the ground begins at 30. After that, it can be expressed by the equation $c(t) = 30r^t$, where r is a constant and t is hours. If the population increases 30% each hour, what is the value of r?

   A) 0.3

   B) 0.7

   C) 1

   D) 1.3

4. Nate was 98 cm tall at the start of 2006. He grew steadily by 7% each year for the next several years. Which of the following functions gives his height h, in centimeters, after the next k years?

   A) $h(k) = 98 + 0.07^k$

   B) $h(k) = 98^k(1.07)$

   C) $h(k) = 98(0.07)^k$

   D) $h(k) = 98(1.07)^k$

5. Which of the following describes a function exhibiting exponential decay?

   A) Each year, 10 percent of the initial value of a house is added to the house's total value.

   B) Each year, 10 percent of the initial value of a house is subtracted from the house's total value.

   C) Each year, $10,000 is subtracted from the total value of a house.

   D) Each successive year, 10 percent of the current value of a house is subtracted from the house's total value.

6. A common formula for annually compounded interest is $A = P(1+r)^t$, where P means principal amount, r means rate as a decimal and t means time in years. What is the significance of the number 1 in the formula?

   A) All interest-bearing accounts gain at least 1% interest.

   B) The principal is always at least $1.

   C) The interest is always taken on 100% of the initial value.

   D) The interest is always taken on 100% of the current value.

7. The population of an invasive pest is predicted to double every year. The initial population is 2,000. How many years will it take for the population to increase to where it is at least 30 times its initial size?

A) 3

B) 5

C) 10

D) 15

8. A marketer estimates that a website will increase its hits by 50% every 12 days. If the site got 200 hits today, which of the following functions estimates how many hits h the site will have d days from now?

A) $h(d) = 200(.5)^{12d}$

B) $h(d) = 200(.5)^{\frac{d}{12}}$

C) $h(d) = 200(1.5)^{12d}$

D) $h(d) = 200(1.5)^{\frac{d}{12}}$

9. The number of deer in Morgan Park is decreasing at the rate of 7.5% per year. There are currently 380 deer in Morgan Park. In how many years will there be fewer than 30 deer in Morgan Park?

A) 15

B) 16

C) 32

D) 33

10. Which of the following is the closest to the difference after 5 years in the amount of money in an account that gains 4% interest compounded annually and an account that gains 5% interest compounded annually if both accounts began with $500?

A) $25.00

B) $25.25

C) $29.81

D) $30.00

11. Which of the following might be modeled by the function $f(x) = 3(2)^{\frac{x}{10}}$?

A) A population of initially three elephants, which will double in size every 10 years

B) A population of initially two lions, which will triple in size every 10 years

C) A bank account with continuously compounding interest, which will double every 10 months

D) A bank account with annually compounding interest, with an interest rate of 50 percent

12. An area entomologist predicted that the population of an invasive insect will triple in size every 6 months. The population density at the beginning of 2015 was estimated to be 1000 insects per acre. If D represents the population density (in insects per acre) n years after 2015, then which of the following equations models the population over time?

A) $D = 1000(3)^{\frac{n}{2}}$

B) $D = 1000 + (3)^{2n}$

C) $D = 1000(3)^{2n}$

D) $D = 1000n + (3)^{n}$

13 What are the domain and range of the function
$y = 3^{(x-5)}$?

A) Domain: All real numbers
Range: All real numbers

B) Domain: All real numbers
Range: $y > -5$

C) Domain: All Real Numbers
Range: $y > 0$

D) Domain: $x > 5$
Range: All Real Numbers

14 A financial institution advertises that you can use the following formula to calculate the amount of money you will have in an account after y years if you invest $1000 and interest is compounded annually: $1000(x)^y$. If one of their funds predicts 6% annual growth, what should be the value of x that is used in the formula?

15 Using the formula, principal and interest rate in the previous question, how much *interest* will be gained by the account after seven years (round to the nearest dollar)?

Additional Functions and Transformations

Though linear functions, quadratic functions, higher-level polynomial functions, and exponential functions are the most commonly tested functions on the SAT, you should be aware of some of the characteristics of other types of functions, and you should know basic function transformation rules as well.

Absolute Value Functions

$y = |x|$ is the parent absolute value function. It behaves like the parent linear function $y = x$ except that negative y-values are reflected to their positive counterparts. Though the domain of an absolute value function is all real numbers, the range, like a quadratic, depends on where the vertex is.

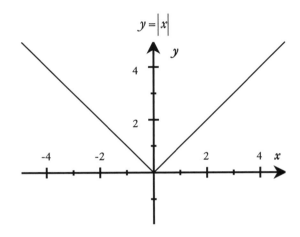

Rational Functions

When a function expresses a fraction of two polynomials, it is called a rational function. These functions can have restricted domains that exclude any x-value that makes the bottom equal zero. Usually, those domain restrictions manifest as vertical *asymptotes*, invisible vertical lines that the graph will bend away from but never cross (though any number that makes both the top *and* bottom of the function equal zero produces a hole in the graph instead of a vertical asymptote). Rational functions, like exponential functions, can also have horizontal asymptotes, which describe the *end behavior* of the graph as x gets very large or small.

Example 1 $\quad y = \dfrac{4x-1}{x^2-x-6} = \dfrac{4x-1}{(x+2)(x-3)}$

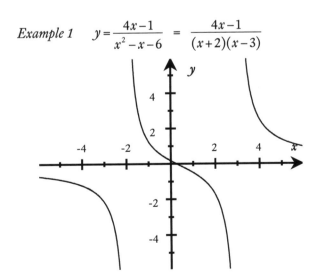

Example 2 $\quad y = \dfrac{x^2+1}{x^2+4x-12} = \dfrac{x^2+1}{(x+6)(x-2)}$

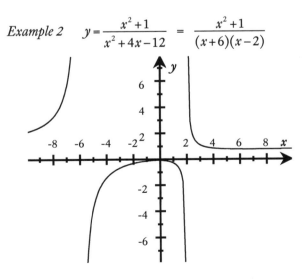

Radical Functions

When a function takes a root of an expression, it is called a radical function. Square root functions are the most common of these. The graph of a square root function looks like half of a rotated parabola. In square root functions, any x-value that makes the expression under the radical negative cannot be in the domain.

Example 6 $y = \sqrt{x+2}$

The domain of this function can be found by setting the inside greater than or equal to zero: $x + 2 \geq 0$, so $x \geq -2$.

The range can be expressed as $y \geq 0$ because the $\sqrt{}$ symbol only calls for non-negative square roots.

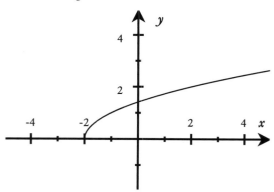

Function Transformations

Graphs of functions are flipped, shifted, stretched, or squeezed by operations on the parent function (its simplest form).

$$y = f(x) \;\rightarrow\; y = a\left[f\big(b(x-h)\big)\right] + k$$

h = horizontal shift

k = vertical shift

$$a \Rightarrow \begin{cases} a > 1 & \rightarrow \text{vertical stretch} \\ 0 < a < 1 & \rightarrow \text{vertical squeeze} \\ a < 0 & \rightarrow \text{reflect over } x\text{-axis} \end{cases}$$

$$b \Rightarrow \begin{cases} b > 1 & \rightarrow \text{horizontal squeeze} \\ 0 < b < 1 & \rightarrow \text{horizontal stretch} \\ b < 0 & \rightarrow \text{reflect over } y\text{-axis} \end{cases}$$

Example 7 $y = x^2$ $\rightarrow$ $y = 2(x-1)^2 - 3$

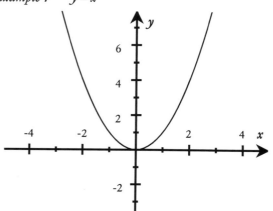
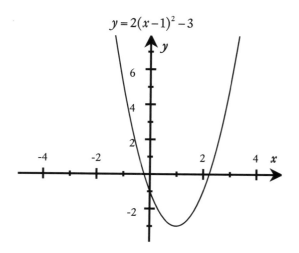

Additional Functions and Transformations Problem Set

1. What is the domain of the function

   $f(x) = \dfrac{(x-7)(x+4)}{(x-7)(x+1)}$?

   A) All real numbers except -1
   B) All real numbers except -1 and 7
   C) All real numbers except -4 and 7
   D) All real numbers except -1, -4, and 7

2. Which of the following is not in the domain of

   the function $y = \dfrac{x^2 - 16}{x + 16}$?

   A) -16
   B) -4
   C) 4
   D) 16

3. What is the equation(s) of any vertical

   asymptotes for the function $y = \dfrac{x-6}{x^2 - 2x - 24}$?

   A) $x = -4$ only
   B) $y = -4$ only
   C) $x = -4$ and $x = 6$
   D) $y = 0$

4. What is the domain of the function

   $f(x) = \sqrt{2x-5}$?

   A) $x \geq 2.5$
   B) $x \geq 5$
   C) $x > 2.5$
   D) All real numbers

5. If $f(x) = \sqrt{x^2 + 1}$ and $g(x) = x + 2$, what is the
   x-coordinate of the point of intersection of f
   and g?

   A) -1
   B) $-\dfrac{3}{4}$
   C) 2
   D) No solution

6. What is the domain of the function

   $f(x) = \dfrac{x-5}{\sqrt{x-2}}$?

   A) All real numbers
   B) $x \geq 2$
   C) $x > 2$
   D) $x > 2$ and $x \neq 5$

7 What is the range of the function
   $f(x) = |x| + 2$?

   A) All real numbers
   B) $f(x) \geq -2$
   C) $f(x) \geq 2$
   D) $-2 \leq f(x) \leq 2$

8 Which of the following functions has two
   distinct x-intercepts?

   A) $y = |2x - 7|$
   B) $y = |2x| - 7$
   C) $y = |2x + 7|$
   D) $y = |2x| + 7$

9 Which of the following functions has no
   positive y-values?

   A) $y = |x| - 1500$
   B) $y = \left|\dfrac{x}{15} - 1000\right|$
   C) $y = |-150x - 10|$
   D) $y = -15|x - 100|$

10 Which of the following functions will have a
   graph that will look like the graph of $y = x^2$
   reflected over the x-axis and shifted 4 units to
   the left?

   A) $y = (-x - 4)^2$
   B) $y = -(x - 4)^2$
   C) $y = (-x + 4)^2$
   D) $y = -(x + 4)^2$

11 If $f(x) = |3x - 12| - 3$, for what value(s) of x
   does $f(x) = 0$?

   A) 3 only
   B) 5 only
   C) -5 and 5
   D) 3 and 5

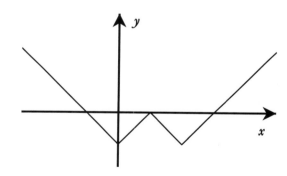

12 For which of the following functions could the
   figure shown above be the graph?

   A) $y = |x - 3|$
   B) $y = |x - 3| - 3$
   C) $y = ||x - 3| - 3|$
   D) $y = ||x - 3| - 3| - 3$

Which of the following has a graph in the *xy*-plane where the value of y is never larger than -3?

A) $y = |x| - 3$

B) $y = -(x-3)^2$

C) $y = x^3 - 3$

D) $y = -x^2 - 3$

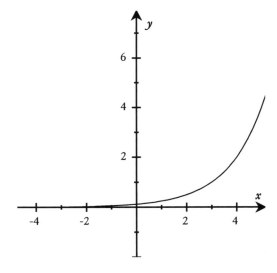

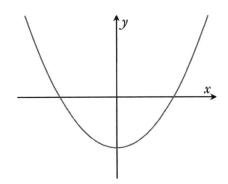

14 The function graphed above is given by the equation $y = x^2 - m$. Which of the following <u>must</u> be true?

A) $m > 0$

B) $m < 0$

C) m is odd

D) m is even

15 Which function is represented by the figure above?

A) $y = 2^x$

B) $y = 2^{(x+3)}$

C) $y = 2^x + 3$

D) $y = 2^{(x-3)}$

16 Which of the following functions will have a graph with a discontinuity?

A) $y = 1.5^{x-3} - 8$

B) $y = -|x - 12|$

C) $y = \dfrac{x-3}{x^2+4}$

D) $y = \dfrac{x+3}{x^2-4}$

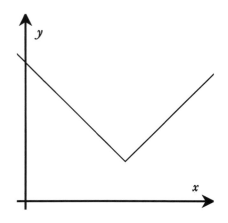

17 Which of the following could be the function represented by the figure above?

A) $y = (x-5)^2 + 2$

B) $y = |x-5| + 2$

C) $y = (x+5)^2 + 2$

D) $y = |x+5| + 2$

18 Which of the following is the equation for an asymptote of the function given by

$y = 3^{3x-2} + 2$?

A) $x = 0$

B) $y = 0$

C) $x = 2$

D) $y = 2$

19 Which of the following functions will have graphs with the same turning point?

    I. $f(x) = -(x+3)^2 - 7$

    II. $f(x) = (x-3)^2 - 7$

    III. $f(x) = |x+3| - 7$

A) I and II only

B) I and III only

C) II and III only

D) I, II, and III

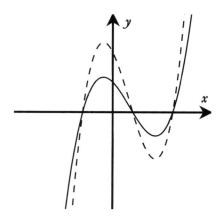

20 The solid curve above is the graph of the function $y = f(x)$. Which of the following could be an expression for the dashed curve in terms of constant a, where $a > 1$, and $f(x)$?

A) $y = f(x+a)$

B) $y = f(x) + a$

C) $y = a(f(x))$

D) $y = \dfrac{f(x)}{a}$

Problem Solving and Data Analysis

Using data to express and predict the complex systems that govern our world is perhaps the most widespread application of mathematics. When you can interpret graphs and tables and synthesize information into statistical measurements or predictive functions, you increase your fluency both in mathematical analysis and scientific and cultural understanding.

The College Board tests these skills in limited ways in the Evidence-Based Reading and Writing sections, and there are no questions in this domain in the No Calculator Mathematics section, but Problem Solving and Data Analysis is the main attraction in Section 4: Math Test—Calculator. Nearly half of all questions in this section will test your ability in the following categories:

- Analysis of tables and graphs
- Probability
- Percent
- Rates and unit conversion
- Statistical measurements of center, correlation, and spread

 Keep in mind that because *all* of the questions you'll find in this chapter would be in Section 4 of the SAT, a calculator can be used on every one of these questions.

Data Analysis and Probability

Tables and Graphs

When answering questions that refer to tables or graphs, actively engage the data. Use your pencil to circle data points that are addressed in tables and to draw lines from relevant positions on axes to their corresponding points on graphs. This will have the effect of siphoning the pertinent information away from the noise of all the other information that is presented.

Some basic measurements can be gathered from data sets whether those sets are presented in lists, tables or graphs. They include:

Mean   the average of a set of numbers, found by dividing the sum of the set by the amount of numbers in the set

Median   the middle number when a set of numbers is placed in numeric order
When there is an even amount of numbers in a set, the median is the average of the two in the middle.

Mode   a number that occurs most often in a set of numbers (there can be more than one mode in a set)

Range   the difference between the highest and lowest numbers in a set

Fractional or Decimal Probability

- A probability is determined by the simple fraction $\dfrac{\text{desired outcomes}}{\text{total possible outcomes}}$.

- This can be converted into a decimal or a percent, but it will always be between 0 and 1.

- The sum of all possible probabilities for an event must add to 1.

- Independent events do not affect each other's outcomes. If you get tails on twenty straight flips of a fair coin, you will still have a one-half probability of it coming up tails on the next flip.

- When an event occurs multiple times "without replacement," meaning that a selection cannot be repeated, you must reduce outcomes by one each time.

Conditional Probability

The probability of an event given that another event has occurred

Often conditional probability questions are asked when a table is given. The condition that is referenced is usually represented by a row or column of the table, so the conditional probability can be found by placing a single data point (cell of the table) over the sum of a row or column.

Example 1   According to the table below, what is the probability that if a boy from Laco High School is chosen at random he will have blue eyes?

Students at Laco High School

	Boys	Girls
Brown Eyes	45	38
Blue Eyes	20	31

Because there are a total of 65 boys at Laco High School (the sum of 45 and 20), the probability of selecting a blue-eyed boy once it is known that a boy is selected is $\dfrac{20}{65}$.

Data Analysis Problem Set

Questions 1–3 refer to the following information

A group of students doing research on stream quality collected and analyzed samples from 6 sites along a mountain stream. The students measured water temperature, and concentrations of nitrates, phosphates, and sulfates in parts per million (ppm). Data collected are shown below.

Site	Elevation (ft)	Water Temp (°F)	Nitrates (ppm)	Phosphates (ppm)	Sulfates (ppm)
1	4310	44	0.0012	0.035	5.76
2	4260	44	0.0032	0.030	5.60
3	3710	46	0.0060	0.025	5.21
4	3240	47	0.0011	0.007	1.24
5	3380	48	0.0213	0.182	4.21
6	2700	50	0.0204	0.180	3.95

[1] Which site had the highest ratio of phosphate concentration to nitrate concentration in the samples?

A) Site 1

B) Site 3

C) Site 5

D) Site 6

[2] Which of the following is closest to the average rate that water temperature, in degrees Fahrenheit, changes with each 100 feet of decrease in elevation?

A) 0.294

B) 0.373

C) 2.68

D) 3.73

[3] One of the students is inexperienced, and accidentally left some distilled water in the collection bottle for one of the sites, which diluted that particular sample. According to the table, which site was most likely the one with water in the collection bottle?

A) Site 2

B) Site 3

C) Site 4

D) Site 6

Questions 4–7 refer to the following information

The table below presents information about elements in Group 1 and Group 7 of the periodic table. Group 1 is the alkaline earth metal elements, and Group 7 is the halogen elements (non-metals).

Element	Atomic Number	Electronegativity	First Ionization Energy (kJ/mol)	Atomic Radius (pm)	Ionic Radius (pm)
Group 1 Metals					
Li	3	1.0	520	152	90
Na	11	0.9	496	186	116
K	19	0.8	419	227	152
Rb	37	0.8	403	248	166
Cs	55	0.7	377	265	181
Group 7 Halogens					
F	9	4.0	1681	72	119
Cl	17	3.0	1251	100	167
Br	35	2.8	1140	114	182
I	53	2.5	1008	133	206

NOTE: kJ/mol means kilo-joules per mole, pm means 10^{-12} meters.

4 For the Group 1 metal elements, as atomic number increases, which of the following two properties display alike trending behavior?

A) Electronegativity and First Ionization Energy

B) Electronegativity and Ionic Radius

C) Atomic Radius and First Ionization Energy

D) Ionic Radius and First Ionization Energy

5 If the table included group 7 Halogen element At, with atomic number 85, what would the electronegativity value of At most likely be?

A) 5.0

B) 2.6

C) 2.2

D) 0.6

6 Ionic bonds form between ions of different elements. The greater the difference in electronegativity between the two elements, the greater the ionic character of the bond. Which of the following bonds would have the LEAST ionic character?

A) Na-Cl

B) K-I

C) Li-I

D) Cs-F

7 How much larger, in pm, is the mean atomic radius of the metals in the table than the mean atomic radius of the halogens in the table?

A) 26.1

B) 98.5

C) 104.75

D) 110.85

Questions 8–11 refer to the following information and figure

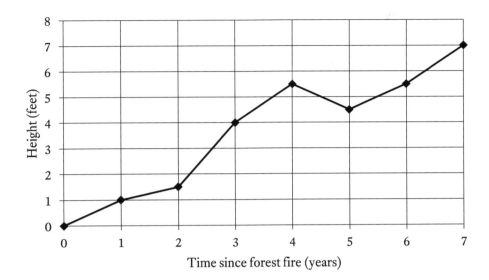

The line graph above shows the average height in feet of vegetation each year after a forest fire.

8 According to the graph, in which two years was the vegetation the closest in size?

A) Year 1 and Year 2

B) Year 2 and Year 3

C) Year 3 and Year 4

D) Year 6 and Year 7

10 Which of the following is closest to the range of vegetation height, in feet, from year 4 to year 7 after the fire?

A) 1.5

B) 2.5

C) 5.5

D) 7

9 According to the graph, what was the greatest change (in absolute value) in vegetation height between two consecutive years?

A) Year 0 and Year 1

B) Year 1 and Year 2

C) Year 2 and Year 3

D) Year 3 and Year 4

11 What is the average rate of increase, in feet per year, from one year after the forest fire to four years after the forest fire?

A) 1.375

B) 1.5

C) 4.5

D) 5.5

Questions 12–15 refer to the following information

The bar graph below shows the average monthly temperature in Celsius over a 12-month period in the town of Rupert.

Average Monthly Temperature (°C)

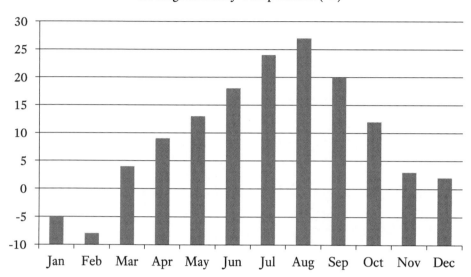

12. Which of the following is the closest to the range of average monthly temperature, in degrees Celsius, in the graph?

A) 15

B) 25

C) 35

D) 45

13. If one month with an average temperature in Rupert under 15 degrees Celsius is chosen at random, what is the probability that it will begin with the letter J?

A) 0

B) $\dfrac{1}{12}$

C) $\dfrac{1}{8}$

D) $\dfrac{1}{4}$

14. A temperature of zero degrees Celsius is considered freezing weather. In how many of the 12 displayed months was the average monthly temperature within 10 degrees of freezing?

A) 2

B) 4

C) 6

D) 8

The formula for converting between degrees Fahrenheit (F) and degrees Celsius (C) is:

$$\frac{5}{9}(F-32)=C$$

15. In which month was the average temperature closest to 25 degrees Fahrenheit?

A) January

B) April

C) August

D) December

Probability Problem Set

1 David has 10 baseball cards, 4 football cards and 5 hockey cards. How many more hockey cards will David need to acquire to have a one-third probability of randomly selecting a hockey card from all of his sports cards?

A) 2

B) 4

C) 7

D) 9

2 A jar contains 20 total jelly beans. 10 of the jelly beans are blue, 7 are red, and 3 are green. Nancy withdrew one jelly bean at random, ate it, and then withdrew another jelly bean at random. What calculation gives the probability that Nancy withdrew two red jelly beans?

A) $\dfrac{7}{20}+\dfrac{6}{19}$

B) $\dfrac{7}{20}\times\dfrac{7}{20}$

C) $\dfrac{7}{20}\times\dfrac{6}{20}$

D) $\dfrac{7}{20}\times\dfrac{6}{19}$

3 A student will be chosen at random to represent a homeroom class in student government. If the probability that a male student will be chosen is $\dfrac{3}{7}$, which of the following could NOT be the number of students in the homeroom class?

A) 21

B) 24

C) 28

D) 35

Questions 4-5 refer to the following information

Number of Frog Species Found in 35 Ponds

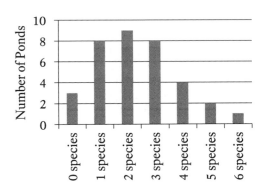

4 If you were to choose a pond at random, which of the following is the probability that the pond would have 5 frog species represented?

A) $\dfrac{2}{35}$

B) $\dfrac{2}{32}$

C) $\dfrac{5}{35}$

D) $\dfrac{5}{6}$

5 If a pond with two or fewer frog species were selected at random, what is the probability the pond would have zero frog species in it?

A) 0

B) $\dfrac{1}{7}$

C) $\dfrac{3}{20}$

D) $\dfrac{1}{3}$

Questions 6–10 refer to the following information

The following table shows absences by class this semester at Rosalind Franklin High School:

Absences	Sophomores	Juniors	Seniors
0	10	7	3
1	12	19	14
2	17	16	22
3	30	17	34
4	25	23	28
5	20	22	19
6	25	25	12
Total:	139	129	132

6. What percentage of the senior class has at least 4 absences this semester?

   A) 21.2%

   B) 35.7%

   C) 44.7%

   D) 55.3%

7. What fraction of all students combined have no absences this semester?

   A) $\frac{1}{100}$

   B) $\frac{1}{44}$

   C) $\frac{1}{20}$

   D) $\frac{1}{10}$

8. Which class has the highest percentage of students with two or fewer absences?

   A) Sophomores

   B) Juniors

   C) Seniors

   D) Both sophomores and seniors (tied)

9. If a student from Rosalind Franklin High School with 1 absence is chosen at random, what is the probability that that person is a Junior?

   A) $\frac{19}{400}$

   B) $\frac{45}{400}$

   C) $\frac{19}{129}$

   D) $\frac{19}{45}$

10. Based on the data, if chosen at random from their respective class, how many times more likely is it for a Senior to not have 6 absences than for a Sophomore to have 6 absences (round the answer to the nearest hundredth)?

    A) 0.51 times as likely

    B) 1.11 times as likely

    C) 4.69 times as likely

    D) 5.05 times as likely

Percent Problems

Percent problems can most easily be solved, when a calculator is available, using the direct translation method, where you convert words into mathematical operators. **What** or **what percent** can be written as x, **of** as a multiplication symbol, and **is** as an equal sign. Remember to write percentages in decimal form when they appear in equations (e.g., $32\% = 0.32$). You can do this by moving the decimal point two places to the left and dropping the percent symbol. Here are a few examples:

Example 1 What is 35% of 50?

What becomes x

is becomes =

35% becomes 0.35

of becomes the multiplication symbol

$x = 0.35 \cdot 50$

$x = 17.5$

Example 2 63 is what percent of 72?

$63 = x \cdot 72$

$0.875 = x$

Since the question asked for a percent, remember to convert 0.875 into 87.5%

Example 3 40% of what number is 80?

$0.40 \cdot x = 80$

$x = 200$

Sales tax   A sales tax is an additional amount you pay for goods or services based on a set tax rate (percent).

Use this formula: **Total Price** = **Original Price** $\times (1 + $**Tax Rate**$)$

Note that the tax rate should be given as a *decimal*.

Example 4 A dress is priced at $229. The sales tax is 5%. What is the total cost of the dress, including tax?

Cost $= 229(1 + 0.05) = 229(1.05)$

$= 240.45$

Discount and mark-up   A discount is a decrease in price and a mark-up is an increase in price.

These work similarly to a sales tax, and you can use the formula **New Price** = **Original** $\times (1 \pm $**%change**$)$.

As with sales tax, the change should be given as a *decimal*.

Example 5 A book that was originally $15 is marked "10% off." What is the new price?

New Price $= 15(1 - 0.10) = 15(0.90)$

$= 13.50$

Percent change   Positive or negative change can be found as a decimal using the formula $\dfrac{new - original}{original}$ and then converted to a percent.

Example 6   A pair of jeans is on sale for $33.75. The usual cost is $45. What is the percent discount?

$$\text{Percent Change} = \frac{33.75 - 45}{45} = \frac{-11.25}{45} = -.25.$$

The percent change is negative because it is a discount, so the jeans are 25% off.

Example 7   Erwin has been a lifeguard the past three summers. In the second summer, his salary increased 5% from the first summer. In the third summer, his salary increased 8% from the second summer. What percent greater was his salary in the third summer than his salary in the first summer?

A) 3%

B) 13%

C) 13.4%

D) 40%

If Erwin's first-summer salary is represented by x, you can calculate the second-summer salary to be $x(1+0.05) = 1.05x$, and, consequently, you can calculate the third-summer salary to be $1.05x(1+0.08) = 1.05x(1.08) = 1.134x$. Since $1.134 = 1+\%change$, the percent change is 0.134 or 13.4%. Erwin's salary in the third summer is a 13.4% increase from his salary in the first summer. Notice, this is different than the straight 13% increase you would get if you simply added 5% and 8%, so the answer is C.

Percent Problem Set

1. What percent of 50 is 20?

   A) 20%

   B) 30%

   C) 40%

   D) 250%

2. What percent of 20 is 50?

   A) 20%

   B) 30%

   C) 40%

   D) 250%

3. 35% of what number is 70?

   A) 105

   B) 200

   C) 350

   D) 2450

4. Puppy food costs $6.75. After sales tax, it costs $7.56. What is the sales tax rate?

   A) 10%

   B) 12%

   C) 15%

   D) 17.5%

5. A cake is cut into M equal pieces, and 12 of these pieces are eaten by guests at a birthday party. In terms of M, what percentage of the cake was not eaten?

   A) $\left(\dfrac{M-12}{M}\right)100$

   B) $\left(\dfrac{M-12}{M}\right)$

   C) $\left(\dfrac{M}{12}\right)100$

   D) $(M-12)100$

6. A video gaming system is selling for $150 after a 25% reduction in price. What was the original price?

   A) $175

   B) $187.5

   C) $200

   D) $225

7 50% of 24 is increased by 50%, resulting in which of the following values?

A) 18

B) 24

C) 36

D) 62

8 The price on a suit is reduced by a $\frac{1}{4}$ for a sale, and then that new price is increased by 25% after the sale. The new price is what percent of the original price?

A) 93.75

B) 97.5

C) 99.5

D) 100

9 What is 20 percent of $15x \cdot 30y$?

A) $3xy$

B) $18xy$

C) $45xy$

D) $90xy$

10 In the 2014 season, the Fairfield Cougars won exactly 36% of their games and had a total of 18 victories. How many games did they play?

A) 36

B) 45

C) 50

D) 72

11 The Merriweather Mockingbirds won 17.5% of their games and lost 33 games. How many games did they play?

A) 35

B) 40

C) 42

D) 50

12 15 students split the bill evenly for their favorite teacher's birthday present and spend $5 each. If there had been only 12 students to pay for the same present, then each student would have paid what percent more?

13 A washing machine is put on sale for 25% off the marked price. Shortly afterwards there is a going-out-of-business sale, so it is again marked down by 25% off the new price. The final sale price is what percent greater than the price of the machine if the initial discount had been 50%?

14 Jamal buys a Chemistry book for $200. After the semester is over, he sells it back to the bookstore for 60% less than his purchase price. If the store marks up the used book by p percent and sells it for $120, then what is p?

15 Sarah has 20 pens and 30 pencils. If 15% of the pens are red and 40% of the pencils are red, then what is the percentage of the writing utensils that are red?

Rate and Unit Conversion

You will often need to convert units or rates in word problems, so pay close attention to the language of a question so you can determine when two measures are linked.

Unit conversion   When a measurement of the same size and quality is related using different units.

Example 1   1 mile = 5280 feet

Rate   When a certain increase in an amount of one unit occurs for every increase of one of an otherwise unrelated unit. The word "per" will often be a signal that a rate is being used, but sometimes rates are described less formally.

Example 2   176 feet per second

Example 3   1 second of video footage costs $2

When you place equivalent measures in a fraction, you get a conversion factor. Since the numerator and denominator are equal, this factor will always be equivalent to 1, so you can always multiply by it:

$$\frac{1 \text{ mile}}{5280 \text{ feet}} \text{ or } \frac{5280 \text{ feet}}{1 \text{ mile}} \qquad \frac{176 \text{ feet}}{1 \text{ second}} \text{ or } \frac{1 \text{ second}}{176 \text{ feet}} \qquad \frac{1 \text{ second}}{2 \text{ dollars}} \text{ or } \frac{2 \text{ dollars}}{1 \text{ second}}$$

Notice the different ways you can arrange each of these conversion factors. The way you choose to arrange each will depend on what conversion you need to make. You will always be looking to eliminate units (cross out on top and bottom) until you get the unit you are looking for.

Example 4   Aunt Betty wants to film her skydive. The cameraman is an expert, so every second of footage costs $2. If a typical skydiver averages a vertical speed of 176 feet per second (free fall and chute time combined) and Aunt Betty jumps from an altitude of 3.4 miles, how much will it likely cost to record her jump?

The starting value is the quantity that is linked to the question and the only measure that doesn't have a partner. In this case it is Aunt Betty's starting height of 3.4 miles. Now that you've identified your starting point, arrange your conversion ratios and perform your calculation until you end up with a monetary unit:

$$3.4 \text{ miles} \times \frac{5280 \text{ feet}}{1 \text{ mile}} \times \frac{1 \text{ second}}{176 \text{ feet}} \times \frac{2 \text{ dollars}}{1 \text{ second}} = 204 \text{ dollars}$$

Notice that every unit that appears in a numerator can be canceled in a denominator except the unit you are looking for, dollars.

A very similar process can be used for converting between different rates.

Example 5   According to the information above, what is the average speed of a skydiver in <u>miles per hour</u>?

$$\frac{176 \text{ feet}}{1 \text{ second}} \times \frac{1 \text{ mile}}{5280 \text{ feet}} \times \frac{60 \text{ seconds}}{1 \text{ minute}} \times \frac{60 \text{ minutes}}{1 \text{ hour}} = \frac{120 \text{ miles}}{1 \text{ hour}}$$

It's important to examine the units and let them serve as a check to see if you did the problem correctly. Above you can see by the different strike marks that *feet*, *seconds*, and *minutes* have canceled to leave you with only *miles* and *hours*, and that the proper configuration of *miles per hour* is in the result.

Rates and Unit Conversions Problem Set

1. Which of the following correctly expresses the weight of a 150 pound person in kilograms (1kg = 2.2 lb) ?

   A) 68.2 kg
   B) 147.8 kg
   C) 152.2 kg
   D) 330 kg

2. How high is a 10 ft basketball rim when expressed in cm?
   (1 in = 2.54 cm)

   A) 47 cm
   B) 254cm
   C) 305cm
   D) 610cm

3. Khalid runs 2 miles in 16 minutes and 36 seconds. Which of the following is closest to his average speed in miles per hour?

   A) 3 mi/hr
   B) 5 mi/hr
   C) 7 mi/hr
   D) 10 mi/hr

4. A length of rope is 5ft 6in long. If it is to be cut into three equal pieces, how long will each piece be?

   A) 1ft 2in
   B) 1ft 6in
   C) 1ft 8in
   D) 1ft 10in

5. A coffee company brews coffee in 20 gallon containers. Approximately how many 12-ounce small-sized coffees can be filled from the container?
   (128 ounces = 1 gallon)

   A) 77
   B) 213
   C) 4096
   D) 30720

6. Nene rode his motorcycle for 4 hours at an average speed of 70 miles per hour. If his motorcycle gets 55 miles per gallon of gas, approximately how many gallons of gas was used during the 4-hour trip?

   A) 3
   B) 4
   C) 5
   D) 6

7   The speed of light is roughly 3.0×10^8 meters per second. What is this speed in miles per hour?
(1 mile = 1609 meters)

A) 5.1×10^1

B) 5.1×10^5

C) 1.3×10^8

D) 6.7×10^8

8   A rocket traveling at 200 meters per second is moving at what speed in kilometers per second?

A)   0.02

B)   0.2

C)   200,000

D)   200,000,000

9   Tara has a 25-meter roll of ribbon and needs to cut it into 6 inch portions to wrap around diplomas. Which calculation can be used to find how many diplomas she will be able to wrap from the roll of ribbon?
(1 inch = 2.54 cm)

A) $\dfrac{25 \times 100}{6 \times 2.54}$

B) $\dfrac{25 \times 2.54}{6 \times 100}$

C) $\dfrac{100 \times 6}{2.54 \times 25}$

D) $\dfrac{25 \times 100 \times 2.54}{6}$

10   David watches too many YouTube videos. If the average video is m minutes long, and he watches videos for an average of 5 hours each day, how many videos does David watch in a week in terms of m?

A) $300m$

B) $60\left(\dfrac{m}{35}\right)$

C) $35\left(\dfrac{60}{m}\right)$

D) $\dfrac{60}{35m}$

11   Robert ran a 40-yard dash in x seconds. What was his average speed in miles per hour?
(1 mile = 1760 yards)

A) $\dfrac{40 \times 1760}{x \times 60 \times 60}$

B) $\dfrac{40 \times x}{1760 \times 60 \times 60}$

C) $\dfrac{x \times 60 \times 60}{1760 \times 40}$

D) $\dfrac{40 \times 60 \times 60}{1760 \times x}$

12 The average gasket produced at the Sarnia MetalWorks Factory weighs 30.6 grams. The loading machinery can load gaskets by weight at a rate of 1.5 pounds per second for a maximum of 4 hours each day. What is the maximum number of gaskets that can be loaded each day (rounded to the nearest thousand)?
(1 pound = 454 grams)

A) 9,000

B) 320,000

C) 2,243,000

D) 8,335,000

13 A candle maker can make 750 candles from 332.8 liters of liquid wax. If each candle is 15 ounces when liquid, how many ounces to the nearest tenth are in 1 liter?

14 The furlong, an imperial unit of length, is approximately equal to 0.125 miles. It is also equivalent to 10 smaller units called chains. Based on these relationships, 16 chains are equivalent to how many feet?
(1 mile = 5280 feet)

The citizens of planet Tehar use the following currencies:

8 Glurfs = 11 Collywobbles

9 Zaps = 2 Dodos

5 Dodos = 7 Glurfs

15 According to the above relationships, how many Zaps are in 3 Collywobbles, to the nearest hundredth?

Statistics and Scatterplots

There are more complex statistical measurements and concepts than the ones mentioned at the beginning of this chapter. Though you will not be asked to calculate these numerically on the SAT, it is important to have a basic understanding of their meaning.

Standard deviation   a measurement of dispersion, or spread, in a set of numbers

- If the numbers in the set are bunched near the mean, the standard deviation will be small, and if they are, for the most part, far from the mean, the standard deviation will be large.

Margin of error   the maximum expected difference between an actual, usually difficult-to-measure, statistic and the estimate determined by a mathematical process

Confidence level   how likely it is that a statistic falls within a given margin of error

- SAT questions will only use 95% confidence levels. That is, a question may say that the *actual* mean, for example, of a large population has a 95% chance of falling between the lowest and highest numbers given by a particular margin of error.

Example 1   If a study shows, by using a random sample of 900 respondents, that the average amount of time adults spend driving each day is 93 minutes, and that study has a margin of error of ±4 minutes with a 95% confidence level, then there is 95% confidence that the true average amount of time adults in the entire population spend driving is between 89 and 97 minutes a day.

> **NOTE:** This does not mean that 95% of *all adults* in the population drive between 89 and 97 minutes a day. That is an example of a common error made with confidence intervals.

Bias   a flaw in the design of an experiment that hinders randomness and causes misrepresentation

Outlier   an observation or number that is very different from others in a group

Scatterplot   a graph of data points, often taken from an experiment or study, which may show trends that indicate a relationship that can be modeled closely by a function (linear, exponential...)

Association (or **correlation**)   two sets of numbers are associated (or correlated) if variation in one set can be used to predict variation in the other (though this doesn't assume one causes the other). This can be seen graphically if a scatterplot of several points appears to closely follow the path of a function graph.

- Association can be strong or weak depending on how closely the points fit onto the graph of the function.
- When association is positive and linear, the points will approximate a positive-sloped line; when it is negative and linear, the points will approximate a negative-sloped line. The points can also approximate exponential growth or decay.
- BE CAREFUL: Association between points does <u>not</u> indicate *causation*, though wrong answer choices will often try to assign a cause/effect relationship.

Statistics Problem Set

[1] Dan's average score on 8 tests is 89. What is the sum of his scores on all 8 tests?

A) 89

B) 77

C) 356

D) 712

[2] If set S consists of three positive integers x, y, and z such that $x < y < z$, which of the following could <u>not</u> affect the median of set S?

A) Decreasing x

B) Decreasing y

C) Decreasing z

D) Increasing x

[3] Leo and Don both receive an 88 on a test. Mike receives an 89 and Rocky receives a 93. April scores a 94. Arrange the mean, median and mode of their scores in ascending order.

A) Mode, mean, median

B) Mode, median, mean

C) Median, mode, mean

D) Mean, mode, median

[4] A is a set of n numbers whose average (arithmetic mean) is 9. B is another set of n numbers, created by multiplying each number in A by 3. What is the average of the numbers in set B?

A) 3

B) 9

C) 12

D) 27

35 ponds were surveyed to see how many frog species were represented in each pond. Data is presented below.

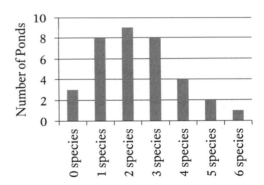

Number of Frog Species Found in 35 Ponds

[5] Suppose 7 additional ponds were surveyed, and each had 5 species of frogs represented. Which of the following measurements of this data would change?

   I.   The median

   II. The mean

   III. The range

A) I only

B) II only

C) I and II only

D) II and III only

The following information and table relate to questions 6 and 7.

St. Sebastian's School held a race to raise money for a charity. The table below lists the number of contestants who completed 1, 2, 3, or 4 miles of the extremely challenging obstacle course.

Miles	Contestants
1	45
2	30
3	20
4	5

6 What is the median number of miles per contestant?

A) 1

B) 2

C) 2.5

D) 25

7 How many miles, on average, did each contestant complete?

A) 1

B) 1.85

C) 2

D) 25

8 Which of the following is most likely to cause bias in a study?

A) The size of the population

B) The ensuring of randomness in selection of a sample

C) The neglecting of randomness in selection of a sample

D) The choice of calculator the researcher uses to work out her conclusions

Heights of Students (in inches)						
38	54.5	55.5	56	56	57	57.5
57.5	58	58	58	58	58.5	58.5
59	59	59.5	59.5	60	61	85

9 The table above lists the heights of the 21 students in Mr. Murray's class. It has been determined that the outlier measurements of 38 and 85 inches are errors. If these two measurements were removed, how would the standard deviation be affected?

A) The standard deviation would increase.

B) The standard deviation would decrease.

C) The standard deviation would remain the same.

D) The standard deviation cannot be measured.

10 A clothing company wants to gather information about the habits of consumers and the effectiveness of its ad campaign by interviewing shoppers at a local mall. Over the course of two weeks, the company interviews 300 people. Why would the information gathered in these interviews not provide accurate information?

A) The population size is too small.

B) The sample size is too small.

C) Interviews are not effective methods of conducting research.

D) The sample of people will not be representative of the general population.

11 A survey was conducted to examine the number of students per class in a certain county. It was found that the mean number of students per classroom was 22, but the median number of students per classroom was 18. Which of the following situations could explain the difference between the mean and median number of students per classroom?

A) Many of the classrooms in the county have between 18 and 22 students.

B) The classrooms have numbers of students that are very close to each other.

C) There are a few classrooms that have a much higher number of students than the rest.

D) There are a few classrooms that have a much lower number of students than the rest.

Rachel	77
Monica	75
Phoebe	81
Joey	97
Chandler	79
Ross	71

14 The table above lists the test scores of 6 friends. If the outlier score is not included, what is the mean of the remaining scores?

A) 63.8

B) 76.6

C) 80.0

D) 81.8

12 If $x+1$ is the average (arithmetic mean) of $20, x, x, 12,$ and 30, what is the value of x?

A) 12

B) 19

C) 20

D) 29

15 A researcher wants to know the opinions of local business owners about a town's recycling policies. The researcher obtains a list of 520 local business owners and mails a questionnaire to 60 businesses located in the downtown area. 4 of the questionnaires are completed and returned. Which of the following factors makes it least likely that a reliable conclusion can be drawn about the opinions of the local business owners regarding the town's recycling policy?

A) Population size

B) Planned sample size

C) Sample size obtained

D) Sample location

13 Which number set below has the largest standard deviation?

A) $4, 5, 4, 5, 4, 5$

B) $6, 6, 6, 6, 6, 6$

C) $17, 18, 17, 18, 18$

D) $1, 4, 5, 6, 17, 18$

16 Rich jogged m days in May, a days in August, and s days in September, averaging x jogging days over those three months. If he jogged j days a month in both June and July, how many days a month did Rich average jogging over the five-month period?

A) $\dfrac{x+j}{2}$

B) $\dfrac{m+a+s+j}{4}$

C) $\dfrac{3x+j}{4}$

D) $\dfrac{3x+2j}{5}$

17 An inspector at a bottling plant for a soda company randomly selects 120 bottles and finds, with a 95% confidence level, that the average volume of soda that the machines are dispensing into each bottle in the plant is between 63.1 and 64.5 fluid ounces. Which of the following conclusions is most reasonable?

A) 95% of all bottles in the plant that day have between 63.1 and 64.5 fluid ounces of soda in them.

B) 95% of all bottles ever filled in that plant have between 63.1 and 64.5 fluid ounces of soda in them.

C) 95% of the capacity of each bottle in the plant is somewhere between 63.1 and 64.5 fluid ounces.

D) It is likely that the true average volume of soda dispensed by all the machines at the plant that day is between 63.1 and 64.5 fluid ounces.

18 The margin of error of a poll conducted to determine apple preference is, with 95% confidence, ±3%. If the poll shows that 32% of people prefer gala apples to all others, what is the range of percentages within which one can be most confident that the true percentage of gala apple lovers will fall?

A) 92% – 98%

B) 32% – 38%

C) 32% – 35%

D) 29% – 35%

19 Data shows that the months in which the highest numbers of ice cream cones are eaten are the same months that have the highest incidence of shark attacks. Which of the following conclusions can be drawn from this?

A) Ice cream causes shark attacks.

B) Sharks are attracted to cone-shaped desserts.

C) The threat of shark attacks causes people to eat more ice cream.

D) No cause and effect conclusion can be made from this information alone.

20 Casey found that there is a strong positive correlation between the number of televisions at area bars and the number of bar patrons. Is he correct in concluding that many televisions in a bar will cause people to visit that bar?

A) Yes, because televisions make bars more popular

B) Yes, because people who like television like bars

C) No, because correlation does not prove causation

D) No, because there are already enough bars with many televisions in that part of town

Scatterplots Problem Set

1   Which of the following scatterplots shows a weak positive correlation between the x and y variable?

A)

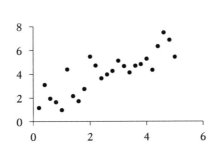

B)

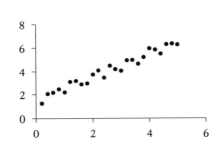

C)

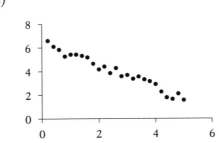

D)

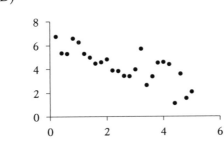

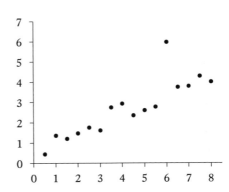

2   What type of association does the above graph have?

A) Strong, positive and linear

B) Strong, positive and non-linear

C) Weak, negative and non-linear

D) Weak, negative and linear

3   In the scatterplot above, which of the following is the x-coordinate of the point that is farthest from the line of best fit?

A) 1

B) 4

C) 6

D) 7

Questions 4–6 refer to the following information

Population density of damselflies was measured at varying distances from a riverbed. The data collected are presented below.

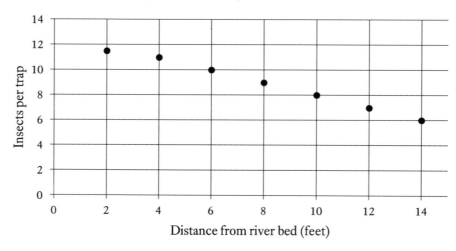

Population Density of Damselflies

4 Which of the following descriptions best describes the data presented?

A) There is a weak positive association between population density and distance from riverbed.

B) There is a weak negative association between population density and distance from riverbed

C) There is a strong negative association between population density and distance from riverbed

D) There is a strong positive association between population density and distance from riverbed.

5 Assume that the relationship is valid for distances beyond what is shown on the graph. Based on the graph, what is the approximate population density of damselflies, in insects per trap, at 18 feet from the riverbed?

A) 4

B) 6

C) 8

D) 10

6 What is the absolute value of the approximate change in population density over distance?

A) 1 per foot

B) 3 per 2 feet

C) 1 per 2 feet

D) 1 per 4 feet

7 Researchers have discovered a strong positive correlation between body mass and fecundity of female spiders. Which of the following scatterplots could show the relationship between body mass and fecundity of female spiders?

A)

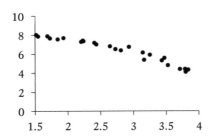

B)

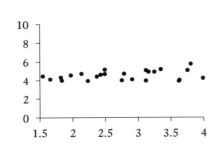

C)

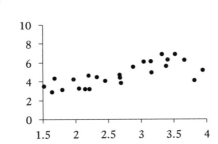

D)

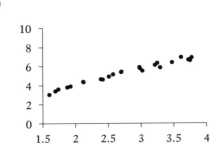

Questions 8–10 refer to the following graph and information

The graph below shows the yield, in thousands of barrels, of corn and soybeans on Good Acres Farm.

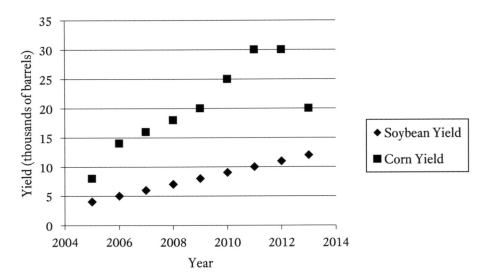

8 Which crop shows a stronger linear correlation with time?

A) Corn

B) Soybean

C) Cannot be determined

D) Neither

9 If the data points from one year were eliminated, which year's removal would best make the case that soybean and corn have similar types of correlation?

A) 2005

B) 2010

C) 2012

D) 2013

10 Which of the following is a reasonable conclusion from the data presented?

A) It is more profitable to grown corn than it is to grow soybeans.

B) The highest combined yield was in 2012.

C) The difference in yield between the two crops is due to disease factors.

D) The farm should devote more acreage to soybeans.

Additional Topics in Math

One of the ways in which the SAT differs from other standardized tests is that it emphasizes a narrower set of mathematical skills, confined mostly to algebra, functions, and data analysis. These are the areas that usually translate most directly to success in college and in the work force, but they don't encompass all of the abstract problem-solving methods that are more prevalent in other mathematical disciplines.

Still, there are six questions on every SAT that do not have a designation in Heart of Algebra, Passport to Advanced Math, or Problem Solving and Data Analysis. These are often referred to as simply "Additional Math Topics" questions, and they include explorations in:

- Basic geometry
- Trigonometry
- Characteristics and graphs of circles
- Complex numbers

Since the majority of Additional Topics questions test geometry, it is important to remember that there is a list of geometry facts and formulas in the beginning of each math section of the SAT. That reference section will look very similar to the following:

REFERENCE

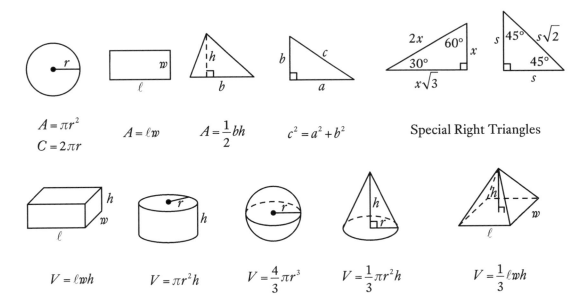

The number of degrees of arc in a circle is 360.
The number of radians of arc in a circle is 2π.
The sum of the measures in degrees of the angles in a triangle is 180.

Basic Geometry

In addition to the given reference information, it is helpful to know a few other angle relationships and geometric characteristics.

Complementary angles   a pair of angles whose sum is 90°

Supplementary angles   a pair of angles whose sum is 180°

     Note that angles in a linear pair (adjacent angles which form a line) will be supplementary.

Parallel lines cut by a transversal   lines ℓ_1 and ℓ_2 on the
     right are parallel. The transversal line that cuts
     through them creates two groups of four congruent
     (equal in measure) angles:

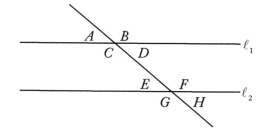

     $m\angle A = m\angle D = m\angle E = m\angle H$ and
     $m\angle B = m\angle C = m\angle F = m\angle G$.
     Also, every angle in the first group is supplementary
     to every angle in the second group.

Isosceles triangle   a triangle with two congruent sides and
     two congruent angles opposite those two congruent
     sides.

Equilateral triangle   a triangle with all three sides
     congruent and, thus, all three angles congruent.
     The angles each measure 60°.

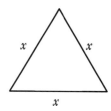

Pythagorean triples   groups of three whole numbers that work in the Pythagorean Theorem, $a^2 + b^2 = c^2$.
     They include 3-4-5, 5-12-13, 8-15-17, and all of their multiples. It is not essential to memorize these,
     but they will save time and reduce errors, especially on the No Calculator section.

Volume

Though all pertinent volume formulas are provided in the reference area, it is helpful to know that all prisms
(3D shapes with two identical base faces, like a cylinder or a rectangular solid) have volumes equal to the area of
the base face multiplied by the height. Pyramidal shapes (including cones), which have only one base face and
come to a point, have volumes equal to one-third of their prism counterparts.

Basic Geometry Problem Set

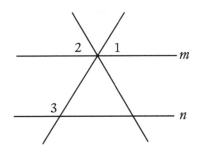

[1] In the figure above, $m \parallel n$. Which of the following statements <u>must</u> be true?

A) $\angle 1 \cong \angle 2$

B) $\angle 2 \cong \angle 3$

C) $m\angle 1 + m\angle 3 = 180°$

D) $m\angle 2 + m\angle 3 = 180°$

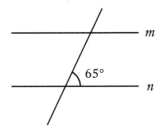

[3] What is one possibility for the difference between the measures of two of the angles in the figure above if the lines m and n are parallel to each other?

A) 25°

B) 50°

C) 65°

D) 115°

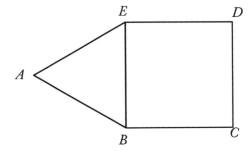

[2] In the figure above, $\triangle ABE$ is equilateral and quadrilateral $BCDE$ is a square. What is the measure of $\angle AED$?

A) 60°

B) 120°

C) 135°

D) 150°

[4] A swimming pool in the shape of the right circular cylinder shown above has a volume of 320π cubic feet. If the height of the pool is 5 feet, what is the area of a circular tarp, in square feet, that just covers the top of the pool?

A) 16π

B) 32π

C) 64

D) 64π

5 In $\triangle ABC$, $\angle A$ and $\angle B$ are congruent. If the measure of $\angle C$ is 98°, what is the measure of $\angle A$?

A) 41°

B) 49°

C) 82°

D) 98°

6 Gatsby leaves his dock and takes his motorboat due east for 0.5 miles to pick up Daisy. Then they motor 1.2 miles north to a private island in the middle of the sound. What is the straight-line distance, in miles, from the island to Gatsby's dock?

A) 0.7

B) 1.2

C) 1.3

D) 1.7

7 A rectangle has a length of 8 inches and an area of 48 square inches. What is the length, in inches, of its diagonal?

A) 6

B) 10

C) 12

D) 16

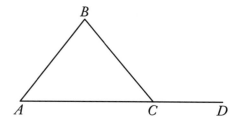

8 In the figure above, $m\angle A = 52°$, $m\angle B = x°$, and $m\angle BCD = (2x - 26)°$. What is the value of x?

A) 52

B) 76

C) 78

D) 102

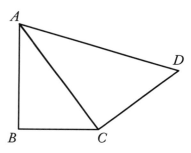

9 In the figure above, both triangles are right. If $AB = 12$, $BC = 9$, and $CD = 8$. How long is AD?

A) $\sqrt{145}$

B) $\sqrt{208}$

C) 15

D) 17

10. What is the length of a side of an equilateral triangle with a height of $4\sqrt{3}$?

A) 4

B) $4\sqrt{2}$

C) $4\sqrt{3}$

D) 8

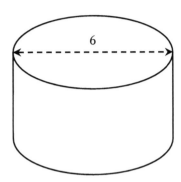

Note: Figure not drawn to scale

11. If the diameter of the right circular cylinder pictured above is half its height, what is its volume?

A) 18π

B) 27π

C) 72π

D) 108π

12. Square $ABCD$ has an area of 100. If E, F, G, and H are all midpoints of the sides of $ABCD$, what is the perimeter of square $EFGH$?

A) $5\sqrt{2}$

B) 20

C) $20\sqrt{2}$

D) $40\sqrt{2}$

13. A rectangle is divided in half, forming two squares. If each square has a perimeter of 36, what is the perimeter of the original rectangle?

A) 72

B) 60

C) 54

D) 45

14. A cone has the same volume as a sphere with radius 3. If the base radius of the cone is the same as the radius of the sphere, what is the height of the cone?

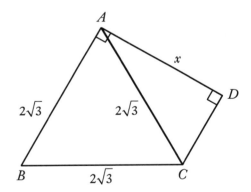

15. ABC is an equilateral triangle with each side equal to $2\sqrt{3}$. If $m\angle BAD = m\angle ADC = 90°$, what is the length of side AD?

Similar Triangles and Trigonometry

Similar Triangles

Two non-congruent triangles that have identical angle measures are *similar* (denoted by the symbol ~), which means they have the same shape but not the same size. Though their corresponding angles are congruent, their corresponding sides are not. Instead, the corresponding sides are in proportion, so you will often have to set up an algebraic proportion to solve for a missing segment. Solve "Special Right Triangles" problems (see the reference information) using proportions in the same way.

Examples

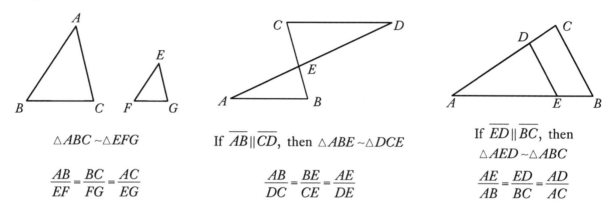

$\triangle ABC \sim \triangle EFG$

$$\frac{AB}{EF} = \frac{BC}{FG} = \frac{AC}{EG}$$

If $\overline{AB} \| \overline{CD}$, then $\triangle ABE \sim \triangle DCE$

$$\frac{AB}{DC} = \frac{BE}{CE} = \frac{AE}{DE}$$

If $\overline{ED} \| \overline{BC}$, then $\triangle AED \sim \triangle ABC$

$$\frac{AE}{AB} = \frac{ED}{BC} = \frac{AD}{AC}$$

Trigonometry

All right triangles with congruent acute angles must be similar to each other. Therefore the ratios of the sides in any right triangle with a certain acute angle are consistent and knowable. The three main trigonometric ratios are called sine, cosine and tangent (abbreviated sin, cos, and tan).

Note that the ratios of sides in right triangles that have 30°, 45°, and 60° angles are given in the reference information at the beginning of each math section. The acronym SOH-CAH-TOA can be used to remember the following:

$$\sin\theta = \frac{\text{opposite}}{\text{hypotenuse}}$$

$$\cos\theta = \frac{\text{adjacent}}{\text{hypotenuse}}$$

$$\tan\theta = \frac{\text{opposite}}{\text{adjacent}}$$

Co-functions   Since switching from one acute angle in a right triangle to the other acute angle (its complement) also switches the "opposite" and "adjacent" sides, $\sin\theta° = \cos(90-\theta)°$.

Radian Measure   Often used instead of degree measure in trigonometry, a radian represents the measure of an angle necessary to intercept exactly one radius-length on the circumference of a circle. Since an entire circle is 2π radii in circumference, 2π radians = 360°.

You can covert from degrees to radians by multiplying by $\frac{\pi}{180}$.

Similar Triangles and Trigonometry Problem Set

1 Mann Park is in the shape of a triangle. On a map, it has borders that measure 5 inches, 7 inches, and 9 inches. If the shortest border of Mann park is 1000 meters long, how long, in meters, is its longest border?

A) 1,004

B) 1,400

C) 1,600

D) 1,800

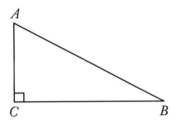

2 In the figure above, $\tan A = \dfrac{15}{8}$. If the length of $\overline{AB}$ is 51, how long is $\overline{BC}$?

A) 24

B) 34

C) 45

D) 49

3 In right triangle JKL, $\angle L$ measures 90 degrees. If $\cos J = 0.25$, what is the value of $\sin K$?

A) 0.25

B) 0.5

C) 0.75

D) 0.97

4 If $0° < x < 90°$ and $\tan x = \dfrac{4}{3}$, what is the value of $\sin x + \cos x$?

A) $\dfrac{3}{5}$

B) $\dfrac{4}{5}$

C) $\dfrac{4}{3}$

D) $\dfrac{7}{5}$

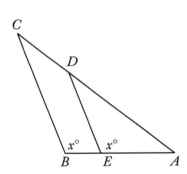

5 In the figure above, $AE = 10$, $DE = 12$, and $CB = 18$. What is BE?

A) 5

B) 6

C) 8

D) 15

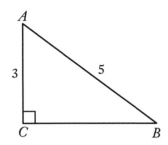

6. In the figure above, which of the following is equal to $\frac{3}{5}$?

A) $\sin A$

B) $\cos A$

C) $\cos B$

D) $\tan B$

8. If θ is an acute angle, then $\frac{\tan\theta\cos\theta}{\sin\theta}$ is equal to which of the following?

A) $\tan\theta$

B) $\sin\theta$

C) -1

D) 1

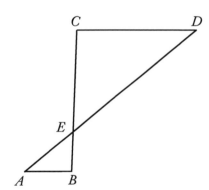

7. In the figure above, $\overline{AB}\parallel\overline{CD}$. If $AB = 12$, $CD = 30$, and $AD = 56$, what is the measure of AE?

A) 16

B) 18

C) 22.4

D) 40

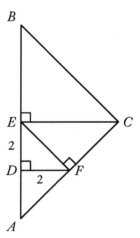

9. If all the right triangles in the figure above are similar to each other, what is the measure of BC?

A) 4

B) $4\sqrt{2}$

C) $4\sqrt{3}$

D) $6\sqrt{3}$

10 What is 210° expressed in radians?

A) $\dfrac{7\pi}{12}$

B) $\dfrac{7\pi}{6}$

C) $\dfrac{7\pi}{3}$

D) 7π

11 In a circle, an arc of length 12 is intercepted by a central angle of $\dfrac{2}{3}$ radians. How long is the radius of the circle?

A) $\dfrac{2}{3}$

B) 8

C) 18

D) 120

12 If $0 < x < 90$, which of the following statements is always true?

A) $\tan x° < 1$

B) $\sin x° + \cos x° < 1$

C) $\dfrac{\sin x°}{\cos x°} < 1$

D) $\dfrac{\sin x°}{\tan x°} < 1$

13 How many degrees are equivalent to $\dfrac{3\pi}{10}$ radians?

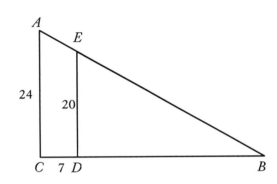

14 In the figure above, $\overline{AC} \parallel \overline{ED}$. What is the length of $\overline{DB}$?

15 If $0 < x < 90$ and $\sin x° = 0.84$, what is $\cos(90 - x)°$?

Circles

In addition to the area and circumference formulas you are given at the beginning of each math section of the SAT, there are other characteristics of circles and their graphs that should be reviewed.

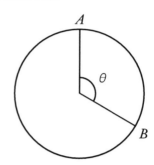

Sectors

Sectors are portions of circles created by the joining of two radii.

Arc length   the portion of the circumference of a circle that a sector

carves out. The length of an arc is given by $\ell = \dfrac{\theta}{360°} \cdot 2\pi r$.

Area of a sector   The area of a sector is given by $A = \dfrac{\theta}{360°} \cdot \pi r^2$.

EQUIVALENCE OF RADII: All radii of the same circle have equal length. This property is often the key to solving a problem. Mark all radii as congruent to each other, and any angle congruence that results, and draw any relevant radii that might help flesh out a diagram.

Graphing Circles

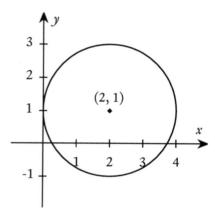

The equation of a circle in the *xy*-coordinate plane with radius *r* and center (h,k) is $(x-h)^2 + (y-k)^2 = r^2$.

For example, the circle on the right has the equation $(x-2)^2 + (y-1)^2 = 4$. This circle has a radius of 2 ($r^2 = 2^2 = 4$) and its center is the point (2, 1).

Example 1   The following equation describes a circle in the regular *xy*-plane: $x^2 - 6x + y^2 + 8y - 11 = 0$. What are the center and radius of this circle?

Here you must *complete the square* in order to get it into your desired form.

Note that $(x-3)^2 = x^2 - 6x + 9$, so $x^2 - 6x = (x-3)^2 - 9$.

Similarly, $(y+4)^2 = y^2 + 8y + 16$, so $y^2 + 8y = (y+4)^2 - 16$.

The equation can be rewritten as $(x-3)^2 - 9 + (y+4)^2 - 16 - 11 = 0$, which is equivalent to $(x-3)^2 + (y+4)^2 = 36$.

Thus the circle is centered on $(3,-4)$ and has radius 6 (since $6^2 = 36$).

Circles Problem Set

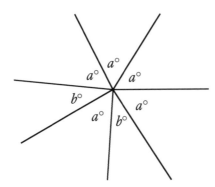

Note: Figure not drawn to scale

1 In the figure, if $a = 58$, what is b?

A) 35

B) 58

C) 64

D) 70

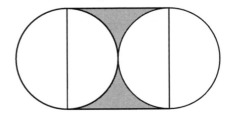

3 The radius of each of the circles above is 1. What is the area of the shaded region?

A) $2\pi - 4$

B) $8 - 2\pi$

C) $4 - \pi$

D) $4 - 2\pi$

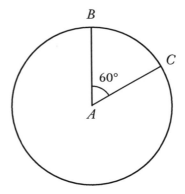

2 In the figure above, two circles are externally tangent at point B and $AC = 9$. If the radius of the larger circle is twice that of the smaller, what is the area of the smaller circle?

A) 3π

B) 4π

C) 6π

D) 9π

4 What is the area of sector ABC pictured in the circle above if A is the center of the circle and $AC = 3$?

A) $\dfrac{3\pi}{4}$

B) π

C) $\dfrac{3\pi}{2}$

D) 6π

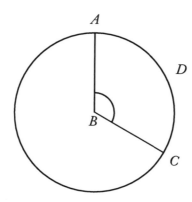

5 What is the length of arc $\overset{\frown}{ADC}$ if B is the center of the circle, $AB = 3,$ and $m\angle ABC = 120°$?

A) 9π

B) 6π

C) 3π

D) 2π

6 What is the equation of a circle in the xy-coordinate plane with a center of $(-7, 10)$ and a radius of 4?

A) $(x-7)^2 + (y+10)^2 = 4$

B) $(x+7)^2 + (y-10)^2 = 4$

C) $(x-7)^2 + (y+10)^2 = 16$

D) $(x+7)^2 + (y-10)^2 = 16$

7 In the xy-coordinate plane, what are the coordinates of the center of the circle whose equation is given by $(x+2)^2 + (y-\sqrt{3})^2 = 25$?

A) $(2, -\sqrt{3})$

B) $(-2, \sqrt{3})$

C) $(2, 3)$

D) $(7, 5)$

8 What is the equation of a circle with a center $(2, 3)$ and which passes through the point $(1, 1)$?

A) $(x+2)^2 + (y+3)^2 = 5$

B) $(x+2)^2 + (y+3)^2 = \sqrt{5}$

C) $(x-2)^2 + (y-3)^2 = 5$

D) $(x-2)^2 + (y-3)^2 = \sqrt{5}$

9   What is the center of the circle given by the
equation $x^2 - 10x + y^2 + 6y + 2 = 0$?

A) $(5, -3)$

B) $(-5, 3)$

C) $(10, -6)$

D) $(-10, 6)$

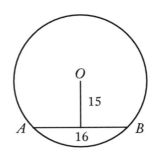

11   In the circle above, the segment extending
from center O is perpendicular to chord $\overline{AB}$.
What is the area of the circle?

A) 34π

B) 64π

C) 256π

D) 289π

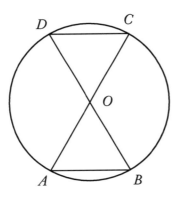

10   In the figure above, points A, B, C, and D
lie on Circle O. If $m\angle DOC = 30°$, what is
$m\angle OAB$?

A) 30°

B) 60°

C) 70°

D) 75°

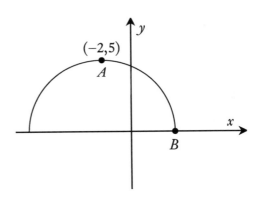

12   In the figure above, the center of the circle lies
on the x-axis, directly below point A. What is
the equation of the circle?

A) $(x+2)^2 + (y-5)^2 = 25$

B) $(x+2)^2 + y^2 = 25$

C) $(x-2)^2 + (y+5)^2 = 25$

D) $(x-2)^2 + y^2 = 25$

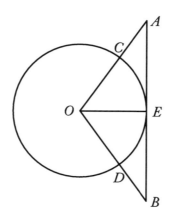

13 In the figure above, $\overline{AB}$ is tangent to circle O at E. If $AC = DB = 4$ and $OE = 6$, what is the value of AB?

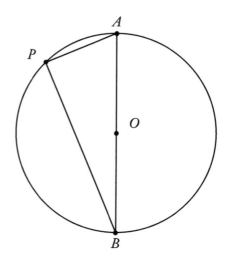

15 In the figure above, points A, B, and P are all on circle O. If $AP = 10$ and $BP = 24$, what is the measure of OB?

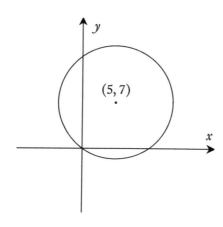

14 The figure above is the graph of a circle which goes through the origin and has a center of $(5, 7)$. If the equation of the circle can be written as $(x-5)^2 + (y-7)^2 = m$, what is the value of m?

Complex Numbers

Complex numbers have the form $a+bi$, where a and b are real numbers, and i is the base of the imaginary number system equal to $\sqrt{-1}$.

Each complex number $a+bi$ has a *complex conjugate*, $a-bi$. When conjugates are multiplied, the resulting product will be a pure real number.

Complex numbers can be added and subtracted just like binomials, but when they are multiplied or divided, the property that $i^2=-1$ complicates things. In particular, whenever anything is divided by a complex number, you should multiply both the top and bottom by the conjugate of the bottom to make the denominator real and

rational. Since you are often asked to leave answers in $a+bi$ form, you may need to split up fractions like $\dfrac{5-3i}{7}$

into $\dfrac{5}{7}-\dfrac{3i}{7}$.

Complex Numbers Problem Set

1 What is the sum of $(3-5i)$ and $(-7-2i)$ if $i=\sqrt{-1}$?

A) $-4+7i$

B) $-4-3i$

C) $-4-7i$

D) $4-3i$

3 What is the product of $(6-3i)$ and $(2+5i)$ if $i=\sqrt{-1}$?

A) $12-15i$

B) $12-9i$

C) $-3+24i$

D) $27+24i$

2 Which of the following results from the computation $(12-11i)-(8-6i)$ if $i=\sqrt{-1}$?

A) $-4-17i$

B) $4-17i$

C) $4+5i$

D) $4-5i$

4 What is the product of $(4-2i)$ and $(4+2i)$ if $i=\sqrt{-1}$?

A) 20

B) 12

C) $16-4i$

D) $12-4i$

5. Which of the following complex numbers is equivalent to $\dfrac{12}{2+3i}$ if $i=\sqrt{-1}$?

A) $6+4i$

B) $-\dfrac{24}{5}+\dfrac{36i}{5}$

C) $\dfrac{24}{13}-\dfrac{36i}{13}$

D) $\dfrac{6}{13}-\dfrac{4i}{13}$

8. What is the value of i^6 if $i=\sqrt{-1}$?

A) -6

B) i

C) -1

D) $-6i$

6. Which of the following complex numbers is equivalent to $\dfrac{3-5i}{2+7i}$ if $i=\sqrt{-1}$?

A) $\dfrac{41}{53}-\dfrac{31i}{53}$

B) $-\dfrac{29}{53}-\dfrac{31i}{53}$

C) $-\dfrac{29}{45}+\dfrac{31i}{45}$

D) $-\dfrac{41}{45}+\dfrac{31i}{45}$

9. What is the value of i^3+i^2+i if $i=\sqrt{-1}$?

A) i

B) -1

C) $-i$

D) 1

7. What is the square of the complex number $(2-i)$ if $i=\sqrt{-1}$?

A) $3-4i$

B) $4-4i$

C) $4-5i$

D) 3

10. If $i=\sqrt{-1}$, and $2i^2-(3i)^3+4i^4=a+bi$, then what is $a+b$?

Essay Manual

The SAT essay question asks you to read a passage and then explain how the author of the passage develops his or her argument to persuade the audience. You must provide evidence from the passage to support your explanation.

Unlike a typical essay that you may write for a class, your job is *not* to agree or disagree with the author's argument. Instead, you must describe the strategies the author uses to build his or her argument.

You have 50 minutes to read the passage and write the essay. The passage will generally be between 650 and 750 words. Passages range from opinion editorials from newspapers such as *The New York Times* to speeches delivered by leaders such as Martin Luther King, Jr.

The Prompt

The prompt shown below, or a nearly identical one, is used every time the SAT is given. Part one of the prompt is provided before the passage, and part two of the prompt is provided after the passage. Read both parts of the prompt before you read the passage.

As you read the passage below, consider how [*the author*] uses:

- evidence, such as facts or examples, to support claims.
- reasoning to develop ideas and to connect claims and evidence.
- stylistic or persuasive elements, such as word choice or appeals to emotion, to add power to the ideas expressed.

Write an essay in which you explain how [the author] builds an argument to persuade [*his/her*] audience that [*author's claim*]. In your essay, analyze how [*the author*] uses one or more of the features listed above (or features of your own choice) to strengthen the logic and persuasiveness of [*his/her*] argument. Be sure that your analysis focuses on the most relevant features of the passage.

Your essay should not explain whether you agree with [*the author's*] claims, but rather explain how the author builds an argument to persuade [*his/her*] audience.

Tackling the SAT Essay

1 Read and annotate the passage

Be sure to read the passage carefully. One of the three sections of the scoring rubric (worth up to 8 points) assesses how well you comprehend the passage, so a close reading is essential. As you read, identify:

① THE AUTHOR'S ARGUMENT. Before even reading the passage, look at the second part of the prompt provided at the end of the passage. The prompt ALWAYS gives you the author's argument in the first sentence. For example, one prompt reads: "*Write an essay in which you explain how Jimmy Carter builds an argument to persuade his audience that the Arctic National Wildlife Refuge should not be developed for industry.*" The prompt will help you see why the author is writing and what he or she wants the audience to believe.

② EVIDENCE the author uses to support his/her argument. Evidence might include:
- Facts or statistics
- Quotations
- Personal experience or anecdotes

③ STYLISTIC DEVICES the author uses to build his/her argument, such as:
- Appeals to emotion
- Word choice
- Tone (See list of rhetorical devices for more examples)

④ REASONING used by the author. Examples of reasoning might be a counter-argument that the author refutes or an explanation of the evidence provided.

Mark up the passage as you read. Write the strategies you see the author using in the margin and underline or circle quotations or facts that you can cite as evidence of your claims.

Remember SOAPS as you read. Write these down as you read:

- **Speaker**   Who is speaking? Consider position, time, context, gender, ethnicity, etc.
- **Occasion**   What is the context/occasion of the speech? How does it affect the purpose, strategy and tone of the speech?
- **Audience**   Who is the target audience? A group of high school students is very different from a group of college professors. How does the audience influence the strategies the author is using to make his argument?
- **Purpose**   What does the author or speaker want?
- **Strategy**   Consider the audience and the purpose—is the author using the right strategy to get his/her message across?

2 Create an Outline

After you have read the passage and before you begin writing, you MUST create an outline. Consider using a classic four or five paragraph structure. In your outline, jot down three literary strategies or techniques you are going to discuss and notes about quotes or evidence you'll use. Here's a sample outline with the information you would include:

1. Introduction
2. Word Choice and examples/quotations from text. How it contributes to argument.
3. Appeals to emotion and quotation from text. Effects on reader.
4. Statistics and how they contribute to argument.
5. Conclusion

3 Write the Essay

A. The Introductory Paragraph

In your introductory paragraph, you want to state the author's purpose and the strategies he or she uses to make his or her argument. You may also want to include relevant SOAPS information, such as the background of the author or speaker if you know it and why it is relevant, the occasion for the article or speech and the intended audience. Finish your introduction with a thesis statement that clearly states how the author builds his argument. Consider choosing three strategies or devices to focus on in your essay and explicitly state these three strategies in your thesis. The following is an example of an SAT essay thesis:

> "Klinenberg uses statistics, hyperbole, and reasonable alternatives to air-conditioning to build his argument that we must reduce our consumption of air conditioning."

Note in the example provided above that the student 1) states the author's argument (we must reduce our consumption of air conditioning) and 2) lists three strategies the author uses (statistics, hyperbole, and alternatives to air conditioning). These strategies will form the basis of her body paragraphs.

Sample Format for the Introduction:

- State the author's argument.
  E.g. "In his article, [*author*] argues that [*author's argument*]. Remember, the SAT will always include the author's argument in the prompt.
- State your thesis, i.e. what strategies or techniques the author uses to make his/her point.
  E.g. [*Author*] uses certain strategies including [*insert your three strategies*] to urge his readers to [*repeat author's argument*]

B. Body Paragraphs

There are two ways to approach the body paragraphs:

1. Focus on one strategy in each body paragraph

   Let's say you have identified in your thesis three strategies or techniques the author uses to make his argument. In each body paragraph, you would discuss one of those strategies. For example, one body paragraph might discuss the author's word choice and the tone it creates in the passage. Perhaps the author uses words that suggest urgency. You would then analyze how the tone contributes to the author's argument. Perhaps the words connoting urgency convince the audience that immediate action is necessary. Make sure to cite specific examples of the strategy or technique you are discussing by using a short quotation from the text or by paraphrasing from the passage. For example, if you are discussing word choice, provide examples of the words used by the author and the effect they have on his argument.

   After discussing one strategy, move on to the next paragraph and discuss the next strategy stated in your thesis. Remember to start each new paragraph with a clear topic sentence that circles back to the thesis.

2. Focus on one paragraph from the passage in each body paragraph

   An alternative way of writing the essay is to choose three paragraphs in the passage and write about the rhetorical strategies used in each paragraph. For example, perhaps the author starts with a personal anecdote in the introductory paragraph of the passage, then progresses to providing statistics in a middle paragraph, and then concludes with an appeal to the audience's emotions. Your first body paragraph would discuss the author's use of the anecdote or personal experience that establishes his credibility on the subject. Your second body paragraph would discuss the evidence he provides in the form of statistics. Your third body paragraph would discuss the appeal to emotion. For each paragraph, be sure to provide concrete examples from the text.

Sample Format for Body Paragraphs:

1. Topic Sentence: e.g. "[*Author*] effectively uses [*strategy*] to advance her argument that [*restate author's argument*]."
2. Provide Example: e.g. "For example, in paragraph two, she comments….[*relevant quotation*]"
3. State Effect of the strategy and why the author uses it: e.g. "The effect of [*strategy*] is …" or "By using [*strategy*], [*author*]…."
4. Explain how the strategy/technique you've identified helps the author promote his/her argument.

Transitions

As you move from one body paragraph to the next, use a transition phrase as part of your topic sentence. Sample transitions:

- In addition to…
- To further support/bolster/promote her argument, [*author*] uses …
- Another way that [*author*] promotes her argument…

Language:

Vary your language. Here are some good alternatives for common words like "argue" and "show":

- Argue: contend, assert, maintain, claim, insist, reason
- Show: reveal, demonstrate, depict, illustrate, portray, express, illuminate
- Tell: convey, impart, communicate, disclose, relate

C. Concluding Paragraph

In the final paragraph, restate your thesis. Summarize the rhetorical devices used in the passage. If you have time, you could comment on whether you feel the author has used the strategies effectively. Even if you're running out of time, just add a sentence or two for the conclusion. You must have a conclusion to get 4 points on the writing portion of the score (see below).

Suggested Timing for the Essay

- CLOSE READING: 10–12 minutes
- OUTLINE: 5 minutes
- WRITING: 30 minutes
- REVIEW: 3–5 minutes

Scoring

There are three categories used to grade the SAT essay. Each category is worth 4 points, and two readers grade each essay. Each essay is therefore given three sub-scores, one for each of the three categories, and these scores range from 2–8, so the total essay score ranges from 6–24.

1. READING: A successful essay shows that you understood the passage, including the interplay of central ideas and important details. It also shows an effective use of textual evidence.
2. ANALYSIS: A successful essay shows your understanding of how the author builds an argument by:
   - Examining the author's use of evidence, reasoning, and other stylistic and persuasive techniques
   - Supporting and developing claims with well-chosen evidence from the passage
3. WRITING: A successful essay is focused, organized, and precise, with an appropriate style and tone that varies sentence structure and follows the conventions of standard written English.

Rhetorical Strategies or Techniques

The following is a partial list of common rhetorical devices and strategies authors use as they build their argument. There are many others. It's not important to pick an obscure rhetorical device to discuss in your essay. You should pick devices or strategies that help build the author's argument and that you can easily discuss.

Evidence   Could come in the form of statistics, facts, quotations, or anecdotes. Evidence is used to lend credibility to an argument. Rather than just giving an opinion, the author is backing up his argument with data.

Appeals to an audience's emotions (*Pathos*)   Does the author's text inspire feelings of pity, sympathy, anger, sorrow, joy, or another type of feeling? How does he do this? By generating an emotional connection, he may be successful in convincing you of his argument.

Logical arguments or Reasoning (*Logos*)   The author is asking the audience to think and use their intelligence to come to the same conclusion as him. Perhaps he provides data and then suggests a way for interpreting this data that supports his argument.

Credibility (*Ethos*)   Ways in which the author establishes his or her own authority to gain the trust of the audience. For example, if the author is writing about a medical issue, perhaps he uses the fact that he is a surgeon to gain credibility with the audience.

Literary Devices

Allusion   a reference to a historical or literary figure, event or subject. An author makes an allusion for a reason, so ask yourself why he or she has alluded to a particular person or event.

Anecdote   a brief story usually about a real person or event.

Analogy   a comparison of two things that are alike in some respects.

Cause–effect argumentation   reasoning that if one thing happens, a particular outcome logically follows.

Diction (word choice)   Look at individual words the author uses. Are there a lot of words that are happy words, sad words, passionate words, or angry words? What tone do these words set for the passage?

Hyperbole   exaggerated statements or words not intended to be taken literally. Again look at the word choice of the author. Are the words over the top? Why might the author be using exaggeration to make his point?

Irony   statement that is characterized by a significant difference between what is said and what is meant. What effect does irony have?

Imagery   sensory details that involve any or all of the five senses. Sensory details can make a passage more vivid or alive. It's like you're experiencing something rather than just reading about it.

Metaphor   figurative language comparing two ideas that are not related. This can help the audience better visualize the author's ideas.

Parallelism   repeating similar components or phrases in a sentence , e.g. "it was the best of times, it was the worst of times…"

Repetition   making the same point over and over.

Satire   use of humor or ridicule to expose the stupidity of an idea.

Tone   the overall mood conveyed by the author of the passage. Tone is generally created by the author's choice of words.

Sample Essay Prompt

As you read the passage below, consider how President Kennedy uses

- evidence, such as facts or examples, to support claims.
- reasoning to develop ideas and to connect claims and evidence.
- stylistic or persuasive elements, such as word choice or appeals to emotion, to add power to the ideas expressed.

Adapted from a speech delivered by President John F. Kennedy at Rice University, September 12, 1962.

We meet at a college noted for knowledge, in a city noted for progress, in a state noted for strength, and we stand in need of all three, for we meet in an hour of change and challenge, in a decade of hope and fear, in an age of both knowledge and ignorance.

No man can fully grasp how far and how fast we have come, but condense, if you will, the 50,000 years of man's recorded history in a time span of but a half-century. Stated in these terms, we know very little about the first 40 years, except at the end of them, advanced man had learned to use the skins of animals to cover himself... Only five years ago man learned to write and use a cart with wheels. The printing press came this year... Last month electric lights and telephones and automobiles and airplanes became available. Only last week did we develop penicillin and television and nuclear power, and now if America's new spacecraft succeeds in reaching Venus, we will have literally reached the stars before midnight tonight.

This is a breathtaking pace, and such a pace cannot help but create new ills as it dispels old, new ignorance, new problems, new dangers. Surely the opening vistas of space promise high costs and hardships, as well as high reward.

So it is not surprising that some would have us stay where we are a little longer to rest, to wait. But this city of Houston, this state of Texas, this country of the United States was not built by those who waited and rested and wished to look behind them. This country was conquered by those who moved forward—and so will space.

The exploration of space will go ahead whether we join it or not...

Those who came before us made certain that this country rode the first waves of the industrial revolution, the first waves of modern invention, and the first wave of nuclear power, and this generation does not intend to founder in the backwash of the coming age of space. We mean to be a part of it—we mean to lead it. For the eyes of the world now look into space, to the moon and to the planets beyond, and we have vowed that we shall not see it governed by a hostile flag of conquest, but by a banner of freedom and peace. We have vowed that we shall not see space filled with weapons of mass destruction, but with instruments of knowledge and understanding.

Yet the vows of this Nation can only be fulfilled if we in this Nation are first, and, therefore, we intend to be first. In short, our leadership in science and industry, our hopes for peace and security, our obligations to ourselves as well as others, all require us to make this effort, to solve these mysteries, to solve them for the good of all men, and to become the world's leading space-faring nation.

Within these last 19 months at least 45 satellites have circled the earth. Some 40 of them were made in the United States of America and they were far more sophisticated and supplied far more knowledge to the people of the world than those of the Soviet Union.

The Mariner spacecraft now on its way to Venus is the most intricate instrument in the history of space science. The accuracy of that shot is comparable to firing a missile from Cape Canaveral and dropping it in this stadium between the 40-yard lines.

Transit satellites are helping our ships at sea to steer a safer course. Tiros satellites have given us unprecedented warnings of hurricanes and storms, and will do the same for forest fires and icebergs…

The growth of our science and education will be enriched by new knowledge of our universe and environment, by new techniques of learning and mapping and observation, by new tools and computers for industry, medicine, the home as well as the school.

And finally, the space effort itself, while still in its infancy, has already created a great number of new companies, and tens of thousands of new jobs. Space and related industries are generating new demands in investment and skilled personnel, and this city and this state, and this region, will share greatly in this growth. During the next 5 years the National Aeronautics and Space Administration expects to double the number of scientists and engineers in this area, to increase its outlays for salaries and expenses to $60 million a year…

I am delighted that this university is playing a part in putting a man on the moon.

Write an essay in which you explain how President John Kennedy builds an argument to persuade his audience that the United States should invest in space exploration. In your essay, analyze how Kennedy uses one or more of the features listed above (or features of your own choice) to strengthen the logic and persuasiveness of his argument. Be sure that your analysis focuses on the most relevant features of the passage.

Your essay should not explain whether you agree with Kennedy's claims, but rather explain how the author builds an argument to persuade his audience.

Answer Keys

Reading Test Manual Answer Key

Special SAT Reading Strategies

Command of Evidence Questions

Practice Passage

1	C	5	A
2	D	6	B
3	B	7	D
4	C		

Words in Context Questions

Practice Passage

1	C	8	D	15	D
2	A	9	A	16	D
3	C	10	C	17	B
4	B	11	D	18	A
5	A	12	D	19	C
6	C	13	A		
7	A	14	B		

Figure-Based Questions

Try It!

1	B

Practice Set

1	C
2	A
3	C

Practice Passages

Social Science

1	A	5	B	9	C
2	C	6	A	10	A
3	D	7	D	11	C
4	C	8	C		

Science

12	B	16	A	20	C
13	D	17	C	21	A
14	C	18	D	22	A
15	C	19	C		

Literature

23	D	27	A	31	C
24	B	28	B	32	D
25	B	29	A		
26	D	30	A		

Challenge

33	C	37	D	41	B
34	A	38	D	42	D
35	A	39	C	43	B
36	B	40	A	44	C

Writing and Language Test Manual Answer Key

Expression of Ideas

Questions without Questions

Try It!

1	A		3	A
2	C		4	D

Practice Set

1	D		6	A		11	A
2	D		7	C		12	B
3	A		8	A		13	D
4	C		9	B		14	C
5	B		10	D		15	B

Writer's Intention Questions

Try It!

1	B

Practice Set

1	A		6	B		11	B
2	C		7	B		12	C
3	D		8	A		13	A
4	B		9	A		14	A
5	A		10	D			

Add/Delete Questions

Try It!

1	C
2	B

Practice Set

1	D		5	A
2	A		6	A
3	B		7	D
4	C			

Ordering Questions

Try It!

1	C

Practice Set

1	C
2	C
3	C
4	A
5	D

Sentence Combining

Try It!

1	B

Practice Set

1	B		6	B
2	A		7	D
3	C		8	B
4	C		9	B
5	A			

Figure-Based Questions

Try It!

1	B

Practice Set

1	A
2	D
3	C
4	D

Standard English Conventions

Sentence Structure

Try It! (other correct answers are possible for many questions)

1. speaker, Jonathan
2. and then
3. However out / be, Crighton
4. Math; however, he
5. making
6. match; hence, / trophy: it
7. I grew
8. game did / play: I
9. NO CHANGE / traumatized because / unexpectedly and
10. of which

Practice Set

1	B	8	A	15	B
2	D	9	C	16	C
3	D	10	C	17	D
4	C	11	A	18	B
5	D	12	B	19	A
6	B	13	D	20	C
7	D	14	B		

Punctuation: Essential and Nonessential Elements

Try It! (other correct answers are possible for many questions)

1. dog that bit my child should never
2. kind woman, gave
3. Humanity, which receives
4. was musically gifted, composed
5. her socks, she walked
6. presidency, who must be at least 35, campaign
7. Teasing that turns into bullying has
8. musician Michael
9. Children interested in helping others are
10. packages, the mailman tripped
11. My sister Lily coaches / players who are injured.
12. sharpener, which I bought online, broke

Practice Set

1	B	5	A	9	C
2	B	6	D	10	B
3	A	7	B	11	D
4	C	8	D	12	C

Punctuation: Other Uses

Commas—Try It! (other correct answers are possible for many questions)

1. fascinating Spanish town, but
2. Intense(,) daily aerobic / blood circulation, heart-health, and
3. way to the friendly neighborhood
4. dark blue Corvette and / new black leather
5. well, but / unique, appetizing dishes / us and

Semicolons, Colons, and Dashes—Try It! (other correct answers are possible for many questions)

1. guitar as if
2. steps, opened the creaky old door,
3. the city: the beach, the architecture,
4. soda: / peer pressure,
5. monuments; however, / architecture, especially / cities like / Vienna, and

End Marks and Quotation Marks—Try It! (other correct answers are possible for many questions)

1. that nobody / known?
2. declared, "The / with respect."

Practice Set

1	B	6	C	11	D
2	D	7	C	12	B
3	C	8	D	13	A
4	C	9	A	14	B
5	A	10	C	15	C

Verb Usage

Try It! (other correct answers are possible for many questions)

1. writes
2. NO CHANGE / must choose
3. rake / tell
4. have / starting
5. are / live
6. should have corrected / was
7. could not have had any / would be
8. had found / would have appealed

Practice Set

1	A	6	C	11	C
2	C	7	B	12	B
3	D	8	B	13	C
4	A	9	D	14	D
5	C	10	C	15	A

Pronouns

Try It! (other correct answers are possible for many questions)

1. of its problems
2. who the robbers / they
3. the police / he or she is.
4. I really need sleep
5. Whom
6. which is / NO CHANGE

Practice Set

1	C	6	D
2	D	7	D
3	C	8	B
4	A	9	C
5	A	10	D

Parallelism and Comparisons

Try It! (other correct answers are possible for many questions)
1. NO CHANGE / skating.
2. fool or playing
3. time management.
4. nor / best sport.
5. to those of working from an office.
6. or in Central America / the US.
7. write, proofread, and e-mail the essay
8. They are paying not only

Practice Set
1	D	5	D	9	D
2	B	6	D	10	C
3	D	7	B	11	B
4	C	8	C	12	A

Apostrophes

Try It!
1. NO CHANGE / amphibian's tail
2. Smiths' friend's dog
3. grassroots bring-out-the vote / its
4. It's / you're
5. You're / her eyes.
6. books' covers were / their
7. NO CHANGE / shops
8. Stephen and Seth's / its / their audience's thinking.
9. NO CHANGE
10. dog's collar / Joan's dogs' collars / their collars.

Practice Set
1	A	4	C
2	C	5	D
3	A	6	D

Modifiers

Try It! (other correct answers are possible for many questions)
1. with no hard wood floors to a family.
2. children brownies
3. John missed the flight.
4. the seven dwarves found the job more manageable.
5. the research center amazed the scientists by still having
6. Steve gave a disgusting and hilarious description of the projectile vomit striking his eyeball.

Practice Set
1	C	5	B
2	C	6	B
3	A	7	C
4	C		

Idioms and Usage

Try It! (other correct answers are possible for many questions)
1. personal computer / necessary for learning
2. fewer advantages at / than students
3. inconsistent with your performance in / direct effect of
4. between two / effect relationships effectively.
5. different from / of Baltimore.
6. from leaving / eluded / many more years.

Practice Set
1	C	5	A	9	D
2	D	6	B	10	A
3	C	7	C		
4	D	8	C		

Mathematics Test Manual Answer Key

Strategies

Backsolving

1	C	6	D	11	B
2	D	7	D	12	A
3	B	8	B	13	D
4	B	9	B	14	D
5	D	10	D	15	D

Plugging in Numbers

Problem Set 1

1	D	6	B	11	A
2	D	7	D	12	C
3	D	8	D	13	B
4	C	9	D	14	B
5	C	10	B	15	A

Problem Set 2

1	C	6	B	11	B
2	A	7	D	12	B
3	A	8	B	13	B
4	D	9	C	14	B
5	A	10	B	15	B

Calculator

1	C	5	A	9	B
2	B	6	B	10	A
3	D	7	C		
4	B	8	C		

Arithmetic Skills

1	57	11	4	21	13.5
2	41	12	20	22	18
3	5	13	1	23	100
4	5	14	4	24	7
5	18	15	190	25	80
6	$\dfrac{11}{9}$	16	7	26	88
		17	9	27	60
7	16	18	20	28	50%
		19	12	29	20%
8	$\dfrac{1}{14}$	20	12	30	125%
9	$\dfrac{25}{9}$				
10	$\dfrac{3}{5}$				

No-Calculator

1	C	6	C	11	D
2	B	7	C	12	C
3	C	8	C	13	D
4	A	9	C	14	B
5	B	10	A	15	D

Heart of Algebra

Algebraic Translation

1	B	8	A	15	C
2	D	9	D	16	A
3	C	10	A	17	A
4	B	11	C	18	B
5	B	12	A	19	D
6	D	13	C	20	D
7	B	14	A		

Solving Linear Equations and Inequalities

1	B	6	A	11	D
2	B	7	C	12	C
3	D	8	C	13	D
4	C	9	B	14	$3/5 < x < 1$
5	C	10	D	15	3001

Functions

Try It!

1	18	5	2.4	9	13
2	16	6	$a^2 + 2$	10	2
3	5	7	$4a^2 + 2$		
4	8	8	$4b^2 + 8b + 6$		

Problem Set

1	C	5	B	9	4
2	B	6	B	10	3
3	A	7	C		
4	C	8	C		

Linear Functions

Try It!

1	B	2	C

Problem Set

1	B	8	A	15	C
2	C	9	D	16	C
3	C	10	D	17	A
4	D	11	A	18	D
5	B	12	D	19	18
6	C	13	A	20	3
7	D	14	B		

Systems of Equations and Inequalities

1	D	8	C	15	D
2	C	9	D	16	A
3	A	10	C	17	2.5
4	B	11	A	18	9
5	C	12	A	19	18
6	D	13	A	20	2
7	C	14	A		

Passport to Advanced Math

Exponents

Try It!

1	9	3	$\dfrac{1}{2^4}=\dfrac{1}{16}$	5	12
2	2	4	8	6	2

Try It!

1	36	2	9

Problem Set

1	B	6	C	11	D
2	B	7	D	12	B
3	D	8	C	13	9
4	D	9	B	14	0
5	C	10	C	15	8

Distributing

1	C	5	C	9	36
2	B	6	D	10	13
3	C	7	B		
4	D	8	B		

Factoring

1	A	6	D	11	C
2	B	7	B	12	C
3	C	8	D	13	9
4	A	9	C	14	2
5	D	10	C	15	7

Radicals and Fractional Exponents

1	A	5	A	9	C
2	C	6	D	10	8
3	A	7	D		
4	C	8	C		

Fractional Operations and Equations

1	D	5	B	9	$\dfrac{1}{4}$
2	D	6	C	10	2
3	D	7	C		
4	B	8	60		

Literal Equations

1	D	6	B	11	D
2	A	7	D	12	D
3	C	8	D	13	C
4	A	9	C	14	A
5	A	10	D	15	A

Quadratic Functions

1	C	8	C	15	A
2	A	9	C	16	C
3	A	10	B	17	B
4	C	11	C	18	D
5	B	12	B	19	0
6	D	13	B	20	12
7	A	14	A		

Polynomial Functions

1	C	7	B	13	$\dfrac{4}{5}$
2	C	8	B	14	3
3	A	9	B	15	$\dfrac{3}{2}$
4	C	10	C		
5	B	11	B		
6	C	12	2 or 3		

Exponential Functions

1	C	6	D	11	A
2	B	7	B	12	C
3	D	8	D	13	C
4	D	9	D	14	1.06
5	D	10	C	15	504

Additional Functions and Transformations

1	B	8	B	15	D
2	A	9	D	16	D
3	A	10	D	17	B
4	A	11	D	18	D
5	B	12	D	19	B
6	C	13	D	20	C
7	C	14	A		

Data Analysis and Problem Solving

Data Analysis

1	A	6	C	11	B
2	B	7	D	12	C
3	C	8	A	13	C
4	A	9	C	14	C
5	C	10	B	15	A

Probability

1	A	5	C	9	D
2	D	6	C	10	D
3	B	7	C		
4	A	8	B		

Percent

1	C	6	C	11	B
2	D	7	A	12	25
3	B	8	A	13	12.5
4	B	9	D	14	50
5	A	10	C	15	30

Rate and Unit Conversion

1	A	6	C	11	D
2	C	7	D	12	B
3	C	8	B	13	33.8
4	D	9	A	14	1056
5	B	10	C	15	7.01

Statistics

1	D	8	C	15	C
2	A	9	B	16	D
3	B	10	D	17	D
4	D	11	C	18	D
5	C	12	B	19	D
6	B	13	D	20	C
7	B	14	B		

Scatterplots

1	A	5	A	9	D
2	B	6	C	10	B
3	C	7	D		
4	C	8	B		

Additional Topics in Math

Basic Geometry

1	C	6	C	11	D
2	D	7	B	12	C
3	B	8	C	13	C
4	D	9	D	14	12
5	A	10	D	15	3

Similar Triangles and Trigonometry

1	D	6	B	11	C
2	C	7	A	12	D
3	A	8	D	13	54
4	D	9	B	14	35
5	A	10	B	15	0.84

Circles

1	A	6	D	11	D
2	D	7	B	12	B
3	C	8	C	13	16
4	C	9	A	14	74
5	D	10	D	15	13

Complex Numbers

1	C	6	B
2	D	7	A
3	D	8	C
4	A	9	B
5	C	10	29

Notes Regarding Score Improvement Table on Back Cover

1. SAT Score improvements = Super-scored SAT – Actual 10th grade PSAT.
   ACT Score Improvements = Super-scored ACT – 10th grade PSAT scores converted to ACT scores or Incoming ACT scores.
   Most tutoring students come to us in the summer before 11th grade. We thus use either an actual baseline SAT or ACT or the 10th grade PSAT as the baseline test. Students who came to us after taking the 11th grade PSAT improved almost as much, and their improvements are available on our website marksprep.com.

2. In 2015, the SAT changed from a 2400-point scale to a 1600-point scale. All data on the first table here is for the pre-2015 SAT on a 2400-point scale. Data on the third table is on a 1600-point scale.

3. In the class of 2017, because of the changes to the SAT, very few of our students took the SAT. Most of our students took the ACT, and we have only shown ACT data for that class.

4. Full score Improvements are available on marksprep.com. Those calculations include data from most respondents, approximately 99 percent of students who have worked with us.

5. On average, students see us for 10–11 tutoring sessions before a first administration of an SAT or ACT and 5–6 tutoring sessions before a second administration, for a total of 15–17 50-minute tutoring sessions.

6. The years in the table refer to the graduating class year of the students not the year in which we tutored them.

Made in the USA
Middletown, DE
03 November 2020